T0367333

Why God Doesn't Hate You

TIA MICHELLE PESANDO,
Consecrated Maiden

Balboa Press books may be ordered through booksellers or by contacting:

Balboa Press
A Division of Hay House
1663 Liberty Drive
Bloomington, IN 47403
www.balboapress.com
1 (877) 407-4847

Printed in the United States of America.

ISBN: 978-1-4525-9366-1 (sc)
ISBN: 978-1-4525-9364-7 (hc)
ISBN: 978-1-4525-9365-4 (e)

Library of Congress Control Number: 2014903596

Balboa Press rev. date: 4/7/2014

Contents

I wish to thank all the theologians with whom I consulted regarding this work, and express my gratitude that I have received the support of them all. In particular, thanks to (in order of consultation) the inspiring United Church Senior Minister Reverend Doctor Jeff Crittenden, my gentle Anglican Dean of Theology Reverend Doctor William J. Danaher, Jr., who has paid such heed and has been so helpful to my cause and my confidence, those in the Eitz Chaim Messianic Jewish Fellowship who helped me better understand Ancient Hebrew, Metropolitan Community Church activists Angel Collie and Reverend Paul Whiting (you magnificent Pastor; I read your book![1]), my correspondent Roman Catholic Priest, who knows perhaps better than anyone in this country the trials of corresponding over the internet on matters regarding the Faith in this time of "siege-mode Christianity" and who edited Chapter the 3rd in late 2012, and finally my own Roman Catholic Priest and a most worthy Bishop so far as I am concerned, Director of Campus Ministries Reverend Doctor Michael Béchard, for also heeding my visions and helping me to enter the Carmelite order like my dear Patron Saint!

Thanks also to my friends Nicole, who showed more faith than I might have imagined possible for this time, beautiful miracle of God Jenna, Minister-in-training-Emily, Isis (not the pagan goddess), London LGBT leaders Lori Ward and Michelle Boyce and a certain someone who released me in Chapter the 7th (you know who you are). *Uruese* also to Roland, Gloria, and all my other friends in Benin City, Nigeria; please give my regards to Oba Erediauwa if you have the chance. *Osanobua kekan ma ga. Iro emwen rue!*

Additional thanks to the country of France, for keeping me very motivated (if somewhat disconcerted) near the end of the book....

Dedicated to the memory of salt mine worker Normand Laberge of Goderich, Ontario...

...and thanks especially to my brother John, who gave me excellent consultation and reassured me with such phrases as "What you're doing is the hardest thing in the world to do," my father and mother, who stood by and encouraged and worried about me through all the strange

---

1 Namely *SACRED JOURNEYS: A Pastor's Memoir with Spiritual Reflections*. Paul Whiting, Edited by Tom Swicegood. 2004 iUniverse, Inc.

and wonderful adventures in my metamorphosis, and my patron *Sainte Thérèse de Lisieux, de l'Enfant-Jésus et de la Sainte Face, dont l'avocat va au-delà la mort. Tu m'a donné une blanc et d'or de rose à 19 ans, et tu donné mes réponses définitives à 33 ans....*

....and of course, my thanks belong most of all to God, yet I assumed that to be self-evident....

Chapter the 1st

For them that feared the Lord, and that thought upon His Name

---

Introduction

A Dark Night of the Soul

Have we been betrayed by the God we love? As children, we received such comfort in knowing that our dark universe was created by a God who loved us; a God who would save us if we but requited His love, regardless of our social status, or our race, or our sex, or...or....

What has become of the Christianity of our childhood? No matter how war-torn, corrupt, or hopeless the world became, we always knew that there were those of God's Church(es) who believed in peace, charity, and love, and who devoted their lives to performing His perfect will. There are a great many who are still upholding such ideals, yet they are not the ones of whom we hear. Theirs is not the Christianity we are permitted to see, and we are at times left to wonder if it does still exist...or if it ever truly existed. If there was a time when "*it was Love alone* that made the Church's members act"[2] and that time has not yet ended, why is it invisible to so many of us? Is it all to be disfigured beyond recognition by a few lines of ancient Scripture which seem to have driven the world mad?

---

2 *L'Histoire d'une Ame;* The Autobiography of St. Theresa of Lisieux. Letter to Sister Marie of the Sacred Heart, September 8, 1896 Manuscript B Chapter IX – My Vocation Is Love (1896). Third Edition, Translated from the Original Manuscripts by John Clarke, O.C.D.. p. 194.

Why do such lines of Scripture even exist, and why are they suddenly given such a position of importance? It seems quite apparent now, for example, that homosexuality is a trait with which one is born, one which is very capable of innocent love, and one which has remained for far too long in the darkness...yet Christians all over the world seem to condemn it. We were taught the teachings of Christ as the source of our understanding of right and wrong, and that the condemnation of the innocent is clearly wrong. Yet the hatred and condemnation of these innocents is said to come from God, as if it were some flaw in His doctrine of Love. Was the very basis for all the ideals of what was once called Christendom – our very civilization – a lie?

How can we believe in a God of Love if He hates His own children for no reason at all..................but for their love?

> "There hath no temptation taken you but such as is common to man: but God *is* faithful, who will not suffer you to be tempted above that ye are able; but will with the temptation also make a way to escape, that ye may be able to bear it." (1 Corinthians 10:13, KJV)

The Seven Accusations

The major criticisms leveled against God may be organized into Seven Accusations or Articles, which are as follows:

ARTICLE 1
God is a tyrannical Emperor, and His rule is and has always been a reign of terror. Treating us as His slaves, God demands that we live in constant fear of Him.

ARTICLE 2
God is a Warrior who loves war. Conflict, bloodshed and sacrifices are immensely pleasing to Him.

ARTICLE 3

God, who views us as His slaves, sees no problem with our enslaving one another. God allows and has always allowed humanity to own and abuse slaves without making any attempt to free them. Furthermore, the decrees made by God and His Son have done nothing to eliminate slavery, but have rather only helped to perpetuate it.

ARTICLE 4

God is racist. Whomever among the peoples of the earth are God's chosen people thereby have every right to destroy or enslave those who are not. On those occasions when God's chosen people come into conflict with one another, then those to whom victory is granted are thereby proven to truly be God's chosen people.

ARTICLE 5

God is male. Being only male, God thus favours the male gender as a superior representation of His image, and considers masculinity to be superior to femininity. This is further revealed by the many misogynist laws throughout history and by His only choosing males to perform His will, especially at the highest positions of authority.

ARTICLE 6

God hates homosexuals. To God, homosexuality is sinful in any and all cases, as His Sacred Scriptures reveal without exception. God considers hatred of homosexuals to be justified. No matter how God chose to cause homosexuals to exist, they are among the "chaff" of which He spoke, and He "will burn up the chaff with unquenchable fire."[3]

ARTICLE 7

God hates transsexuals. Let us instead call ourselves "transgender" or simply "transpeople" if we wish, it matters not; God gives only one gender, and He reveals this gender to us only by the flesh between our thighs. Even to dress in a manner which does not conform to this flesh is dissolute and could never be pleasing to God. Far from any similarity

3 Matthew 3:12, King James Version.

to the image of the androgynous angel, we are instead nothing more than deluded abominations in the eyes of the LORD our God.

The Seven Accusations are all based either on misinformation, incomplete information, or combinations of both. This is especially apparent with the first four Accusations, the responses to which are so well-studied that they tend to be used only by those who bear a more deeply-seated disenchantment. These appear especially often in online forums where the religious can clash with the anti-religious in relative anonymity:

> "**Maidenpaladin** – 3:05 PM
> As I have said before, neither the President of France, nor the Archbishops of Paris and Lyon, nor the new Pope himself will bring peace to France. Peace shall only be gained through understanding and love; for God is Love.
> **freedom4allau** – 3:19 PM
> lol
> **Max Supernova** – 6:22 PM
> Yeah, like when God commands the slaughter of whole cities, or even of all of humanity...I can feel the Christian love!"
> (Excerpt from the comments section of an April 21st, 2013 Huffington Post article titled "French Gay Marriage Opponents Demonstrate In Paris")

Christianity has always been a question of sacrifice, either made for or by the Christians themselves. Christianity's self-sacrificing nature has always conflicted with what seems practical for survival in this world, and thus even early theologians found themselves forced to dismiss certain ideals of Jesus such as poverty, pacifism, and sometimes even universal love. It is such sacrifice that has often tainted Christianity ever since.

Fortunately, society has generally reached a level of enlightenment at which certain things once thought impossible to discard – such as slavery – are realized to be unnecessary; as God always knew they were. As a result, the first four Accusations are more easily dealt with.

However, if these Accusations seem at all easy to deal with, it is only when they are compared to the final three. Women and the LGBT

(Lesbian, Gay, Bisexual and/or Transgender) community have long been mysterious to a civilization which has generally been governed by heterosexual males, and thus we have been severely misunderstood.

In their zeal to please God, there are those who are tempted to condemn because they lack wisdom. In their belief that we are condemned, there are those who are tempted to abandon God because they lack hope. Yet God has made a way for all of us to escape, for deep within His Sacred Scripture He has enabled us to know the truth, and the truth shall make us free.[4]

One may then ask why the transgendered – who are neither mentioned nor condemned anywhere in the Bible, unless it be by association with cross-dressers – would be the subject of the seventh and final Accusation. Ours is a guilt-by-association through the LGBT community, yes, but we are also generally the most-invisible and least-acknowledged part of the community.

This became especially apparent when I first tried to publish this book through a Christian publishing house. An agent from this publisher telephoned me with the results of their theological evaluation of the manuscript with rather surprising results. Amazingly, the conservative Christian publishing house found my defense of homosexuality and even of the "Matter of France" ('gay marriage') quite convincing, and the agent told me when I asked that such was not the problem! Rather, the publisher was simply concerned with my defense of the trans community and of alternative gender expression. I asked the agent about this also, and she informed me that the only quality of *Why God Doesn't Hate You* which renders it "unacceptable for a Christian publisher" was that "it seemed to regard [being transgender] as an acceptable lifestyle choice."

However, perhaps due to the rest of the book's content, the publishing conglomerate's stance was, according to the agent, that "they did not want to lose it," and that it was recommended as a self-help-style book. Thus I was given the options of either a) recanting and changing the content of the book, or b) letting it be turned over to the secular arm.

I chose the latter.

---

4 John 8:32.

Such was the journey I took in my transition of body, mind, and soul. Assigned first the wrong gender marker and then the label of 'transsexual', I spent most of my life feeling that I had been trapped outside; shut out from the supposedly loving Christian community. Isolated because my innocent thoughts were nonetheless forbidden, I felt unworthy even to hear Mass or attend Church service, because of what I was born to be. There are a great many others enduring similar situations.

So it was that the resignation of His Holiness Pope Emeritus Benedict XVI actually brought rejoicing from those who protested his policies. These included the 'feminist activists' of Femen, who painted slogans upon their topless bodies as they rushed to ring the bell celebrating the 850th anniversary of Notre Dame Cathedral. The most mysterious of these slogans was *"Crise de Foi"* or "Crisis of Faith". What did it mean? Was its wearer hoping to, in the words of a former friend of mine in the Gothic subculture, "dance on the grave of the Faith?" Or did the message run deeper than the naked skin upon which it was written? Did it suggest a crisis of the protester's own faith; a feeling of loss which came from no longer being able to believe in what she was brought up believing was the force of Good?

We thus have one answer to the question of why such a frighteningly-huge number of people (the majority of the population in some formerly-Christian countries) are losing faith in God, or have never found reason to seek faith in Him. Ironically, in my experience such "godless" people have often been among the most decent ones I have ever known; people who otherwise would seem best-suited to be inhabitants of Heaven.

Yet it is difficult to blame them for their lack of belief in a world in which the most publicized examples of "religious" people are murdering innocent civilians or condemning innocent minorities. When such things happen all around them, one can find it all-too-easy to stop believing in Jesus Christ's story, for one can stop believing in Jesus Christ's most prominent teaching: that God loves you.

I fear those words may sound hollow to many of you reading this, as at times they almost did to me. After all, is the Bible not a collection of ancient books which contradict one another and are collectively used to condemn whomever and whatever religious authorities choose to persecute? To quote Galileo:

> "...they would have us altogether abandon reason and the evidence of our senses in favour of some biblical passage, though under the surface meaning of its words this passage may contain a different sense." – Galileo Galilei, *Letter to the Grand Duchess Christina, 1615*

We live now in a world in which atheists and other detractors accuse Christians of not having read the Bible and/or not understanding the Scriptures while they themselves fail to understand the Scriptures also. At times it nearly seems that noone living on this earth has truly read the Bible or understands the Scriptures contained therein.

Indeed, with over one thousand pages which often seem filled with descriptions of ancient lineages, archaic laws and horrific occurrences, even reading the Scriptures can seem like a long journey beneath a dark and oppressively-heavy cloud. Yet as one continues to look toward the heavens one can begin to see openings of azure through which shafts of brilliance reveal the truth and give hope. In that sense it is much like life itself in this world, and as with life here the journey is necessary to truly understand it.

To seek understanding myself, I entered a deep contemplation of God, and after an especially spiritual experience (related and analyzed as part of the final chapter) I came to the conclusion that if we could somehow still believe that He could hate any innocent person then there must be something in the Scriptures which we have missed.

For me to have arrived at this idea may seem strange to some readers. Why would I consult documents which have been so heavily-processed by religious authorities in the hope that they somehow miraculously still possess content capable of countering the condemnation condoned by so many of these aforementioned authorities? To answer this, I turn to the "catch-all" response that truly does catch all: faith.

Thus it was that pure faith drove me to pore over the entire Holy Bible anew, despite my Catholic school upbringing and having taken university courses on the Bible (and related texts), and research the Scriptures and their origins to an extent I had never before realized.

Yet this time I did so while attempting to maintain the innocence of a child even while I retained the knowledge (and cognitive ability) of an adult; a child seeking consistent indication of the love of her Heavenly Father, the Father of us all. I thus discovered intensely that those who scour the Scriptures for condemnation and hatred will find them – from humanity – and those who search the Scriptures for acceptance and love will find them – from God.

I have met with remarkable success in this endeavour, and my discoveries have gained the support of clergy from across the denominations of Christianity; from the United Church to the Anglican Church to the Roman Catholic Church. In so doing, I have been shown how small the differences separating these denominations truly are, and thus the folly of conflict between them. Nevertheless, these differences have had a great deal of effect upon a very large portion of humanity, and thus it is addressing those areas of controversy – namely women and the LGBT community – to which the majority of this book is devoted.

> "For God sent not His Son into the world to condemn the world; but that the world through Him might be saved." (John 3:17, King James Version)

We have as a species always been inclined to ascribe/assign mortal human qualities such as envy, wrath, and even hatred to our own man-made gods and limit their motivations to those which we can understand from our own human perspective. This is entirely appropriate, because these false deities were of human origin. The LORD God is rather the origin of humans, however, and thus to assume He can be petty or hateful is an unimaginable disservice to Him. Yes, He can be a jealous God – and who among us has not experienced jealousy who has also known love? – for He is capable of feeling the same full spectrum of emotions as we, yet Love is mightiest among them.

> "Whoever does not love does not know God,
> because God is love."
> (1 John 4:8, New International Version)

The Fear of God[5]

"How can I fear one whom I love?"– Saint Theresa of Lisieux, on her deathbed[6]

Why then, one might ask, does it seem like God demands fear from His subjects like some sort of tyrant? Why is the final reckoning of Revelation 20:12 at the end of the New Testament apparently based upon these requirements written at the end of the Old:

> "Then they that feared the LORD spoke often one to another: and the LORD hearkened, and heard it, and a book of remembrance was written before him for them that feared the LORD, and that thought upon His name." (Malachi 3:16, KJV)

The classical explanation is that of the disciplinary parent: that the immature child operates on a reward-and-punishment level of morality and is thus at risk of being swayed by negative influences such as envy, greed, pride, falsehood, etc. If this is the case, then at least negative reinforcement may be used to guide them in a positive direction:

> "It is good, however, that even if love does not as yet restrain you from evil, at least the fear of hell does. The man who casts aside the fear of God cannot continue long in goodness but will quickly fall into the snares of the devil."
> – *The Imitation of Christ* (ca. 1427 A.D.), Bk. I, Ch.24: Judgment and the Punishment of Sin

---

5 **The term "Theophobia", which appears to be fairly new in common usage, originally meant "Fear of God", but is defined now as "morbid fear or hatred of God."** "theophobia." *Collins English Dictionary - Complete & Unabridged 10th Edition.* HarperCollins Publishers. 05 Dec. 2012. <Dictionary.comhttp://dictionary.reference.com/browse/theophobia>.

6 *L'Histoire d'une Ame;* The Autobiography of St. Theresa of Lisieux. Spoken to her sister, Mother Agnes of Jesus in July of 1897. Manuscript C Epilogue. Third Edition, Translated from the Original Manuscripts by John Clarke, O.C.D.. p. 263.

This approach to failure to achieve the true ideal – settling for something far darker indeed – is lamentably one which appears often-used in Christianity. However, it is not appropriate to the Sacred Scriptures.

> "There is no fear in love; but perfect love casteth out fear: because fear hath torment. He that feareth is not made perfect in love." (1 John 4:19, KJV)

One may point out that this appears to be an example of Biblical contradiction; the Old Testament says one thing, but the New Testament says quite another. It is a very positive message, but doesn't it go against what the All-Knowing, Unchanging LORD said earlier?

No; actually it is a matter of mistranslation due to misinterpretation. It is extremely important to properly analyze Scripture in its original languages, as failure to do so is the source of the most brutal Biblical misunderstanding of our times.

The Ancient Hebrew word translated as "fear" is ארי ("*yir'ah*" or "*yare*"). Its root meaning is "to flow" as rain, water in a stream, or the emotions which flow forth from the heart. In Hebrew thought it has two possible meanings; it can mean "fear" as what is felt when in danger, or as those emotions felt when in the presence of an awesome sight or being of great authority. The overall context of this word's appearance in the Bible suggests that "reverence" is usually a more apt interpretation of it, as do the Ancient Hebrew characters that compose it: *yad resh el*, the meanings of which are in this case most accurately interpreted as "worship (י) the Top (and First) (ר) Power (who is the Strong Leader) (א)." (Hebrew is normally read from right to left.)

His Hallowed Name

This logographic method of interpreting a word based on the characters within it also works when thinking upon His name. From a Christian (or Messianic Jewish) perspective, the background to this is the most significant of all such interpretations.

Names in the ancient world were considered to have supernatural power, and to know or use a being's true or secret name was thought to grant one influence over said being. This is why the demon in Mark 1:24-25 attempted to ward off Jesus' power by invoking His precise name/title with the statement, "I know thee who thou art, the Holy One of God" (KJV), why when Jesus asked the demon his name in Luke 8:30 he would not provide Him with a straight answer, and why it was so significant that no one would know the name written in the white stone of Revelation 2:17 except the one who received it. Thus when a friend of mine named Isis consulted me regarding the origins of her namesake I began to look up "the Secret Name of Ra;" the story in which the aforementioned mythological character gained power over the entire Egyptian pantheon by using a poisonous serpent to wrest the secret name from its ruler, Ra. I shifted focus, however, when I learned of the "Secret Name of God," which is not a method of gaining power over the Supreme Being but rather a means of understanding His faith and Love.

As suggested above when translating the word ירא ("*yir'ah*"), Ancient Hebrew is a uniquely intriguing language in that each word has meaning not merely in itself but also in the pictographic letters from which it is constructed. The Name of God, which is translated as LORD in most English Bibles and known as the Tetragrammaton due to its containing four characters, as a word means "I AM" or literally "the existing One", suggesting a universal Presence and consciousness. However the characters that compose it point to another complementary meaning. יהוה "*Yad He Waw He*" (pronounced "Yud Hey Waw Hey") contains the following pictographs: י *Yad* (masculine), a (closed) hand; ה *He* (feminine), which in its most ancient form depicted a robed man seated with their right side visible and their arms raised in the declaration, "Look!"[7]; and ו *Waw* (masculine), a tent peg or nail. Taken together, they reference that instruction so famously given by Jesus Christ to the ("doubting") Apostle Saint Thomas[8], which in common speech has often been shortened to, "Behold the Hand, Behold the Nail." Such is the Hallowed Name spoken of in the Lord's Prayer (Matthew 6:9-13, Luke 11:2-4), and it reveals that God's Love was thus written from the

---

7 This is reminiscent of the angel(s) declaring Jesus' resurrection in Matthew 28:2-6, Mark 16:5-6, and John 20:12-13.

8 In John 20:25-27. This instruction is addressed to the Apostles in general in Luke 24:39.

beginning, and expressed most overtly by the sacrifice of His Son Jesus Christ. (John 15:13)

Of all the Commandments, which were intended to promote safety and mutual love between God and the community and within the community itself, those of Jesus Christ are both the most desirable and the most difficult. In a world of violence and cruelty, we are to "turn the other cheek"[9]. In a world of ambition and tyranny, we are to keep a submissive heart. In a world of greed and thievery, we are to practice charity. In a world of deceit and illusion, we are to believe without having seen.

The very fact that these commandments were seemingly-impossible to keep in a more ancient society reveals that they transcend time and civilization. Therefore once one is at the pinnacle of the loving goodness we have received, what feels right to oneself is indeed right to God. Violence, slavery, racism, misogyny, and homophobia are not truly what He desires. Rather, the Scriptures have been misinterpreted and at times been horribly misused, for even the Devil himself quoted Scripture (when attempting to tempt Jesus Christ in such passages as Luke 4:9-13[10]). Yet the Scriptures are greater than those who would use them for evil.

---

9 Matthew 5:39, Luke 6:29.

10 Wherein he alludes to Psalm 91:11-12.

Chapter the 2nd

Thou Shalt Not Kill

Issues of Biblical Violence

> "The Christmas message sounds like mockery to a world at war, but those of us who wished and still wish for peace may surely offer a solemn greeting to such of you who feel as we do."
>
> – Emily Hobhouse, "The Open Christmas Letter" for the International Congress of Women (distributed amongst nations of all sides during World War I), November 1914
>
> (The particular importance of the role of women in obtaining and maintaining peace shall be elaborated upon in Chapter the 5th)

In this world of religious schisms and "holy wars", how does one reconcile the Fifth Commandment ("Thou shalt not kill"[11]) with all the horrific violence committed in God's name and supposedly with His blessing? Even the more educated arguments I have encountered always state that such violence was necessary due to the prevailing conditions of the time; if those surrounding/threatening us are hostile, then we have every right to defend ourselves. However, if this were an acceptable historical and even scientific justification-by-necessity, why does it nevertheless feel so wrong to so many of us?

I recall a kingdom strategy/war game I once played online. As with so many games of its ilk, it began with my being inserted with no power whatever into a land surrounded by intimidating empires. These players considered me too weak to ally with them and once they learned that I

---

11 Exodus 20:13.

never attacked anyone without provocation, they laughed at me for being a dove in a game of war. Nevertheless my strategy worked – though I had to journey far and wide for suitable "level 10" land unclaimed by other players and even then needed to clear out its computer-controlled indigenous people – and eventually my tribe went from a populace of tent-dwelling nomads to a mightily-fortified kingdom. Numbers were impressive in all branches of the military (40,000-strong dragon cavalry, etc.), massive and powerful alliances were competing for my potential allegiance, and I was able to erect golden hanging gardens just like those of the surrounding nations. I ceased playing, however, once a new expansion was released in which maximum power over one's enemies was promised only to those who would sacrifice human souls upon the altar to an enormous spirit of death; this was all beginning to feel a little too familiar. Though this was but a frivolous video game, it nevertheless served as a small reminder that human nature may have changed precious little since the time of Ancient Egypt and Babylon.

Perhaps the apparent universality of warfare lends itself to such ease of parallel, yet in any case the Tribes of Israel did in fact endure a similar journey to the establishment of their kingdom and the Temple of the LORD in a harsh and brutal reality.

In Numbers 12:3, Moses is described as very humble and meek, perhaps the meekest man on the face of the earth; a statement which coincides well with the numerous other pieces of Biblical evidence that such people are favoured by God. However, the Israelites under him were religiously zealous even to the point of brutality, for God was the Force that united them...and One whom they failed to understand. Understanding of the intricacies of the Creator was not the goal at this point of these desperate people in the desert, however; their perception of Him was limited, perhaps inspired by the Pagan people's perceptions of their own false gods, and of a familiar image:

> "The LORD is a man of war: the LORD is his name." (Exodus 15:3, KJV)

Passages such as this are what has led to the faulty belief that God somehow changed between the Old and the New Testament, becoming more gentle in His approach to humanity. This is pure projection;

humanity assigning its own hidden desires and impulses – however base – to its Creator, and believing that He shares its subjective mental life. Surely God does not change[12], but human understanding of Him does, and it has been thus changing since the time of the Old Testament, as evidenced in the later Deuterocanonical passage:

> "You, the LORD, crush warfare; LORD is your name." (Judith 9:8, NAB)

However, to the Israelites at the time written of in the Torah, devotion was sufficient, along with the assurance that their God would use His power to grant them success in establishing a realm for themselves.

This attitude is spelled out quite clearly in Deuteronomy 7:1-11, which promised that although the Israelites were "the fewest of all people" (v. 7) their soldiers would fight and God would grant them the victory. This was because "the LORD thy God hath chosen [them] to be a special people unto himself" (v.6) and their loyalty needed to remain true, necessitating the total destruction of foreign influence. In short, the conditions for military conquest required cultural conquest.

Thus this passage is among the most frightening in the Bible, and it is quite fitting that it also occurs fairly early in the Good Book. It presents God in a manner which the people of the time could understand, and as we shall see in the forthcoming chapters, much of the Scriptures to follow serve the purpose of showing how very limited and inaccurate this perspective is.

In fact, the perspective of God revealed here is an excellent example of the first level of Lawrence Kohlberg's stages of moral development, which are based not on adherence to any particular religious doctrine but rather upon capacity for thought, altruism, and empathy, and find that this process of moral development is principally concerned with justice. This first stage, wherein moral views are driven by obedience simply as a means by which to avoid punishment, is clearly evidenced in the passage previously referenced: serve only God and you will be rewarded; betray Him and you shall feel His wrath. Though this personal- rather than society-focused level of morality is most typical

---

12 Malachi 3:6.

of children, in the case of the Ancient Israelites this pre-conventional approach was employed due to the fact that the social conventions (ie. The Commandments and the Mosaic Law) of Israel were still being established at the time of Deuteronomy.

The second stage is selfishness regardless of consequence, but higher stages of moral development move past blind obedience and self-interest, though they still involve operation within the conventions of established society. At stages three and four people are concerned with conformity/pleasing others and a sense of duty, respectively, yet both of these rely on established social conventions and the law. Only at the final levels do people eventually transcend these conventions and are truly freed from the law (as Christ freed us according to Galatians 2:16 and 3:13), allowing for the improvement of human understanding (this occurs at stages five and six, which are concerned with societal human rights and universal human ethics, respectively). God operates on the otherwise semi-theoretical seventh stage of morality; that of universal principles, including transcendental morality which cannot yet be fully fathomed. (It is between the 4th and 5th stages, concerned with the fulfillment of duty and what is thought best for a society as a whole, that people generally are possessed by the audacity necessary to attempt to morally place God on trial).

Thus we began with a fairly simple concept which everyone could understand; the Israelites' defeat of nations greater and mightier than they is provided as proof of God's favour as well as of His power. The Israelites' devotion to the First Commandment ("Thou shalt have no other gods before me"[13]) and thus to Him as the first and only God was used to explain the utter destruction of these heathen nations. Having noted this, however, there remained the Fifth Commandment, which simply stated that one was not to kill and which thus offered no exceptions despite Moses' insistence that at times absolute destruction must be visited upon the Israelites' enemies. Perhaps this baffled the aforementioned Israelites...or perhaps it was reflected in how they offered even some of the Pagan peoples they encountered the opportunity to let them pass in peace:

13 Exodus 20:3, KJV.

> "And Israel sent messengers unto Sihon king of the Amorites, saying,
>
> Let me pass through thy land: we will not turn into the fields, or into the vineyards; we will not drink of the waters of the well: but we will go along by the king's high way, until we be past thy borders.
>
> And Sihon would not suffer Israel to pass through his border: but Sihon gathered all his people together, and went out against Israel into the wilderness: and he came to Jahaz, and fought against Israel.
>
> And Israel smote him with the edge of the sword, and possessed his land from Arnon unto Jabbok, even unto the children of Ammon: for the border of the children of Ammon was strong." (Numbers 21:21-24, KJV)

Nevertheless, conflict and bloodshed were still deemed necessary and continued on for generations through the time of Joshua and the Judges. At the end of the latter book, the Israelites even found themselves turning upon one another, as the other tribes took vengeance upon that of Benjamin for a heinous crime committed in their city of Gibeah. This violent crime, which was very similar indeed to the mass-gang rape attempted by the Sodomites in the 19th chapter of Genesis, occurs in the 19th chapter of Judges and is followed by a war within Israel described in the following two chapters. At the end of this, the following statement is made:

> "The people were still disconsolate over Benjamin because the LORD had made a breach among the tribes of Israel." (Judges 21:15, New American Bible)

Here the New American Holy Bible (School and Church, 2003-2004 Edition) offers in its footnote an explanation of how the ancient people of Israel, not yet grasping the full extent or ramifications of their God-given free will, apparently assumed that every act of violence they perpetrated was the will of God:

> "...what is here attributed to God was in reality the free and deliberate act of the Israelites and happened only by the permissive will of God. The ancients attributed to the first primary cause what is more directly due to secondary causes." (p. 237)

Eventually, after enduring the mad Saul – whom David repeatedly insisted upon sparing[14] despite Saul's trying to kill him – as its first king, Israel rose to greatness with King David, a shepherd and neglected son from Bethlehem who won legend in a titanic duel with the Philistine champion Goliath. This led to further military victories which further impressed the Israelites; David's people heaped praise upon him for slaying "his ten thousands"[15]. The LORD was – due to the free will He gave us – willing to allow all of this to happen, but did He truly desire it?

Was He not pleased that those who did not know or love Him were dispatched with such efficacy? After all, it was always His intention that we....

> "Hear, O Israel: The LORD our God is one LORD: And thou shalt love the LORD thy God with all thine heart, and with all thy soul, and with all thy might." (Deuteronomy 6:4-5, KJV)

Thus we have a question that has burned down across the millennia: was it ever truly acceptable to ignore other Commandments out of zeal for the First?

No. No it was not. As has often been the case, the LORD was of an opinion differing from that of His followers, as He made quite clear to King David:

> "But the word of the LORD came to me, saying, Thou hast shed blood abundantly, and hast made great wars: thou shalt not build an house unto my name, because thou hast shed much blood upon the earth in my sight." (1 Chronicles 22:8, KJV[16])

---

14 1 Samuel 24 & 26.

15 1 Samuel 18:7.

16 See also Psalm 11:5. David's son Solomon is praised for being a peaceful man,

Blood Sacrifices and Burnt Offerings

Unfortunately, many of the kings who came after David resorted to bloodshed of a somewhat different sort, and one which some people even in modern times seem to believe that God endorsed: sacrificial offerings. After all, a great many verses of the Torah books of the Bible are devoted to precise descriptions of what is to be sacrificed, when and how such things are to be sacrificed, and by whom such things are to be sacrificed. In reality, this practice was by no means unique to Israel, but was quite common in the Ancient World. As the 5th -Century B.C. Greek historian Herodotus wrote:

> "In the temple of Babylon there is...a great seated cult-statue of Bel[17], all of gold on a golden throne.... Outside the temple is a golden altar...reserved for the sacrifice of sucklings [lambs]...."
> (*The Persian Empire: A Corpus of Sources of the Achaemenid Period*, Volume 1, by Kuhrt, p. 249)

While the continued practice of sacrificing animals may seem cruel, it was in fact intended by God as a substitute for a far more horrific form of sacrifice.

The kings who succeeded David often took to imitating the idolatrous practices of the surrounding nations and even their form of religious extremism: the sacrifice of human life – even those of their own children – to false gods. This was acceptable to – and encouraged by – the surrounding nations, but it was never acceptable to God[18].

This almost-unimaginably foul practice was never intended by God. This is shown very strongly in Jeremiah 32:35:

---

and according to the NAB even his name is a play on "Shalom", the Hebrew word for peace.

17 Marduk/Merodach, whom I shall elaborate upon in the following chapter. One familiar with ancient mythology might imagine that a woman named "Tiamat" has some choice words regarding that particular false god....

18 Leviticus 18:21.

> "And they built the high places of Baal, which are in the valley of the son of Hinnom, to cause their sons and their daughters to pass through the fire unto Molech; which I commanded them not, neither came it into my mind, that they should do this abomination, to cause Judah to sin." (KJV)

We are reminded that these practices are foreign in origin even by the Hebrew word translated as "abomination": הבעות *tow'ebah*, which refers specifically to heathen undertakings. Such practices thus may be considered to be human in origin, so one may wonder what inspired them in the first place.

The presumed need for sacrifice appears to stem from some aspect of human nature that urges people to prove their devotion by offering up something most dear to them (typically a firstborn son or virgin daughter). It is disturbingly common historically and still practised even today. A friend of mine from Nigeria recently drew to my attention an article in the newspaper/blog *Talk of Naija*[19] on the sacrifice of a baby girl by what are now called "ritualists" (whose action has made them criminals in the Christian region in which the diabolical deed was performed). Rather than describe for the reader the disturbing and grisly details of the infant's death, suffice it to say that this was by no means an isolated incident.

It was because of the ubiquitous nature of this horror that the Patriarch Abraham did not seem surprised when it appeared that God demanded the sacrifice of his only son in the 22nd chapter of the Book of Genesis. This well-known story frightened me considerably as a seven-year-old child when first I heard it; I recall thinking to myself, *what if MY father decided one day that God wanted ME to be a burnt offering?!?* The request was of course intended as an opportunity for Abraham to prove his faith and loyalty to the LORD. Still, it was probably quite a traumatic experience for both father and son, and one which issued the question of: how many others have gone through with such deeds without the benefit of Divine intervention to stay their hands?

---

19 http://www.talkofnaija.com/News/newsdetailsone.aspx?NewsId=73209CEF-C7A1-4DD2-BAB0-82C19C93045E (Retrieved Sunday, August 19th of 2012.)

Thus it was that God prescribed a system wherein certain animals would be sacrificed in lieu of human beings. This was described in great detail early in the Bible, yet it was intended not to be everlasting but rather merely a progressive measure – a baby-step, if you will – toward the ultimate end of all such material demonstrations of obedience, loyalty, and love.

Indeed, all of the reams of Scripture describing details of this barbaric practice are countered by one line from a "minor prophet":

> "For I desired mercy, and not sacrifice; and the knowledge of God more than burnt offerings." (Hosea 6:6, KJV)

This passage is used by Jesus Christ to thwart the Pharisees on two separate occasions. The first occurs in Matthew 9:9-13, when He defends His befriending of tax collectors and "sinners" with the assurance that He has "not come to call the righteous, but sinners to repentance." The second occurs in Matthew 12:1-8, when He defends His own disciples after they have broken a Pharisee-prescribed rule concerning the Sabbath. Both deal with Jesus' breaking down of ritualistic practices in favour of the true Spirit of God's plan.

A vital part of God's plan – as was revealed in the first chapter of this book through the secret meaning of His name – involved Jesus' sacrificing Himself as an offering for our sins, and this fact gives the aforementioned 22nd chapter of Genesis a quality of severe foreshadowing:

> "And Isaac spake unto Abraham his father, and said, My father: and he said, Here am I, my son. And he said, Behold the fire and the wood: but where is the lamb for a burnt offering?
> And Abraham said, My son, God will provide **himself** a lamb for a burnt offering: so they went both of them together." (Genesis 22:7-8, KJV, emphasis mine)

This leads into another question I have been asked, or more precisely two questions. The first, a question over which I agonized as a teenager and another questioning of the veracity of God's love, was "If God is so loving, why didn't He sacrifice Himself rather than His Son?" and it is answered most satisfactorily by Jesus' statement in John 10:30:

"I and my Father are one." (KJV)

Unfortunately, the next question then becomes a possible multitude of questions, such as "How can the Son be One with the Father?", "If Jesus and the Father are One, then how could Jesus not know the precise time of the destruction of the Temple (and/or the time of His own Second Coming) even though His Father did?"[20], and "How could the Holy Trinity of Father, Son and Holy Spirit be God in Three Persons if there is only One God?"

Let us consider the dream. The dreamer exists outside the dream, yet their mind encompasses the entirety of the dream. Nevertheless, the dreamer can also exist as a being within the dream, who can access amazing supernatural power therein, yet still is not consciously aware of the course the dream will take. Despite this, we do not consider the dreamer, the dream, and the dreamer within the dream to be three separate entities. So it can be with God.[21]

It was in this meekness, this self-sacrifice, that God chose to manifest Himself to show His Supreme Devotion to us. In fact, upon detailed examination there are evident possible parallels between the components of the Holy Trinity and the three major types of sacred[22] sacrificial animals[23]. The Father is often referenced with the Ancient Hebrew character א "*El*"[24] which in its most ancient form is intended to represent the head of an ox or bull (sacrificed significantly in Leviticus 8:14). The Son, as previously-mentioned, is specifically referred to as

---

20 Matthew 24:36, Mark 13:32.

21 Ephesians 4:6-7.

22 These animals are sacred as opposed to the goat, which was also given to Azazel; who is generally regarded as a fallen angel or evil spirit (Leviticus 16:8-10).

23 Leviticus 1.

24 This is also the case in the names of Biblical figures such as the Archangels Gabriel ("God is my strength"), Raphael ("God heals"), and Michael ("Who is like God?"). Logographically, the word "*El*" is spelled "*El lam*" (Modern Hebrew אל "*Aleph lamed*") to include both the ox's head and the shepherd's staff.

the Lamb of God[25] as a reference to the sacrifice of Passover[26]. The omnipresent Holy Spirit descended in a bodily form like a dove upon Jesus in Luke 3:22 (as well as in Matthew 3:16 and John 1:32), and is a sacrifice especially notable in Luke 2:24 as the 'sin offering' for bringing Jesus Christ into the world[27]. Jesus Himself makes the value of such ultimate sacrifice intimately clear with His statement that....

> "Greater love hath no man than this, that a man lay down his life for his friends." (John 15:13, KJV[28])

This inclination toward self-sacrifice was long kept a mystery, for it was difficult for humanity to understand and to accept, given the world to which they were accustomed. As Mohandas K. Gandhi (better known as Mahatma Gandhi, who himself tried to join a Christian church but was rejected due to racism) noted to a Christian missionary:

> "To live the gospel is the most effective way...Not just preach but live the life according to the light.... But you quote instead John 3:16...and that has no appeal to me, and I am sure people will not understand it...the Gospel will be more powerful when practised and preached."[29]

Knowing the willingness of God to suffer with us and even sacrifice Himself for us goes quite a long way toward understanding the enigmatic verse that is John 3:16, for in Jesus He both preached and practised the Gospel:

---

25 John 1:29.

26 Exodus 12:21.

27 Leviticus 12:1-8, NAB.

28 Though the Greek pronouns used here (*oudeis* (1st "man"), *tis* (2nd "man"), and *autos* ("his")) are generally considered masculine by default, they include the feminine equivalents as well.

29 Samuel, Dibin. "Mahatma Gandhi and Christianity." *Christian Today.* 2008. http://in.christiantoday.com/articledir/print.htm?id=2837 Retrieved 02/10/2012.

> "For God so loved the world, that he gave his only begotten Son, that whosoever believeth in him should not perish, but have everlasting life."[30]

Jesus Christ, the ultimate sacrifice for (and of) God, also provides the most well-known and important understanding of God's desire for peace. This is shown not only in the Saviour's life, but also in that which was and that which was (and is) to come.

Final Justice

Jesus' message in Matthew 26:52 (and God's message in Genesis 9:6), that "all they that take the sword shall perish with the sword" (KJV), so universal that Martin Luther King, Jr. referred to the verse not only regarding his own situation but also that of Gandhi[31], is displayed no less in Biblical Israelite history. God promised the Israelites that they would possess dwelling places which were not theirs[32], and while He would not punish them for that alone after He had given them such a promise, after they had unrepentently turned from Him this conquest would be an action returned by the Chaldeans/Babylonians[33]. Those who had taken with the sword were themselves taken by the sword, yet even when God promised to reverse their fortunes again with the end of the Babylonian exile[34], the lesson had not yet been learned. The Israelites expected another (regime) change of fortune from God regarding the Roman Empire which later occupied them...and they expected this change to come from the Messiah; Jesus Christ.

By the traditional Jewish understanding of the Messiah, He was expected to be a military leader of sorts who would free Israel from the

---

30 KJV.

31 *The Martin Luther King, Jr. Papers Project.* "Palm Sunday Sermon on Mohandas K. Gandhi, Delivered at Dexter Avenue Baptist Church." 22 March 1959, Montgomery, Ala. http://mlk-kpp01.stanford.edu/primarydocuments/Vol5/22Mar1959_PalmSundaySermononMohandasK.Gandhi,DeliveredAtDext.pdf Retrieved Friday, December 7th of 2012.

32 Deuteronomy 6:10-12.

33 Habakkuk 1:6, 2:8-12.

34 Jeremiah 50:2.

captivity of occupying forces. He did so, though He freed not only Israel, but all of humanity on an eternal level far beyond human comprehension. His doctrine was Love, which had nothing to do with war, yet would eventually triumph over all else.

> "He that leadeth into captivity shall go into captivity: he that killeth with the sword must be killed with the sword. Here is the patience and the faith of the saints." (Revelation 13:10, KJV)

This passage from the Bible's final book offers hope of final justice, though sadly we must wait a little while longer for its final resolution. Just as in Jesus' time upon the earth, this message would not be understood by most of humanity, as it was not in the time before, when conquest was met with conquest and faithlessness with faithlessness. Instead more traditional and violent means were favoured over those of Christ. So it was that those who instead chose the rebellious, violent way of Barabbas took action resulting in the Romans' retributive destruction of the temple, where its conquerors made an idol of "the abomination of desolation"[35]: Zeus Olympios, just as the Babylonians had done centuries earlier with Bel Marduk[36].

35 Matthew 24:15, Mark 13:14, KJV.

36 2 Kings 17:30, NAB. See also Jeremiah 50:2, KJV, etc..

Chapter the 3rd

The Golden Calf[37]

Issues of Biblical Slavery

William Lynch, a man who made his living off of his attempts to perfect the enslavement of Africans in southern North America, was one of a number of more-recent historical villains to draw inspiration from Biblical ones. In peddling his supposedly-foolproof method of control, titled *The Making of a Slave*, he spoke of how much they all cherished the King James Bible and in the same breath made the statement that....

> "Ancient Rome would envy us if my program is implemented. ... While Rome used cords of wood as crosses..."

Lynch (from whose name we derive the term "to lynch") immediately and without a hint of irony compared the Roman practice of crucifixion with the hanging of black slaves. He then lamented that such practices have led to uprisings and exoduses before explaining his tactics for preventing such things.

When he spelled out these tactics in 1712, he promised that they would keep the "uncivilized nigger (sic)" under control for at least 300 years, and they had nothing to do with Biblical values. Instead, he sought out differences among the slaves and magnified them. Rather than love and charity, Lynch advised all who would listen to...

> "use fear, distrust, and envy for control purposes. ...distrust is stronger than trust, and envy is stronger than adulation, respect, or admiration."

---

37 Exodus 32, Deuteronomy 9:7-29.

To coincide with his psychological approach, Lynch recommended the use of other techniques employed by the Roman Empire: striking fear into the hearts of slaves while also giving them a contained hope of 'mercy'. His instructions involved setting the most rebellious male slave on fire while having horses pull him apart in front of the women and child slaves. However, the other males were not to be treated in the same manner, but rather beaten almost to death by a bullwhip, for the object was not to kill them but rather to "put the fear of God" in them.

Which 'god' would that be, then? The belief that slavery was a divine institution is a myth...in the most literal sense of the word.

Marduk, God of Slavery

The Ancient Mesopotamians (such as the Ammonites, Canaanites, and other peoples mentioned previously) consolidated their mythology into one in which slavery was more than merely an institution: it was the very reason for humanity's existence. By the time of Ancient Babylon, the "Baals/Bels" ('Lords') of the various peoples often-referred to in the Old Testament had united with the Empire, into a false god whose name evokes a common graven image of worship related to masculinity and strength: Marduk (in Sumerian/Akkadian literally *Amar-Utu;* "Solar (ie. Golden) Calf")

Bel-Marduk's violent rise to power is detailed in the *Enuma Elish*, the Babylonian creation epic written upon seven clay tablets which predate the Book of Genesis by approximately a millennium. It required him to overcome and pull apart Tiamat, the female entity responsible for creation. Unable to actually create anything himself, Marduk sculpted humanity out of clay from the body of Tiamat and combined it with the blood of her second husband, Kingu, who had sided with her bearing the Tablets of Destiny in the war, yet been shaken at the sight of Marduk, captured and slain thereafter. The attitude this new ruler had towards humanity is revealed in his stated intentions for it:

> "I will establish a savage, 'Man' shall be his name.
> Verily, savage-man I will create.
> He shall be charged with the service of the gods

> That they might be at ease!"
> (Tablet VI, Lines 3-6, Pritchard translation)

It is again worthy to note that like Zeus, Marduk is a true abomination to God, and that there is much confusion between the Babylonian idol and the LORD our God, especially after the Kingdoms of Israel and Judah were conquered by and its people absorbed into the Babylonian Empire. Indeed, thousands of years prior to the penning of William Lynch's *The Making of/Let's Make A Slave*, the Babylonians were utilizing his philosophy that slaves must be completely severed from their original beginnings through the annihilation of their mother tongue upon the captive Hebrews. In order to operate safely within even Persian society, the Biblical Hadassah[38] found it necessary to assume the name Esther (derived from the Babylonian fertility goddess of love and war, "Ishtar"[39]) at the advice of her uncle Mordecai (whose name is Aramaic for "[servant/follower/devotee] of Marduk")[40]. Mid-19th-Century American slave Lucretia Alexander stated clearly what has been the case throughout history, that when one is a slave one has to go by one's owner's name, and here one's 'owners' included the Babylonian pantheon.[41]

Mordecai's name gains additional irony when one considers that he gained great favour with Ahasuerus a.k.a. Xerxes I, whose violent seizure and melting down of the famed golden statue of Bel[42] in 484 B.C.

---

38 "Myrtle", coincidentally enough considered sacred to Ishtar and the Greek goddess of love she inspired, Aphrodite. (*Harper's Dictionary of Classical Literature and Antiquities.*) Further information on this name's etymology is found at http://www.babynamer.com/esther and http://chaldeanhistory.blogspot.ca/2006/09/country-study-iraq-library-of-congress.html

39 Esther also has a meaning in Hadassah's mother tongue, for it is derived from the Hebrew verb *lehastir* (meaning "to hide"). http://www.palmtreeofdeborah.blogspot.ca/2012/02/sequel-to-amalek-alive-and-well-pt-3.html Retrieved Sunday, October 28th of 2012.

40 Esther 2:5-10.

41 *Voices from Slavery: 100 Authentic Slave Narratives.*

42 Marduk, of course; the hands of which the rightful king of Babylon was required to clasp each New Year's Day.

precipitated revolt among the Babylonians.[43] This destruction of the idol occurred in the very same year in which the Book of Esther begins, with the (Greek) Prologue featuring Mordecai's dream of clashing dragons and a flood of water ending when "The light of the sun broke forth; the lowly were exalted and they devoured the nobles."[44]. Bel-Marduk himself was always clearly a Biblical enemy, and is mentioned by name both regarding the conquest of Israel....

> "But these peoples began to make their own gods in the various cities in which they were living; in the shrines on the high places which the Samarians had made, each people set up gods. Thus the Babylonians made Marduk and his consort..." (2 Kings 17:29-30, NAB)
>
> ...and also regarding the Jews' eventual freedom from Babylonian captivity:
>
> "Declare ye among the nations, and publish, and set up a standard; publish, and conceal not: say, Babylon is taken, Bel is confounded, Merodach[45] is broken in pieces; her idols are confounded, her images are broken in pieces."
>
> (Jeremiah 50:2, KJV)

I must admit that I find it almost perplexing that, despite all the Biblical evidence to the contrary, there are those who adhere to the

---

43 R. Ghirshman, *Iran*, p.191. The passage from Herodotus' *Histories* referenced in the previous chapter concludes with the mention of Xerxes/Ahasuerus' seizing of the statue (and also of his slaying the priest of Marduk who tried to stop him) without making reference to the resulting Babylonian revolt.

44 Esther A:10.

45 The Biblical Hebrew spelling of "Marduk" (מרדך *Mem resh dal kaph*). This name could be interpreted logographically as something along the lines of "The Mighty/Chaos (מ) at the Top/Beginning (ר) Moves (or is Hung (ד)/Bent/ Opened/Allowed to Enter) to a state of Tameness (כ)", yet it may be reasonable to assume that even in so ancient and mystical a language as Hebrew not every word has a deep and significant logographical interpretation. However, the meaning of the whole word is "thy rebellion." See Isaiah 63:10 for God's attitude regarding rebellion.

belief that God Himself endorses slavery. However, if the belief is present then it must be addressed, and it must be understood to have been entirely foreign in origin.

The Babylonians, as with so many ancient peoples, worked explanations for their own ways of life into their mythology. In this case said way of life involved a cruel system of forcing disenfranchised people to perform those tasks which those of higher station in society did not wish to do.

The LORD as God of Freedom

What a mystery the ways of the LORD must have seemed to these ancient peoples! How strange and perplexing it must have been that He would be more concerned with love and all its resulting vulnerabilities than with mindless, unquestioned compliance! How difficult they must have found it to believe in a God who wished to serve His creation rather than simply be served by it! However, such is the nature of the One who has overcome the world by peaceful means; the One who has no true rival for His position because He is truly Almighty.

> "Jesus called them together and said, 'You know that those who are regarded as rulers of the Gentiles lord it over them, and their high officials exercise authority over them.
>
> Not so with you. Instead, whoever wants to become great among you must be your servant,
> and whoever wants to be first must be slave of all.
> For even the Son of Man did not come to be served, but to serve, and to give his life as a ransom for many.[46]'" (Mark 10:42-45, New International Version)
>
> "And all things, whatsoever ye shall ask in prayer, believing, ye shall receive." (Matthew 21:22, KJV)

---

46 The value/price placed upon Him by the sinful – 30 silver shekels – (Zechariah 11:13, Matthew 26:15) being that of a slave gored by an ox according to Exodus 21:32.

Still, much as was the case with ritual sacrifice, slavery was assumed by the Ancient Israelites and their ancestors to be a normal part of society. Thus it was that even Noah, by far the most noble and faithful man in a society of wicked ones[47], endeavoured to invoke that institution of said society to punish his son Ham by cursing his offspring:

> "he said:
> 'Cursed be Canaan!
> The lowest of slaves
> Shall he be to his brothers.'
> He also said:
> 'Blessed be the LORD, the God of Shem!
> Let Canaan be his slave.
> May God expand Japheth,
> so that he dwells among the tents of Shem;
> and let Canaan be his slave.'" (Genesis 9:25-27, NAB)

However, when one considers that Noah's attempt to issue the Bible's first recorded decree of slavery was intended as retribution upon Ham/Canaan, his dictate was destined to backfire somewhat spectacularly. Not only was Ham's son Mizraim the founder of Egypt[48], but his son Cush became the father of Nimrod, "the first potentate on earth...a mighty hunter by the grace of the LORD..." and the founder of Babylon[49]; both nations that would eventually enslave and/or conquer Israel. In his vengeful effort to make slaves, the otherwise-virtuous Noah instead made enemies and conquerors of his chosen sons.

(As an aside, it may be noted that alcohol was involved in Noah's situation and possibly in his decision, just as it was in the decision to elect Marduk champion of the Annunaki Babylonian deities.)

Noah's attempt to re-instate a horrific quality of the society eradicated by God, to which he formerly belonged, proved disastrous as part of God's grand-scale plan, and God never failed to remind His

---

47 Genesis 6:5-8.

48 Genesis 10:5-6; see footnote in New American Holy Bible (School and Church Edition).

49 Genesis 10:8-10.

people of that fact. Even the preamble to the Ten Commandments makes it clear that the LORD is a God of freedom:

> "I am the LORD thy God, which have brought thee out of the land of Egypt, out of the house of bondage.
> Thou shalt have no other gods before me."
> (Exodus 20:2-3, KJV, the former verse reiterated in Deuteronomy 5:15)

However, slavery as an institution already existed and thus was acknowledged quite soon thereafter, though its approach became less harsh compared to that of the surrounding nations, and it would eventually improve. Due to a similarity of antecedents and of general initial intellectual/cultural outlook, Israel's original rules involving slavery possess parallels with those of Hammurabi, first ruler of the Babylonian empire (whose famous code of laws carved in a stone slab begins with "Anu and Bel called by name me, Hammurabi, the exalted prince, who feared Marduk, the chief god of Babylon, to bring about the rule in the land."[50]). The Code of Hammurabi involved scaled punishments for transgression depending upon social status (such as whether one was a slave or a free man) and allowed a man to sell their daughters (or even wives) into slavery.

The Mosaic law described in Exodus 21 also reveals that a Hebrew man could be enslaved against his will, though only for a limited duration[51], and while women were still to be permanent slaves, the details of their slavery indicate a preference toward them either going free or becoming legal members of their owners' families:

> "And if a man sell his daughter to be a maidservant, she shall not go out as the menservants do.
>
> If she please not her master, who hath betrothed her to himself, then shall he let her be redeemed: to sell her unto a

50 Barton, G.A.: *Archaeology and the Bible.* University of Michigan Library, 2009, p. 406.

51 Exodus 21:2.

> strange nation he shall have no power, seeing he hath dealt deceitfully with her.
>
> And if he have betrothed her unto his son, he shall deal with her after the manner of daughters.
>
> If he take him another wife; her food, her raiment, and her duty of marriage, shall he not diminish.
>
> And if he do not these three unto her, then shall she go out free without money. [ie. She shall go out free without having to pay money for her freedom.]" (Exodus 21:7-11, KJV)

Still, despite these amendments, the Israelites retained the institution of slavery, and it remained an unfair and wretched practice no matter how accustomed to it they were. Perhaps Moses realized this, and entreated God for a superior compromise between His desires and those of His people. In any case, the law was changed in Deuteronomy prior to Moses' death:

> "For the poor[52] shall never cease out of the land: therefore I command thee, saying, Thou shalt open thine hand wide unto thy brother, to thy poor, and to thy needy, in thy land.
>
> And if thy brother, an Hebrew man, or an Hebrew woman, be sold unto thee, and serve thee six years; then in the seventh year thou shalt let him go free from thee.
>
> And when thou sendest him out free from thee, thou shalt not let him go away empty[53]:
>
> Thou shalt furnish him liberally out of thy flock, and out of thy floor, and out of thy winepress: of that wherewith the LORD thy God hath blessed thee thou shalt give unto him.

52 In the ancient world, it was not uncommon for the desperately impoverished to sell even themselves into slavery; see Deuteronomy 28:68.

53 Cf. Exodus 12:35-36.

> And thou shalt remember that thou wast a bondman in the land of Egypt, and the LORD thy God redeemed thee: therefore I command thee this thing to day. ...
>
> ...And also unto thy maidservant thou shalt do likewise.
>
> It shall not seem hard unto thee, when thou sendest him away free from thee; for he hath been worth a double hired servant to thee, in serving thee six years: and the LORD thy God shall bless thee in all that thou doest." (Deuteronomy 15:11-18, KJV)

One must ask: does this passage come from a God who is fond of slavery, or One who seeks to gradually lead His people – who have free will and thus a capacity to create such terrible things as slavery – away from such foul ways? I invite the reader to compare this to Marduk's statement earlier in this chapter, and note that this passage too is accompanied by God's reminder that the Israelites were once slaves themselves in the land of Egypt–until God delivered them.

Perpetuation of Slavery in Biblical Times and Beyond

This reminder also has great importance when we return to the enslavement of African-Americans referred to at the beginning of this chapter. As noted before, in his advice as to how one is to make a slave, William Lynch overtly compared the situation of slave-owners in the southern United States with that of the enemies of the Israelites in the very Bible he presumed to cherish. Thus it was only fitting that the slaves who served such slave-owners compared their own situation with that of God's chosen people in that same text.

The story of Exodus – of the Israelites' escape from slavery into the Promised Land – was a story quite inspirational to the African-Americans of the South, and this inspiration often appeared in the spiritual songs they employed to encourage one another. Songs such as "Wade in the Water" and "Go Down Moses" give strong indication of the significance of the Bible in inspiring those seeking emancipation, as they are filled with lyrics that encourage those singing to flee from bondage and be free in Christ.

Frederick Douglass, an escaped slave, abolitionist author, supporter of women's suffrage, and cautious Methodist offered explanation of the dual-meaning behind slaves' singing of such songs. He noted that keen observers might have detected more than just a recollection of the sufferings of God's chosen or an expression of the hope of reaching heaven. The stories of the Bible must endure because they must inspire, and that is exactly what they did for the slaves: the North was their "Canaan"; their Promised Land in which they would escape the evils of slavery.

Another Methodist, Sojourner Truth, who simply explained her abolitionist preaching as being because, "The Spirit calls me, and I must go," herself led an "Exodus" to Kansas in an effort to find available land for former slaves. So strong was the Biblical parallel to them that these slaves even became known as "exodusters".

To truly bear witness to the full effects that Judeo-Christianity has had upon the world, one must at times go beyond the Bible and gaze as we have begun to do across the time that has passed since its writing. In this case, it is useful to examine how Scriptural debate effected attitudes regarding slavery. As slavery was already the bedrock of Roman world society, there existed an inherent temptation for the emerging Christians to maintain the status quo of the civilization from whence they came. However, this is precisely the same reason why slavery was practised in the Old Testament, save that rather than doing as the Romans did the Israelites instead imitated Babylon. Regardless of the era, God's attitude toward slavery did not change.

> "Now when all the princes, and all the people, which had entered into the covenant, heard that every one should let his manservant, and every one his maidservant, go free, that none should serve themselves of them any more, then they obeyed, and let them go.
>
> But afterward they turned, and caused the servants and the handmaids, whom they had let go free, to return, and brought them into subjection for servants and for handmaids.

Therefore the word of the LORD came to Jeremiah from the LORD, saying:

Thus saith the LORD, the God of Israel; I made a covenant with your fathers in the day that I brought them forth out of the land of Egypt, out of the house of bondmen, saying,

At the end of seven years let ye go every man his brother an Hebrew, which hath been sold unto thee; and when he hath served thee six years, thou shalt let him go free from thee: but your fathers hearkened not unto me, neither inclined their ear.

And ye were now turned, and had done right in my sight, in proclaiming liberty every man to his neighbour; and ye had made a covenant before me in the house which is called by my name:

But ye turned and polluted my name, and caused every man his servant, and every man his handmaid, whom he had set at liberty at their pleasure, to return, and brought them into subjection, to be unto you for servants and for handmaids.

Therefore thus saith the LORD; Ye have not hearkened unto me, in proclaiming liberty, every one to his brother, and every man to his neighbour: behold, I proclaim a liberty for you, saith the LORD, to the sword, to the pestilence, and to the famine; and I will make you to be removed into all the kingdoms of the earth.

And I will give the men that have transgressed my covenant, which have not performed the words of the covenant which they had made before me, when they cut the calf in twain, and passed between the parts thereof,

The princes of Judah, and the princes of Jerusalem, the eunuchs, and the priests, and all the people of the land, which passed between the parts of the calf;

> I will even give them into the hand of their enemies, and into the hand of them that seek their life: and their dead bodies shall be for meat unto the fowls of the heaven, and to the beasts of the earth.
>
> And Zedekiah king of Judah and his princes will I give into the hand of their enemies, and into the hand of them that seek their life, and into the hand of the king of Babylon's army, which are gone up from you.
>
> Behold, I will command, saith the LORD, and cause them to return to this city; and they shall fight against it, and take it, and burn it with fire: and I will make the cities of Judah a desolation without an inhabitant." (Jeremiah 34:10-24 (KJV))

I humbly submit that, given the evidence of the preceding passage, it is reasonable to assume that God is not terribly fond of slavery. However, as slave-owners and those benefiting from them doubtless found this truth tremendously inconvenient, there continued to be argument – even within the Church – as to whether or not such 'Christians' could rationalize slavery into perpetuation.

Slavery and Christianity

Though the nature of Roman society seemed to dictate the necessity of slavery, there was opposition to it from within the Christian community from very early on. A number of prominent Catholics campaigned against slavery from as early as the 5th Century (the decline of the Western Roman Empire). Some of these Catholics had even been slaves themselves, such as St. Patrick, who had served Pagan owners in Ireland from a young age, and St. Balthilda, who used her royal stature to abolish the trading of Christian slaves and dedicated her efforts to buying and freeing children who were already enslaved. This attitude toward the practice remained Saintly, as even at the end of the 1800s (and her life) The Little Flower, Saint Theresa of Lisieux, insisted that any money that otherwise would have been spent attending to her funeral instead be spent "rescuing poor little negroes from slavery."[54] (This was by no means a derogatory term, for everything in the world was "poor" and "little" to Ste. Thérèse; herself most of all). However, though by the end of the Medieval Period the slavery of Christians was largely abolished, there was a history of Catholic clergy, religious orders, and even Popes owning slaves. Nevertheless, throughout its history the Catholic Church has constantly endeavoured to alleviate the evils of slavery and repeatedly denounced the mass enslavement of conquered populations and the slave trade (thereby undermining slavery at its sources)[55], and by 1538 Pope Paul III had made three major pronouncements against the very institution of slavery.

Why, one asks, was there such ambiguity in the attitudes of Christianity? In addition to human corruption, it was also due to apparent ambiguity within the Scriptures. In the words of His Eminence Cardinal Avery Robert Dulles:

> "Throughout Christian antiquity and the Middle Ages, theologians generally followed St. Augustine in holding that although slavery was not written into the natural moral law it was not absolutely forbidden by that law."
>
> ("Development or Reversal?" Review of *A Church That Can and Cannot Change: The Development of Catholic Moral Teaching* by John T. Noonan, Jr. (University of Notre Dame Press))

Saint Augustine of Hippo, who lived from 354-430 and was quite taken with the writings of Saint Paul the Apostle, endeavoured to balance the evils of the age with virtuous conduct (just as he balanced his Platonic education with the teachings of Christianity, of course heavily favouring the latter) so that a greater good might eventually be achieved. This is evidenced by his attempt to reconcile the obvious evils of war with said institution's apparent necessity in his framing of the concept of a Just War and its requirements, and he took the same

---

54 Rev. Albert M. Hutting. *The Life of the Little Flower.* 1942. http://www.jesus-passion.com/LittleFlower7.htm Retrieved Thursday, November 15th of 2012.

55 From the statements of His Eminence, Cardinal Avery Robert Dulles, S.J.

approach to slavery. Such an approach to the supposedly-vital institution of slavery (presumed so vital, in fact that it was present even in the 'ideal cities' of Plato's *Laws* or *Republic*) in the civilizations of the time was taken not only by him, but also by those who preceded him.

With the coming of Christ, God's desires for His people – the people of the world – became more apparent, and no longer did their foreign policy involve thousands of warriors accompanied by a storm of hail or pounding rain. Instead the Apostles were given the difficult task to "Go therefore and make disciples of all the nations"[56] without conquering these nations in the traditional manner. Thus the Apostles found it necessary to exert their influence diplomatically, being respectful of even the more abhorrent traditions of other cultures until such time as it became possible to abolish such practices entirely. This was also the approach of the highly-influential Apostle Paul, and just as he permitted God's worship to be explained as that of the "Unknown God" amongst the Roman idols of Athens in Acts 17:23, so too did he take a careful approach to the potentially society-threatening statement of Jesus in Matthew 23:10 (KJV):

> "Neither be ye called masters: for one is your Master, even Christ."

In their meekness and humility, the Apostles of the Epistles held to this teaching especially faithfully with regards to their own selves; even referring to themselves as *doulos* (Greek for "slaves" or "bondservants") of Jesus Christ and/or God in the very first of the verses of Romans, Philippians, Titus, James, 2 Peter, Jude, and Revelation. However, in certain other Epistles slaves are admonished to obey their "masters according to the flesh"[57] faithfully even though they are being treated unjustly[58] as though they were obeying God[59] so that His worship would be well-received by their cultures[60], and to take comfort in the fact that

---

56 Matthew 28:19, New American Standard Bible.

57 Ephesians 6:5, KJV.

58 1 Peter 2:18-20.

59 Ephesians 6:7.

60 1 Timothy 6:1.

they would be saved despite being of the lowest of castes[61]. In his Epistle to Philemon, the Apostle Paul actually returns a fugitive slave named Onesimus to the aforementioned Philemon, albeit with exhortations to receive him...

> "Not now as a servant, but above a servant, a brother beloved, specially to me, but how much more unto thee, both in the flesh, and in the Lord?
>
> If thou count me therefore a partner, receive him as myself." (Philemon 1:16-17, KJV)

It may be worth noting that while this Epistle also does not contain Paul's referring to himself as a *doulos*, it does contain in its first verse and elsewhere his describing himself as a *desmios* (Greek for "prisoner") of Jesus Christ. Among the Epistles in which the writers refer to themselves as *doulos*, there is one which has been used in the argument of advocates for the institution of slavery:

> "Exhort servants to be obedient unto their own masters, and to please them well in all things; not answering again;
> Not purloining, but shewing all good fidelity; that they may adorn the doctrine of God our Saviour in all things." (Titus 2:9-10, KJV)

This passage seems to contradict Jesus' teaching, and thus was utilized effectively against those who oppose slavery as He does; though to be perverted in such a manner it needed to be utilized without drawing attention to that fact. Such a doctored approach (which favourably ignored such passages as Paul's First Epistle to the Corinthians 7:21, which encouraged slaves to seek their freedom whenever possible) inspired the necessity to distinguish between "Master's Preaching" and "Real Preaching":

> "'The preacher ... he'd just say, 'Serve your masters. Don't steal your master's turkey. Don't steal your master's

---

[61] Colossians 3:22-25, Ephesians 6:8.

> chickens...hogs...meat. Do whatsomever your master tells you to do.' Same old thing all the time..... Sometimes they (the slaves) would ... want a real meetin' with some real preachin'...."
>
> (Lucretia Alexander, quoted from *Slave Religion: The 'Invisible Institution' in the Antebellum South*)

In the early stages of His plan for absolute salvation and emancipation of all who suffer in bondage, God dictated that even slaves should be introduced into His covenant, as indicated in Genesis 17:12 and Exodus 12:43-44. Thus Christian slave-owners found themselves torn between the commandment to spread God's word and the evil desire to retain the obedience and free labour of their slaves. Some utilized the technique of Scriptural vitiation described above, whilst others thought it safer to simply forbid the faith from being spread amongst the slaves.

Former slave John Brown described two harrowing extremes from his own experience. When interviewed, he spoke of how Sunday was a great day for everyone on the plantation where he worked. The Sabbath day of rest meant that the slaves did not need to work in the fields, and thus they hurried through the light chores and everyone prepared for the church meeting. This took place outside, where Brown's 'Master' John's wife would lead the meeting; with a prayer followed by the singing of what Brown described as "old timey" songs. However, on the neighbouring plantation the white folks would beat their slaves for trying to imitate those on Brown's. Neither praying nor singing were permitted there. Some slave-owners not only did not allow their slaves to go to church but also ridiculed the very notion of permitting slaves to partake of religion, for they refused to believe that Negroes even had souls. Others had a more pragmatic reason for forbidding their slaves to attend church: as an ex-slave explained, they were afraid that the slaves would begin to think themselves free if they had such things as churches.[62]

Rather than driving the enslaved Africans away from Christ, however, such harsh tyranny had a different result. As Lucretia

---

62 *Slave Religion: The 'Invisible Institution' in the Antebellum South.*

Alexander noted, slaves would instead pray and sing their songs in a whisper to avoid detection, just like the early Christians under Roman rule.[63] Christianity is a dangerous religion to have if one wishes to oppress others.

> "Then said Jesus to those Jews which believed on him, If ye continue in my word, then are ye my disciples indeed;
>
> And ye shall know the truth, and the truth shall make you free.
>
> They answered him, We be Abraham's seed, and were never in bondage to any man[64]: how sayest thou, Ye shall be made free?
>
> Jesus answered them, Verily, verily, I say unto you, Whosoever committeth sin is the servant of sin.
>
> And the servant abideth not in the house for ever: but the Son abideth ever.
>
> If the Son therefore shall make you free, ye shall be free indeed."
>
> (John 8:31-36, KJV)

Roman Catholic Father Chris Pietraszko noted the connection between spiritual slavery and its manifestation in the world with regard to human beings enslaved for labour, stating that "scripture is not plainly dealing with legal-slavery but something much more destructive and the actual root of slavery itself: sin." Romans 6:12-22 and 8:21 elaborate upon this, revealing that God has freed us from mortal corruption so that we may help to fulfill His purpose.

Still, some slaves also took Jesus' statements in the above passage (and its final verse in particular) to mean exactly and literally what it

---

63 Ibid.

64 The New American Holy Bible (2003-2004 Edition) refers to this statement as "Johannine irony" because the Jews were almost continuously enslaved throughout Biblical history.

appears to mean: that those who become Christian are freed from all slavery. They thus met with amazing results in their belief. In Virginia in 1656, Elizabeth Key, the illegitimate daughter of a slave woman, successfully sued for her freedom from slavery on grounds which included her having been baptized. Twelve years earlier in 1644, "a mulatto named Manuel[65]" who had been purchased "as a Slave for Ever," was instead:

> "by the Assembly adjudged no Slave and but to Serve as other Christian servants do and was freed in September 1665" *(Virginia Magazine of History and Biography,* Vol. XVII, No. 3 (July 1909))

Such events as these had become so prevalent by 1666 that the Virginia Assembly was prompted to issue a law in the following year specifically declaring that baptism of slaves did not exempt them from bondage:

> "Whereas some doubts have risen whether...slaves...by the charity and piety of their owners made pertakers of the blessed sacrament of baptisme, should by vertue of their baptisme be made free; *It is enacted*...the conferring of baptisme doth not alter the condition of the person as to his bondage or ffreedome...."
>
> (*Slavery and the Rise of the Atlantic System*, edited by Barbara L. Solow, 1993, p. 271, chapter by David W. Galenson)

Such legal interventions were not isolated to this one act. In 1671, the Maryland Assembly enacted a parallel law; this one specifically intended to ensure that slave-owners would not be so discouraged at the thought of their property being freed by Jesus that they would stop importing slaves altogether.[66]

---

65 Whose name itself reminds one of the song lyrics, "O come, o come, Emmanuel, and ransom captive Israel..." referencing the Roman occupation of which William Lynch appeared so fond.

66 *Slavery and the Rise of the Atlantic System*, edited by Barbara L. Solow, 1993, p. 272, chapter by David W. Galenson

There you have it: all Christians have to do to perpetuate slavery is **outlaw the teachings of Christ!**

> "No longer do I call you slaves, for the slave does not know what his master is doing; but I have called you friends, for all things that I have heard from My Father I have made known to you." (John 15:15, NASB)

By 1682, the Christian tide against slavery had risen so high that there actually was a notable and permanent concession made. An act was released that year stating that "all servants...which shall be imported into this country either by sea or by land, whether Negroes, Moors [Muslim North Africans], mulattoes or Indians" should be considered slaves according to all laws *unless said people were Christian prior to their "first purchase"*.[67]

The actual attitude of Christianity was well-described by Pope Paul III over a century earlier, as he forbade the enslavement of the First-Nations peoples of the Americas (called "Indians of the West and the South" at the time) and with them all other people in the Papal bull *Sublimus Dei.* Written in 1537 A.D., *Sublimus Dei* openly condemned slavery as an instrument of Satan, intended by the Devil to both impede the preaching of the Word of God to the nations and to cause the beloved human race to "be reduced to our service like brute animals". His Holiness also specifically stated in this bull that "by our Apostolic Authority [we] decree and declare by these present letters that the same Indians and all other peoples – even though they are outside the faith – ...should not be deprived of their liberty."

Among Christians, the Catholic Church was to find herself by no means alone in her anti-slavery position. It has been noted previously that some of the most prominent ex-slave proponents of abolition – such as Sojourner Truth – were Methodists, and there was good cause for such a selection. John Wesley, founder of the Methodist movement, led his followers to become leaders in abolitionist movements and the propagation of Christianity, holding to the belief that all people have

---

[67] *Through the Storm, Through the Night: A History of African American Christianity* by Paul Harvey

the opportunity for salvation through faith. Wesley himself was a keen abolitionist, famously remarking in one of his tracts against the slave trade:

> "Liberty is the right of every human creature[68], as soon as he breathes the vital air; and no human law can deprive him of that right which he derives from the law of nature." (*Thoughts Upon Slavery*, circa 1774)

I have thusfar made much mention of slavery in the United States of America, and I would that in reference to this I could recount some of my own ancestors' experience with African-American slavery. I had non-European ancestors in Brazil during the time of the slave trade, however (though I am not certain if they were slaves or not), for Brazil was the last country in the Western world in which slavery was abolished. The slave trade there received stiff opposition from the Jesuit missionaries as early as the 17th Century along with other evangelical groups throughout its history, yet it would not see the final destruction of the institution until the arrival of the very-unambitious yet very-Christian Princess-Imperial nicknamed "the Redemptress".

Dona Isabel was the heiress presumptive to the throne of the Empire of Brazil after the deaths of her two brothers in infancy. However, her otherwise-loving father, Emperor Dom Pedro II, could not bring himself to believe that a single woman could be a viable ruler. Fortuitously, a Higher Power than the emperor was of a different opinion, and the latter fell ill in March of 1887 and was advised to seek medical help in Europe, leaving the devoutly-Catholic Isabel as Regent of Brazil. Isabel, as she herself stated, "became ever more convinced that some action had to be taken" to expand the emancipation program there. After the police of Brazil's current government mishandled a pro-abolition demonstration in early 1888, Isabel replaced it with one which would swiftly introduce legislation for unconditional abolition. In a manner inviting comparison with the heroic actions of the Biblical Queen Esther, on the 13th of

68 It is probably safe to assume that this phrase was the inspiration for *Transformers* protagonist Optimus Prime's famous statement that "Freedom is the right of all sentient beings."

May 1888 Isabel took an action which would place her at considerable personal risk: signing a document enabling the complete cessation of slavery which was known as *A Lei Aurea*; the Golden Law (for which she was given a Golden Rose by the Pope). She and her father lost the support of slave-owning plantation owners and the great political, economic and social power they held. Additionally, Isabel had no interest in the machinations and intrigues of politics, and her religious zeal was distrusted. On 15 November 1889, Pedro II and his family peacefully responded to a military coup by going into exile in Europe, and on the following day Isabel wrote,

> "If abolition is the cause for this, I don't regret it; I consider it worth losing the throne for."
> (Barman, Roderick J. (1999). Citizen Emperor: Pedro II and the Making of Brazil, 1825-1891. Stanford, California: Stanford University Press. p. 249.)

Jesus Christ is clearly of the opinion that absolute servitude to a human being, or in fact anything other than the LORD, is wrong:

> "No servant can serve two masters: for either he will hate the one, and love the other; or else he will hold to the one, and despise the other. Ye cannot serve God and mammon[69]."
> (Matthew 6:24 & Luke 16:13, KJV)

The fact that in this verse Jesus is referring to wealth is of particular note due to the pro-slavery argument used by Lynch and his many predecessors throughout history: that of 'good economics.' It is quite evident, however, that economics matter not to the One who is truly Good, and that slavery is despised by Him. It is thus unfortunate indeed that His followers were more ambiguous on that issue, and could issue such statements as those referenced earlier along with such ones as the first verse of the fifth chapter of Saint Paul's Epistle to the Galatians:

---

69 "*Mammonas*"; Aramaic personification of wealth.

> "Stand fast therefore in the liberty wherewith Christ hath made us free, and be not entangled again with the yoke of bondage." (KJV)

Such confusing contradiction is found in the Bible! Whose words are we to heed: those of the Apostles and Saints (when they still walked the earth), or those of Jesus Christ and the LORD our God?!?

This is, of course, a rhetorical question.

As such, let this chapter end with another verse penned by Paul, and one by which the entire purpose of this book is supported:

> "There is neither Jew nor Greek, there is neither bond nor free, there is neither male nor female: for ye are all one in Christ Jesus." (Galatians 3:28, KJV)

Chapter the 4th

The Holy Race[70]

Issues of Biblical Racism

As their collective name suggests, the Abrahamic religions (Judaism, Christianity, and Islam) began with God's revelation to one person – Abraham – so that they might miraculously spread to all the peoples of the world. This is a symbolic and appropriate approach to a universe such as ours, which is 95% dark energy and dark matter; just as the warmth of a single candle flame is sufficient to keep everything in the universe from becoming frozen at absolute zero[71], a tiny point of light was destined to illuminate everything. However, in a universe that is so dark, cold and empty, competition for resources can easily become fierce between peoples. This produces a clan mentality that pits the familiar against the unfamiliar, and thus racial hatred is born. Case in point:

> "And Haman said unto king Ahasuerus, There is a certain people scattered abroad and dispersed among the people in all the provinces of thy kingdom; and their laws are diverse from all people; neither keep they the king's laws: therefore it is not for the king's profit to suffer them." (Esther 3:8-9, KJV)

The Biblical passage above refers to the Jewish people and could easily be Nazi propaganda, were it not approximately 23 centuries too early. Nevertheless, even this immense span of time was unable to keep it from becoming Nazi propaganda.

---

70 Ezra 9:2.

71 The basis for the Kelvin scale, absolute zero is the theoretical coldest temperature which anything could possibly reach; at absolute zero, atoms simply and utterly cease to move. It is the equivalent of -273 degrees Celsius.

On January 30th of 1944, Adolf Hitler gave a radio-broadcast speech to the German folk in which he, like William Lynch before him, openly identified with a Biblical villain. In this case, the role-model was Haman from the Book of Esther. Accusing the Allies of "submissive petting" on this issue, Hitler gave an apocalyptic imagining of the future in which they had failed to "detoxify the Jewish bacteria." If Jews were permitted to compete freely – if Germany did not win – Hitler stated that the fate of the Americas and the entire western world would be decided in a matter of months. Even more preposterous, he predicted that ten years later European culture would have been erased, and that the spiritual leadership of these nations would at best be exiled to the forests and swamps of Siberia. Finally, he referred to the Jewish people collectively as Ahasuerus [the Persian king who heeded Esther and punished Haman], suggesting that they might at this point celebrate all of this in a new Purim[72] festival.[73]

Hitler effectively united the ancient hatred with his own hateful cause, using the standard techniques of relying on the fear and ignorance of his audience to support his patently ridiculous claims. He was not alone in embracing the parallel between Haman and himself, either. Julius Streicher, publisher of the anti-Semitic Nazi newspaper *Der Sturmer*[74] ("The Stormtrooper"), maintained this connection even unto his final moment. Seconds before he was hanged as a war criminal on October 16, 1946, he looked down at the witnesses present and shouted, *"Purim Fest 1946!"*[75]

---

72 Purim is a Jewish early-spring celebration of Esther's God-given strategic and diplomatic triumph over Haman's attempted destruction of the Jews (Esther 9:17-22).

73 *Wolfsschanze*, January 30, 1944. http://der-fuehrer.org/reden/english/44-01-30.htm Retrieved Tuesday, October 2nd, 2012.

74 *Literally, "The Stormer," "The Stormtrooper," or "The Attacker." Published weekly in tabloid-format from 1923 until the end of World War II,* it was also anti-Catholic and for a time echoed the idea proposed by Adolf Hitler in his book *Mein Kampf*: that Jews should be deported and left "alone in this world...[to] exterminate one another." Claudia Koonz, *The Nazi Conscience*, pp. 225-236.

75 According to "The Execution of Nazi War Criminals" by Kingsbury Smith (*The Nuremberg Trials: Newspaper Accounts*, http://law2.umkc.edu/faculty/

It may seem a strange phenomenon when supposed Christians identify themselves with Biblical villains. Hatred is so adept at obfuscating the truth, however, that it can cause almost anything to seem sensible in its heat. So widely-acknowledged were these Biblical parallels that they became entirely intertwined with the Nazi movement.

*The Nazis often deliberately scheduled their attacks for Jewish holidays in an effort to make mockery of celebrations of sacred history. The final destruction of the Warsaw Ghetto began on the first night of Passover, 1943. On Purim,*1942, ten Jews were hanged in Zdunska-Wola to avenge the hanging of Haman's ten sons (Esther 9:13; though unlike Esther Hitler clearly demanded that these people be hanged while still alive). This latter act of brutality was intended as a retroactive undoing of the Purim miracle, and the Jews present were even told that they constituted a minyan.[76] The following year in Zdunska-Wola saw the hanging of another ten Jews; this time on Shavuot, festival of Sinai, in revenge for the Ten Commandments. Though officially the vengeance was ironically for "the arrogance of believing that they are the chosen

---

projects/ftrials/nuremberg/NurembergNews10_16_46.html Retrieved 02/10/2012) "Streicher was swung suddenly to face the witnesses and glared at them. Suddenly he screamed, 'Purim Fest 1946.'", then "shouted" at the American officer standing at the scaffold, "The Bolsheviks will hang you one day." Finally, when "the black hood was raised over his head, Streicher's muffled voice could be heard to say, 'Adele, my dear wife.'" Thus "Purim Fest 1946" was apparently his third-to-last statement and his final "scream."

76 A minyan is defined as the number of people required, according to Jewish law, to be present for the conducting of a communal religious service. Traditionally this is a minimum of 10 Jewish males at least 13 years of age. http://dictionary.reference.com/browse/minyan?s=t Retrieved 03/10/2012. A more in-depth account of the event is found here: "Flanked by German officers, he was forced to stand on [a] stepladder and deliver a speech justifying the hangings." He spoke in Yiddish, clarifying before each statement that the Germans ordered him to say that: "The Jews [are] being hanged for their crimes against Germany, they [are] being hanged in revenge for Haman, they constituted a minyan, and this was how Purim should be celebrated." Neuman, Isaac (with Michael Palencia-Roth). *The Narrow Bridge: Beyond the Holocaust.* "Purim Revenge", p. 81.

ones", considering the behaviour of the Nazis it might aswell have been upon the Ten Commandments themselves.[77]

There are those who claim that the events of the Book of Esther never happened; that the story was some form of Biblical fairy-tale. However, whatever one may believe, clearly Esther was real enough for the Nazis, as it was for those who did indeed have cause to celebrate a second Purim.

Adolf Hitler sought to unite his desperate country and used a hideously-easy way to do so: through common hatred. Like Haman and Willie Lynch before him, he attempted to magnify apparent differences and reassure the majority that it could use such differences to somehow improve its situation. He then fanned the hate until it obscured all reason, for hatred is a fire; it can be one's warmth, and it can be one's hell.

> "But more fiery is the Love of thy God" - St. Theresa of Lisieux[78]

Integration of Foreign Elements in Ancient Israel

Such intense examples of national hatred serve as a reminder that racism transcends time, place, culture and race. In the case above and also in the prevailing attitude among Old Testament writers, the exclusivity of racial identity found its basis in all of these things, though in the latter case the emphasis was placed on service to the LORD. Yet was such racial exclusivity ever truly acceptable service to Him?

No. No it was not. This was evident quite early on indeed.

God's revealing Himself and establishing Israel as a nation of His chosen people involved – through necessity at this early point in human history so far as Moses was concerned – removing the influence of Pagan cultures, even through the destruction of said cultures. As was noted in the 2nd chapter of this book, this at the time included the forbiddance

77 "Survival" by Yossi Klein Halevi, Arthur Allen Cohen, *20th Century Jewish Religious Thought:Original Essays on Critical Concepts*, pp. 948-949.

78 *Joan of Arc Accomplishes Her Mission*, Part II: The Captivity. The Martyrdom. Scène 11.

of mixed marriages[79], and the slaughter demanded by Moses for the enforcement of this may best be described as ruthless:

> "And Israel abode in Shittim, and the people began to commit whoredom with the daughters of Moab.
>
> And they called the people unto the sacrifices of their gods: and the people did eat, and bowed down to their gods. ...
>
> And Moses said unto the judges of Israel, Slay ye every one his men that were joined unto Baalpeor.
>
> And behold, one of the children of Israel came and brought unto his brethren a Midianitish[80] woman in the sight of Moses, and in the sight of all the congregation of the children of Israel, who were weeping before the door of the tabernacle of the congregation.
>
> And when Phinehas, the son of Eleazar, the son of Aaron the priest, saw it, he rose up from among the congregation, and took a javelin in his hand;
>
> And he went after the man of Israel into the tent, and thrust both of them through, the man of Israel, and the woman through her belly...." (Numbers 25:1-2, 5-8, KJV)

As was addressed earlier, God was willing to accept a certain measure of zeal for His name[81], yet since the expression of this zeal also broke His Commandments it became necessary for His people to be subtly shown the error of their ways. God's chosen people were possessed of a fear of contamination by foreign elements, yet when these same foreign elements took the form of people who feared and loved Him, He granted them not only acceptance but also choice positions of lineage indeed. Of particular note are two Moabite women, the first being Rahab[82], ancestress of the Prophets Jeremiah and Ezekiel, and

---

79 Deuteronomy 7:3-4.

80 Moabites were in league with Midianites; see Numbers 22:4-7.

81 See also Numbers 31:1-18.

82 Joshua 2:9-13.

Ruth, ancestress of King David and (legally if not biologically) Jesus Christ. Indeed, the entire Book of Ruth is a story of how one woman's faith and love of the LORD transcended the boundaries of culture and race, as its heroine abandoned her heathen people to embrace those of Israel despite the threat of danger and poverty.

Psalm 45, a Song for a Royal Wedding, reveals requirements for full integration into Ancient Jewish society:

> "Listen, my daughter, and understand;
> pay me careful heed.
> Forget your people and your father's house,
> that the king might desire your beauty.
> He is your lord;
> honor him, daughter of Tyre. ..." (Psalm 45:11-13, NAB)

This passage suggests that there was little desire to have the princess/queen serve diplomatically to promote harmony between her culture of origin and that of her new husband (though that would later prove to be secretly the department of Esther and also be such without resulting in cultural sacrifice). It also reveals, however, that Israel's fear of cultural infiltration and infestation was slowly beginning to ebb. Kings could marry foreign wives, even at the risk of the kings being influenced by the Pagan practices of such wives. Nevertheless, the Song of Solomon (also titled the Song of Songs) provides considerable validation of the taking of foreign wives, for the singer is not truly Solomon but rather the Lord. It offers a poetic form of the sublime and mutual love between the Lord and His people; the Lord is represented by the Lover (Bridegroom) while His people are represented by the beloved (Bride).

Whom does the Lord select to represent His beloved? The woman in question describes herself thusly:

> "I am black, but comely, O ye daughters of Jerusalem, as the tents of Kedar, as the curtains of Solomon.
> Look not upon me, because I am black, because the sun hath looked upon me: my mother's children were angry with me; they made me the keeper of the vineyards; but mine own vineyard have I not kept." (Song of Solomon 1:5-6, KJV)

The Bride's self-description makes it clear that she is a foreigner... and that her appearance is different from that of the "daughters of Jerusalem." It is thus an especially intriguing question why even if the majority of translations are as this one, such translations as those of the Common English Bible, Contemporary English Version, GOD'S WORD Translation, and Young's Literal Translation give the opening of verse five not as "I am black, *but* comely" but rather as "I am black/ dark *and* beautiful/lovely...." Is this so because, in the name of modern political correctness, these versions have altered the Word of God?

NO.

Rather, God's original message – one which of course was *against* racism – was corrupted in the translation of the most-circulated Bible (the King James Version) by a sheer lack of understanding. This becomes apparent when one comprehends the original text (one of the Five Megillot Scrolls along with the Books of Ruth, Lamentations, Ecclesiastes, and Esther) in its original language of Ancient Hebrew. The original Hebrew did not distinguish a connecting word akin to the English "and" or "but" between its word for "black" ("*shachor*"[83]) and its word for "beautiful" ("*na'veh*"[84]). The original text simply read, "*Shachor 'aniy na'veh*", literally, "Black, I am beautiful."[85]

What we have in these two controversial verses is really an extolling of African skin tone despite its apparent unfamiliarity. The Bride explains her difference and reminds the daughters of Jerusalem that it is a thing of rare and exquisite beauty, like the riches of King Solomon. When it is translated in such a derogatory manner as it sadly was in the King James Version, such is entirely due to human prejudice. One could more accurately insert the word "and" than "but", or perhaps

---

83 Pronounced "shaw-khore."

84 Pronounced "naw-veh."

85 In his Foreword to the Book of [Jesus, Son of Eleazar, Son of] Sirach, the author's grandson wrote, "...words spoken originally in Hebrew are not as effective when translated into another language. That is true not only of this book but of the law itself, the prophets and the rest of the books, which differ no little when they are read in the original."

translate the section, "I am black, therefore beautiful...." However, in failing to consider this possibility, the caucasian Europeans who translated the King James version of the Bible perpetuated a lie for four centuries[86]. This was the sort of lie which contributed to others, such as those referenced in enslaved poetess Phillis Wheatley's *On Being Brought from Africa to America* (circa 1773). In it she notes that some scorn African Americans, considering their colour "a diabolic dye." She herself, however, refers to it as the valuable "sable" and reminds Christians that even if Cain was black (as Adam and Eve would logically be), those who shared such skin tone could be refined and join the angels.

Truly, Phillis Wheatley's parallels with the above verses are such that she could have *been* the Bride chosen of the Song of Songs. All human suffering stems from a lack of understanding. We must not let deceivers claim that which is fuel for our faith's flame.

It was not merely through intermarriage with women that God planned to expand the race of His chosen people. The LORD always actively encouraged the inclusion of foreigners:

> "But the stranger that dwelleth with you shall be unto you as one born among you, and thou shalt love him as thyself; for ye were strangers in the land of Egypt: I am the LORD your God." (Leviticus 19:34, KJV)[87]

Racial Prejudice in the New Testament and Later

This was the beginning of God's plan for His message to be spread to all peoples. It began with the Israelites, who struggled with God (the literal meaning of the name "Israel" being "God prevails") until His relationship with them was firmly established and the time of the arrival of Jesus Christ the Messiah had come:

> "And he said, It is a light thing that thou shouldest be my servant to raise up the tribes of Jacob, and to restore the

86 The King James Version of the Holy Bible was first published in 1611.

87 This is also reiterated in Numbers 9:14, Deuteronomy 10:19, and Ezekiel 47:23.

> preserved of Israel: I will also give thee for a light to the Gentiles, that thou mayest be my salvation unto the end of the earth." (Isaiah 49:6, KJV)

This passage is quoted in the Acts of the Apostles, though under less than pleasant circumstances:

> "Then Paul and Barnabas waxed bold, and said, It was necessary that the word of God should first have been spoken to you: but seeing ye put it from you, and judge yourselves unworthy of everlasting life, lo, we turn to the Gentiles.
>
> For so hath the Lord commanded us, saying, I have set thee to be a light of the Gentiles, that thou shouldest be for salvation unto the ends of the earth." (Acts 13:46-47, KJV)

Thus herein we find a triumphant statement overcoming racial exclusivity for the cause of good, though it has here been affected by sensations of bitter disappointment and bold judgement. While the Apostles themselves were entirely peaceful in their dismissal and departure from the Jews of that time, those who came after would use those particular Jews' rejection of Christ as an excuse to target them with hatred. We are creatures who stumble, and even a course taken with the best of intentions can lead into some foul places when a wrong turn is selected.

I needn't elaborate further upon the level of anti-Semitism that would be reached; I have referenced it at the beginning of this very chapter. It, like all true and persisting hatred, came from an exclusively human source, and as such it manifested also in racism against other peoples.

For instance, earlier in this book I alluded to Mahatma Gandhi's encountering a racial barrier which prevented him from becoming Christian. Biblical teachings had long acted as a panacea to many of India's problems during its freedom struggle, and Gandhi intently studied the Bible and the teachings of Jesus when he was a young man practicing law in South Africa. Seriously exploring becoming a Christian, Gandhi discovered a small church gathering in his locality and decided to attend service there.

Instead, he was stopped at the door and asked by a belligerent English man where a "*kaffir*" like him thought he was going. Gandhi replied that he would like to attend worship there. At that, the church elder snarled that there was no room for a '*kaffir*' in the church, ordered him to leave, and threatened to have his assistants throw Gandhi down the steps if he did not.[88]

Kaffir is a term used all-too-often to denote those with dusky skin – particularly those of African or Indian heritage – and, as hatred and ignorance go hand-in-hand, very few who employ it seem to know what it actually means. As an example, I recall watching part of *Serafina* (a feature film about apartheid South Africa starring Whoopi Goldberg) on *Youtube* three years ago and encountering a highly disturbing comment. It was left by someone who stated that he was so angry at his treatment by westerners (including their calling him *kaffir*) that he was going to join terrorist organization Al Qaeda. I endeavoured to remind this person that *kaffir* was actually an Arabic word meaning literally "nonbeliever" (it is also the title of the 109th *shura* of the Muslim *Quran*) and that thus if he were a *kaffir* then Al Qaeda was not the place for him!

As for Gandhi, he was no *kaffir*, though so-called Christians conquered by racism did their best to make him one. Gandhi himself stated to missionary E. Stanley Jones that, if Christians would truly live according to the teachings of Christ found in the Bible, all of India would be Christian now.[89] Gandhi's story thus brings to mind a particular teaching of Jesus Christ:

> "Whosoever therefore shall humble himself as this little child, the same is greatest in the kingdom of heaven.
>
> And whoso shall receive one such little child in my name receiveth me.
>
> But whoso shall offend one of these little ones which believe in me, it were better for him that a millstone were hanged

88 Samuel, Dibin. "Mahatma Gandhi and Christianity." *Christian Today.*

89 Samuel, Dibin. "Mahatma Gandhi and Christianity." *Christian Today.* 2008. http://in.christiantoday.com/articledir/print.htm?id=2837 Retrieved 02/10/2012.

> about his neck, and that he were drowned in the depth of the sea.
>
> Woe unto the world because of offences! for it must needs be that offences come; but woe to that man by whom the offence cometh!" (Matthew 18:4-7, KJV)

Instinctual Causes of Hatred

If hate comes not from God, from whence comes hate? Hatred may trace its biological origins to a perceived "survival instinct" of competitiveness for existence. To use a simple example from nature, the coral snake is a beautiful red, yellow/white, and black-banded creature possessing one of the most potent venoms of any North-American snake. The milk snake, however, is harmless; it produces no poison but rather is avoided merely because it closely resembles such venomous serpents as the coral snake. Intelligent humans have developed a mnemonic rhyme so that they might distinguish the two varieties[90] and thus become more confident of their safety. However, what if one were to have a friend slain by a coral snake without then having been given a precise visual description of it? Would one not – just to be safe – avoid (or even kill) a milk snake, if it were encountered? Indeed, would one not develop a fear of ALL serpents, regardless of their individual natures?[91]

Thus it is that hatred relies on intense emotion, prejudice, and the absence of understanding. After all, it requires ever so much less thought – and is thus easier to make split-second decisions – if one prejudges based upon a characteristic common to a large number of creatures, even when this characteristic is not the cause of the original shunning of the object of hatred. As with so many things that seem "necessary for survival" in this dark universe, it goes against the grain of Christ's teachings.

---

90 Specifically, "If red touches yellow, you're a dead fellow, but if red touches black, you're OK, Jack." I am left to assume that this works even if one is not named Jack.

91 To provide another example, the Viceroy butterfly also employs a technique of mimicry so that it may resemble the Monarch butterfly (as a prey animal the latter is poisonous only to those who eat it).

The Jews were God's original priority and the source of the original circulation of His Word amongst humanity. Without them there would be no Christianity, nor the mysteries of the Hebrew language which are still being discovered. Indeed, to even refer to the Jews as "them" can be considered folly, for given the clear desire of God to accept the alien people living among them as their own, it is quite clear that God's policy was always one of inclusion rather than exclusion. Thus only those who exclude are themselves excluded.

We know the maxim: "Never tell anyone they are the chosen people of God; it goes straight to their heads." However, all people are the chosen people of God so long as they are a people who choose God. The Jews are indeed God's chosen people, for spiritually we are all of the Jewish race.[92] I thus happily defer to Saint Paul with the verse immediately following the one with which the previous chapter of this book concluded:

> "And if ye be Christ's, then are ye Abraham's seed, and heirs according to the promise." (Galatians 3:29, KJV)

92 It was in fact a Jewish transwoman who helped me change my name to Tiamat, though I am not certain of whether at the time either of us knew that it was in fact Hebrew as well as Babylonian.

Chapter the 5th

O Woman, Great is Thy Faith![93]

Issues of Biblical Misogyny and Feminism

When the Little Flower of Jesus (Saint Theresa of Lisieux) was making her pilgrimage to the Vatican, she noted how practically every minute women were threatened with excommunication if they but entered into a place where they were not permitted. Lamenting how much women are misunderstood, she wrote of some intriguing qualities regarding their relationship with God. Firstly, women love God in much larger numbers than men do. Secondly, during the Passion of Our Lord, women displayed more courage than even the apostles, for they braved the harassment of the soldiers and dared to wipe the adorable Face of Jesus.

The Little Flower concluded that these were undoubtedly the reasons why Jesus allows misunderstanding to be the lot of women on earth...

> "...since He chose it for Himself. In heaven, He will show that His thoughts are not men's thoughts,[94] for then *the last will be first.*[95]"
>
> – *L'Histoire d'une Ame* (Story of a Soul: The Autobiography of St. Theresa of Lisieux))[96]

---

93 Matthew 15:28, KJV.

94 Isaiah 55:8-9.

95 Matthew 20:16.

96 Manuscript A, Chapter VI – The Trip to Rome (1887). Third Edition, Translated from the Original Manuscripts by John Clarke, O.C.D.. p. 140.

An alternate title I considered for this chapter was Matthew 26:10, "Why do you make trouble for the woman?"[97] This simple question asked by Jesus Christ essentially sums up the problem many seem to have with the apparent sexism of Christianity, and indeed I have even known a number of people who chose Paganism because it was said to include a 'balance between male and female' and the presence of a 'divine feminine' which Christianity supposedly lacks. "But Wisdom is vindicated by all Her children," as Jesus Christ Himself said[98], and from them one learns that any problems with religion are not in fact problems with God.

Vocal (and textual) misogynists have blamed women for much in religions throughout history. In the Bible, instead of a simple condemnation of women in general for some perceived vice possessed universally by the entire sex, one singular woman – that is, Eve – is blamed for opening up the path to evil, as is the case in the Greco-Roman myth of Pandora. This has nevertheless not stopped later preachers from wielding the story against the whole of femaleness, which raises the question: how can it be reconciled by those who desire sexual equality in a religious environment?

The simplest solution is to dismiss the story as fiction. After all, the story of a woman originating from the rib of a man[99] bears a striking similarity to the earlier-recorded Sumerian myth in which the goddess Ninhursag created a beautiful earthly garden called Edinu and charged her husband Enki with its care, eventually creating for him a new goddess named Ninti from his rib (*Nin* being the word for "lady" and *ti* being the word for both "life" and "rib"; an ancient pun). It also may seem to contradict the Biblical First Story of Creation, which in contrast is unique among creation stories and (despite a few discrepancies in the

97 New American Bible (NAB).

98 Matthew 11:19, Luke 7:35, NAB.

99 In response to the archaic suggestion that this origin somehow made women inferior by composition, it should be noted that women were nevertheless given physical components lacking in men – such as breasts and a womb – and that our bodies are otherwise fairly similar in content (I have grown intimately familiar with what differences *do* exist, as we shall see in the 7th chapter).

order of stellar and evolutionary events) bears an uncanny resemblance to current scientific understanding of the creation and development of the universe.

However, I recommend against dismissal of the Second Story of Creation for three reasons of increasing importance. Firstly and most conservatively (in every sense of the term), as fabulous as some of the stories in the Bible may often appear, to utterly deny even one may render one more vulnerable to temptation to deny them all, even in the face of supporting outside evidence of their veracity. Secondly, however historically inaccurate the story may or may not be, it nevertheless provides intriguing insight which shall be elaborated upon momentarily. Thirdly, it is important to remember that with God all things are possible[100], and thus even if there is no scrap of available evidence outside of the text itself to support it, that is yet not absolute proof that there is no truth within the text.

Thus we are left to deal with a story which at first glance could easily be misinterpreted as that of the sinfulness of seeking knowledge and man's folly of listening to woman, yet one which does not truly provide satisfaction until examined more deeply. Eve was innocent and thus unfamiliar with deception, and likely did not know whom to trust implicitly and of whom to be suspicious. Nevertheless, even in her impulsive and disobedient action a self-sacrificing virtue was revealed in her; she ate of the fruit of the Tree of the Knowledge of Good and Evil[101] – which she had been forewarned would bring about her death – first. Had she truly been a vile temptress, she would have endeavoured to convince Adam to be the one to risk death before her, rather than choosing to wait until her own failure to immediately drop dead suggested that the serpent may have been telling the truth. The serpent was in fact lying, of course: Adam and Eve did die after eating the forbidden fruit, though it took far longer than either likely initially expected. There is no question that their rebellion against God and ambition to be like Him demonstrated sinfulness, however it was a necessary part of God's plan for humanity, as Jesus Christ stated:

---

[100] Luke 1:37.

[101] Genesis 3:6.

"Be ye therefore perfect[102], even as your Father which is in heaven is perfect."[103]

To ingest the knowledge of good and evil was to start humanity down the path to the species' maturation into saintly perfection, indeed a perfection which shall enable humans to judge even angels[104], for they will know both good and evil...and choose good.

"For when for the time ye ought to be teachers, ye have need that one teach you again which be the first principles of the oracles of God; and are become such as have need of milk, and not of strong meat[105].

For every one that useth milk is unskilful in the word of righteousness: for he is a babe.

But strong meat belongeth to them that are of full age, even those who by reason of use have their senses exercised to discern both good and evil." (Hebrews 5:12-14, KJV)

Why, one asks, did God warn Adam and Eve not to eat of the Tree – after placing it within easy reach of them – knowing that their human nature would bring about their defiance of Him? This is due to the fact that unfortunately to truly know good and evil one must "know" them in every sense of the word, which means one must experience both. Thus to start down this road, and to accept this heavy burden – and all the risks and suffering it entails – needed to be humanity's choice.

"When God, in the beginning, created man, he made him subject to his own free choice.

If you choose you can keep the commandments; it is loyalty to do his will.

---

102 Originally transcribed as the Greek word *teleios*, which in addition to "perfect" also means "fully grown", "mature", "adult", "brought to its end", and "finished."

103 Matthew 5:48, KJV.

104 1 Corinthians 6:3.

105 In Greek *stereos trophe*, also translated "solid food."

> There are set before you fire and water; to whichever you choose, stretch forth your hand.
>
> Before man are life and death, whichever he chooses shall be given him." (Sirach 15:14-17, NAB)

Yet in the end humans shall thank Eve for setting all of this in motion, for once we have passed through this crucible, we shall have peace, and believe[106].

Like Eve, those women who came after her have had more than their fair share of negative depiction, yet the all-too-often-cited negative examples of women in the Bible are actually fairly few and far-between.

These women tend to take the roles of faithless (often-foreign) foul foils to pious Biblical heroes. These include such characters as Lot's wife, who failed to heed the angels' warning by turning back to look in the direction of Sodom and Gomorrah before it was safe to do so[107], Samson's wife Delilah[108], who like a sort of antithesis to Ruth sided with her own society rather than the man whom she professed to love, and Job's wife, who actually advised her afflicted husband to "Curse God and die"[109]. On very rare occasions they can be power-hungry murderesses such as Athaliah, who attempted to slaughter all male heirs to assure her absolute rulership of Israel, and who might have succeeded had it not been for the heroic actions of the princess Jehosheba[110] (regarding the misogyny inherent in a patriarchal monarchy, one should recall that God was against Israel having a king in the first place[111]).

Perhaps the most famous Biblical villainess falls into both categories, however: Athaliah's mother Jezebel[112], the wife of the Israelite King

---

106 Zechariah 13:9.

107 Genesis 19:15-26.

108 Judges 16:4-20.

109 Job 2:9, NAB. This was before any universal belief in the resurrection of the dead.

110 2 Chronicles 22:9-12.

111 1 Samuel 8:6-9.

112 1 Kings 16:31, 2 Chronicles 21:6.

Ahab; whose Pagan influence upon her husband made her a sort of archenemy of the Prophet Elijah[113].

Incredibly enough, in recent years Jezebel has actually come to be seen by some as a symbol of feminism (even being given her own namesake website, a feminist celebrity/news blog called Jezebel.com[114]). As with all misinterpretations of the Scriptures, this is due to neither knowing nor understanding the whole truth. Those who idolize Jezebel seem either to have forgotten or to have never been told that she is justly vilified not because she was an empowered female, but because she used her power to corrupt Israel's faith to the point of trying to exterminate all those who were still faithful to the LORD!

Jezebel too is a character often used by misogynists as an example of the dangers of listening to women and/or of giving them power, and when attempting to paint the erroneous picture of her deceitful and manipulative qualities being universal among women they often take care to pair her with other rare Biblical villainesses such as King Herod's lover Herodias and her daughter (who seduced him with what would become known as the 'Dance of the Seven Veils'). There are distinct similarities in the sense that female allure was employed to influence a corrupt king here as well; in this case to slay John the Baptist. The parallel is especially intriguing when one considers Jesus Christ's suggestion that both Jezebel and Herodias persecuted precisely the same being!

> "For all the prophets and the law prophesied until John:
> And if you will receive it, he is Elias [Elijah] that is to come."
> (Matthew 11:13-14, Douay-Rheims 1899 American Edition)

---

113 1 Kings 19:1-2.

114 However, despite the site's poor choice of name and at-times haughty tone to its articles, it is nevertheless a useful and professional one, the articles of which have reported upon everything from the mistreatment of imprisoned transpeople (http://jezebel.com/5880990/in-nypd-custody-trans-people-get-chained-to-fences-and-poles) to the preternaturally-warm winter/spring of 2012 which has baffled scientists and brought about the continent-wide drought which afflicts us even as I write this (http://jezebel.com/5895272/eerily-gorgeous-weather-finally-convinces-people-that-global-warming-is-a-thing). Both articles retrieved 27/08/2012.

Perhaps due to the false prophet Jezebel of Revelation 2:20-23 being a fornicator and adulteress coupled with all the misinformation that has been spread regarding the Bible, Jezebel has also been widely misunderstood to be a positive symbol of proud promiscuity or unrestrained female sensuality. This is of course absurd; for adultery is every bit as sinful and painful to the betrayed spouse regardless of the gender of the one committing it. In the case of both Jezebels, however, the crimes of power abuse were the same as those of male tyrants, the many Kings of Israel who "did evil in the sight of the LORD."[115]

At the other end of the Biblical gender-political spectrum we have Esther, who was taken as a harem girl for the powerful King Ahasuerus and eventually became his queen, and from this position saved the entire Jewish people (thus beginning the tradition of the holiday Purim). Esther in a sense may be considered a sort of anti-Jezebel, for she provides stark contrast with her due to the similarity of their political positions.

Each one was beautified with expensive cosmetics and jewelry, married a foreign king with a foreign system of belief, and used her feminine wiles and allure to achieve what she wanted. Growing more specific in similarity, each also proclaimed a fast for the Jews[116] and influenced letters sealed with the king's seal[117], however the nature of these letters differed tremendously. Jezebel used negative tactics of insult and take-charge aggressiveness to brow-beat King Ahab into giving her control[118] – albeit to fulfil his own desire for the vineyard of Naboth's heritage – over the whole affair and used quite sinister means to bring it to fruition. To eliminate Naboth,

> "...she wrote in the letters, saying, Proclaim a fast, and set Naboth on high among the people:

---

115 As found in such verses as 1 Kings 11:6, 14:22, 15:26 & 34, 16:19, 25 & 30, 22:53, 2 Kings 3:2, 8:18 & 27, 14:24, 15:9, 18, 24 & 28, 17:2, 21:2 & 20, 23:32 & 37, 24:9 & 19 and 2 Chronicles 21:6, 22:4, 33:2 & 22, 36:5, 9 & 12, NAB, each verse in these respective titles referring to a different king. This, I believe, may be taken as evidence of power's ability to corrupt.

116 1 Kings 21:9 and Esther 4:16, respectively.

117 1 Kings 21:8 and Esther 8:3-8, respectively.

118 1 Kings 21:7.

> And set two men, sons of Belial[119], before him, to bear witness against him, saying, Thou didst blaspheme God and the king. And then carry him out, and stone him, that he may die." (1 Kings 21:9-10, KJV)

Thus even in the story of such a wicked woman as Jezebel, there is present a lesson which might have prevented many innocent women from later suffering a fate disturbingly similar to that which befell the prophets of the LORD in Jezebel's time[120]. She relied upon the zeal of those loyal to the LORD to be such that they would carry out sentence without even requiring proof of the veracity of the prosecution's claims, thus allowing her deception to triumph. This story reveals quite clearly that ulterior motives may cause people to accuse one another of crimes against God, and to recall it would likely have saved many lives during the witch-trials of the centuries to follow.

Alas, such Sacred Scripture went unheeded even in the definitive text on the subject: the *Malleus Maleficarum*, a 15th Century guide to witch-hunting. This work described a witch as being a committer of high treason against God's majesty, and gives this as the reason why...

> "...the laws allow that **any witness whatsoever** is to be admitted as evidence against them. ... And the same procedure is allowable in a charge of heresy."
> (*Malleus Maleficarum, ("The Hammer of (ie. For Use Against) Witches")* circa 1486 A.D.. Part the First, Question I, p. 3, emphasis mine.)

Clearly fear, suspicion, and prejudice led to this lesson not being learned.

Now as for Esther, she feared for her own life and was not about to try to brow-beat her spouse. The intriguing quality of her story is how she instead met with amazing success using only purely and traditionally feminine means. Though these means included so much

---

119 *Be'li-al,* from Hebrew meaning "Good for Naught" (*beli'*: "not, lacking," and *ya-al'*: "be of benefit; be beneficial"). Belial is usually concluded to be synonymous with Satan, as in 2 Corinthians 6:15.

120 1 Kings 18:4 & 13.

more besides, they also included that much-studied, much-stereotyped, and much-sought-after quality of allure.

Therein dwells the difference between the two: what it was that each wanted to gain through their feminine wiles. Jezebel wanted to revel in wealth[121] (while Esther reviled wealth[122]) and to have all who opposed her brutally murdered. The same was true with her symbolic successor, Herodias (and her daughter), yet it should be noted that Herod and Ahasuerus were so enamoured/in love with Herodias' daughter and Queen Esther (respectively) that they, in an age-old tradition of kingly bravado, offered them *precisely the same thing:*

> "And he sware unto her, Whatsoever thou shalt ask of me, I will give it thee[123], unto the half of my kingdom." (Mark 6:23, KJV)

> "Then said the king unto her, What wilt thou, queen Esther? and what is thy request? it shall be even given thee to the half of the kingdom." (Esther 5:3, KJV. See also 5:6 and 7:2)

Esther wanted simply to save the Jewish people from annihilation. Such is the importance of this tale of one whose "firmness is surprising in light of her training to be a submissive and sensual harem girl..."[124] a role which might by society be considered that of weak, degraded, and even shameful objects of predation, for she possessed little to no official authority. It is sad indeed that people would attempt to distort Scripture for so long as they did in an attempt to justify slavery while simultaneously ignoring God's subtle-yet-clear message in the story of Esther: misogynist political and legal traditions that limit women's

---

121 2 Kings 9:30.

122 Esther 2:13-15 (Hebrew text), C:27 (Greek text).

123 This statement of confidence is similar to that which God gave to Solomon in 2 Chronicles 1:7; his answer being **wisdom** (v.10), and to what Jesus offers the entirety of His people in the very book in which Herod issues his offer: Mark 11:24.

124 Alice Mathews. *A Woman God Can Use.* pp. 148-149. Indeed, Esther's passive docility is further proof of her strength, for brazen boldness did not come naturally to her.

sphere of influence and keep her from being an equal partner can place His entire people in mortal jeopardy.

It was because of this double standard that I was actually mildly annoyed with the Book of Esther when first I read it as a teenager. Having been taught to view things from a man's perspective, I found that Mordecai's second letter to Esther made her appear vacillating[125]; shouldn't she have simply and immediately stated that she was prepared to perish for God and country? Ah, but she *was* prepared to perish[126]; she merely wanted to be certain Mordecai understood the gravity of the situation and to receive reassurance that it would do some good for her to potentially perish. In his feelings of helplessness and frustration, Mordecai emotionally projected; probably because he inwardly blamed himself for the situation. The Prayer of Mordecai found in the Greek Septuagint[127] makes this explicit:

> "You made heaven and earth and every wonderful thing under the heavens. You are LORD of all, and there is no one who can resist you, LORD. You know all things. You know, O LORD, that it was not out of insolence or pride or desire for fame that I acted thus in not bowing down to the proud Haman. Gladly would I have kissed the soles of his feet for the salvation of Israel. But I acted as I did so as not to place the honor of man above that of God. I will not bow down to anyone but you, my LORD. It is not out of pride that I am acting thus." (Esther C:3-7, NAB)

Despite the heroic actions of the woman for whom the book is named, such was the sexism of society in ancient times that Esther was not readily acknowledged for her contribution. This is apparent in

---

[125] Esther 4:13-14. I have often been told that "a leader can afford to be wrong, but they cannot afford to be indecisive." Unfortunately this attitude has led to much horror throughout history, and thus it must fall to the followers to ask themselves whom they would rather serve: one who is boldly wrong, or one who is open to suggestions. Such is the very ideal of democracy: let they (the people) who have wisdom understand.

[126] Esther 4:16.

[127] 3rd Century B.C. translation of the Hebrew Old Testament. It's name is taken from the Latin "translation of the seventy interpreters."

the Bible itself; specifically in the 2nd Book of Maccabees, which took place approximately 300 years later. After Judas Maccabeus ("Judah the Hammer")[128] had inspired the Israelites with the holy sword from his dream-vision[129] and led them to victory against Nicanor and his tens of thousands in the Battle of Adasa, his followers chose to keep this day as one of celebration on the eve of Purim...which they called "Mordecai's Day."[130]

Patriarchal Attitudes and Their Effect on the Position of Women

Both Queen Jezebel and Queen Esther were symbols of female empowerment using charming feminine allure (as well as a bit of forcefulness on the part of Jezebel). This is perhaps a difficult subject to address from a moral standpoint, but really no more so than the exercise of deadly violent force (if Samson, for example, had not used his strength for God and His people, would he have been any better than Goliath?). Allure has been considered a feminine power, and as Esther has shown it can be more effective than even Samson's strength, and unfortunately it can be equally feared. As is the nature of any power, allure can corrupt and be horribly misused. As I know from my experiences in the places where men have their private discussions, abuse of allure is used to justify abuse of physical strength; one may recall that Jezebel met a very brutal and violent end (and at the hands of eunuchs, no less).[131]

Donatien Alphonse Francois, Marquis de Sade, from whence we derive the word "sadism", was an 18th Century French aristocrat whose libertine nature demonstrated this abusive attitude in a most severe and disturbing manner. In his 1785 piece *The 120 Days of Sodom,* a story of four wealthy anti-Christian sadists who forcibly assemble a "seraglio" to

---

128 Hebrew: *Y'hudhah HamMakabi.*

129 2 Maccabees 15:11. In this dream, the Prophet "Jeremiah presented a gold sword to Judas" saying "Accept this holy sword as a gift from God; with it you shall crush your adversaries...." (2 Maccabees 15:15-16, NAB)

130 2 Maccabees 15:36.

131 1 Kings 21:23, 2 Kings 9:30-37.

torture in a secluded castle, de Sade wrote of the uselessness of feminine allure in such an overcompensatory manner as to suggest pure hatred. His 'protagonists' recommend obedience as that one virtue that befits the present state of their slaves (yet it is obedience to the male leads, as they "have no god but their lubricity"), mock even the position of women in the 18th Century as a "ridiculous ascendancy", and express their loathing for womankind and for God in the same breath, using the one as justification for the other.[132] The reaction of the Marquis is an extreme example, however, and Esther's approach has proven quite useful in the modern world. After all, violence is considerably more likely to cause destruction than diplomacy, save in extreme cases such as that of Jezebel.

However, while Jezebel (like Herodias and her offspring) used her diplomatic allure for evil, Esther managed to use hers for good. It should be noted also that both were examples of a woman remaining true to her beliefs despite immersion in a foreign society, with their respective tendencies toward brutality and salvation. Additionally, one may note how both needed to appeal to men, who held the official and legal power. The general prevalence of patriarchy shall continue to be an issue throughout this chapter.

An exception to this rule (no pun intended) was Deborah, Fourth Judge of Israel. When one considers that Athaliah found it necessary to maintain power by steeping her hands in more blood than Regan, Goneril, and Lady MacBeth combined[133], it is remarkable that Judges 4:4 casually mentions Deborah's rulership[134] of Israel as though it were the most ordinary thing in the world for a female to have. Indeed, having neither been born nor married into a family of noble birth, Deborah operated well beyond traditional conventions, for she was a woman chosen to rule literally by an act of God.

---

132 *The 120 Days of Sodom*, 1785 A. D., pp. 47-48.

133 I am referring of course to the Shakespearean characters; counters for the Bard's numerous females who are misjudged/mistreated by men such as Juliet, Desdemona, and Calpurnia (whose portentous dream Julius Caesar really should have heeded....)

134 The specific Hebrew word used here is *shaphat*, which means to rule, govern, judge, and also to plead.

This Divinely-appointed ascendancy to power was likely wisdom-based, and Deborah clearly possessed enough wisdom to be well aware of sexist social attitudes toward women. Still, she was able to use even these to her advantage, that she might teach her people the importance of faith. In Judges 4:6-8, the military commander Barak was ordered by Deborah to march forth against the enemy's forces led by Sisera, but Barak refused to do so unless the Prophetess herself accompanied him. This she agreed to do, yet she assured Barak that because of his ultimatum, he would not receive the honour of slaying Sisera but rather that the LORD would instead give this to a woman; specifically Jael, who drove a tent peg through Sisera's skull[135]. According to Biblical scholar Michael D. Coogan, Jael being a woman "is a further sign that Yahweh ultimately is responsible for the victory: The mighty Canaanite general Sisera will be 'sold' by the Lord 'into the hand of a woman' (Judges 4:9) - the ultimate degradation."[136] Of course, such a sexist attitude was not limited to Israelite culture, and in fact it invites comparison with a shaming statement used in the Babylonian *Enuma Elish* to encourage Marduk to take up arms when all of the other Annunaki were afraid to do so[137]:

> "What man is the cause of the battle which [forced thee to] go forth?"
>
> "...Tiamat...a woman, pursueth thee with weapons."
>
> (Tablet II, Lines 121-122 (translation by E.A. Wallis Budge))

In the somewhat-masculinized world in which we now live, it is easy to fall into the trap of believing that Deborah, this ancient ruler of Israel, was strong and empowered due to her military might, much as

---

135 Judges 4:17-22.

136 Coogan, Michael D. (2009), *A Brief Introduction to the Old Testament: The Hebrew Bible in its Context*, Oxford University Press, p. 180

137 This being due in part to so many remaining on Tiamat's side, and her having given birth to scorpion-people, merfolk, terrifying serpents with poison rather than blood, the Whirlwind, etc. However, like Deborah, Tiamat had no initial desire to go to war herself (First Tablet, Lines 33-43).

is so often the opinion regarding Saint Jeanne d'Arc (known in English as Joan of Arc[138]).

Indeed, such is the masculinization of our society that at times truly ridiculous acts can seem "liberating" or even "empowering". As a case in point, I submit for example the one segment I have ever watched of the reality television show *Fear Factor*, in which the challenge presented involved the eating of live worms. Despite the grotesque childishness of the proceedings, the one female contestant felt it necessary to deliver a spiel about how success therein would prove herself to those men who "underestimated (her) because (she was) a woman." When she proved unable to swallow even her first shot-glass-full of worms and was thus immediately eliminated, the false glory of the men present was undiminished by the absence of the woman, because she had unwittingly *validated their sense of superiority by treating their invertebrate-eating as though it were a worthy achievement.* Never did it appear to occur to her to point out that such an activity was unladylike, unhealthy, and unkind to creatures of God, but had she elected to do so a distinctly and much-needed feminine perspective would have been provided.

Deborah, for her part, was an exemplar of this feminine perspective. She showed that God is entirely willing to choose a woman to rule His people in a time of strife, even if it means defying established social norms. However the duties of war did not supplant those more traditionally fulfilled by women. In a sense, Deborah was an ideal example of the "modern woman" approximately three thousand years before such a concept would become vogue, for she balanced (the LORD's) work with a family, and even combined the two occupations. She still, for example, was able to be a traditionally-feminine married

138 Male attitudes toward women of war had not changed by her time (and in my experience, they remain in place somewhat even to this day). According to Louis de Contes, Joan's page, she met with similar difficulties in Orléans. When she went to a Boulevard which the French were occupying, opposite one garrisoned by English soldiers, she told the latter to retire in God's Name or she would drive them away. The appropriately-titled Bastard of Granville instead viciously asked her if she wished them to surrender to a woman. http://www.stjoan-center.com/Trials/null07.html Retrieved Thursday, October 4th of 2012. This attitude, of course, never stopped God from raising up those who would challenge such stereotypes.

woman[139], though there can be no question that it was she and not her husband whom God had chosen to rule the nation.

There has been some speculation regarding Deborah's home life, yet considering the Prophetess' rather gentle personality it seems more likely that she was wed to a supportive spouse rather than a "hen-pecked" one. We can be thankful in this case for the scribes' tendency to record any and all male names, for it is reason why we even know of the existence of Deborah's husband Lapidoth, whose name means "torches" in Hebrew. Deborah's name means "bee"; fitting for a busy mother of Israel[140]. She lived a married life, led and advised her people in wisdom, and when necessary commanded them in times of war to the extent of calling down the atmokinetic Wrath of God to annihilate all who opposed her[141], even as Moses and Joshua did...and Elijah would eventually do[142]. Indeed, Deborah more than fulfilled all of the requirements considered necessary in an Ancient World leader: as the wisest in her community, she received revelations from God and interceded with Him on behalf of the people, whom she guided in their struggle against nature and their enemies.[143]

Deborah, however, appeared to have no desire to engage in warfare herself – even if to do so would have meant being paraded home in the glory of a conquering hero(ine) – and would have been quite happy remaining beneath her palm tree administering judgement[144] in her nation-mothering role had she not been called to war by a general

---

139 Judges 4:4.

140 Judges 5:7. This is of course figurative, for no children of Deborah's were recorded. Unlike so many women of the time, the Prophetess apparently did not feel the pressing need to bear a son....

141 Judges 4:14-16, 5:4 & 20-21.

142 Moses: Exodus 9:13-33, Joshua: Joshua 10:11, Elijah: 1 Kings 17:1 & 7, 18:1-45, 2 Kings 1:10-15. However, despite the tremendously epic displays of power described therein, it is wise to recall Jesus' response to the question of the "Sons of Thunder" (Mark 3:17) in Luke 9:54-56 (KJV): "Ye know not what manner of spirit ye are of. For the Son of man is not come to destroy men's lives, but to save them."

143 Mikhail Rostovtzeff, *A History of the Ancient World: The Orient and Greece*, Chapter III: Earliest History of Mesopotamia and Egypt, pp. 18-19.

144 Judges 4:5.

unwilling to fight without her[145]. Like Joan of Arc, Deborah partook of military action only because it was necessary to the situation at hand; she did what she had to do because, like any Biblical heroine, she possessed sufficient faith. God chose her to rule in the most direct fashion, and thus she serves as a reminder for all time that to deny women the opportunity to gain leadership positions – any leadership position, no matter how high – is to risk rebelling against the will of God.

It is not my desire to detail here all of the many positive female characters in the Bible, for even in the Scriptures written by men they are so numerous that to do so would be a book unto itself. It also remains unknown how many women have been given spiritual gifts from God yet been unable to make full use of them due to their roles in society; such as the faithful "little maid" from 2 Kings 5:2-4 who identified and proclaimed the significance of another servant of God (Elisha), but who was quite limited in what she was able to do because of her status as a slave. These women all remind us that, while males may be the subject of the vast majority of the words and deeds set down by the inspired men who wrote the Bible, when it came time for an act of singularly-pivotal importance to the whole of Judaism and/or Christianity, God often chose a woman for the task.

A great irony is that these Biblical women of note gained their renown in such a rigidly male-dominated society, and one containing draconian laws regarding adultery determination[146] and precious little mention of women in its lengthy lists of lineage (not that it matters biologically in the bloodline of Jesus[147], as the only human genetic contributor was the Blessed Virgin Mother Mary). An explanation for this masculine focus is given quite clearly in the Census which begins the Book of Numbers and the Preparation for the Departure from Sinai.

> "Take ye the sum of all the congregation of the children of Israel, after their families, by the house of their fathers, with the number of their names, every male by their polls[148];

[145] Barak, whose name in Hebrew translates to "Lightning."

[146] Numbers 5:11-31, Deuteronomy 22:13-21.

[147] Matthew 1:1-16, Luke 3:23-38.

[148] "every male by their polls;" in the original Hebrew "*kol zakar gulgoleth*"

> From twenty years old and upward, all that are able to go forth to war in Israel: thou and Aaron shall number them by their armies.[149] (Numbers 1:2-3, KJV)

This passage shows a focus on males based on eligibility for military service. These terms are repeated (to include all twelve tribes of Israel) in every other verse from 20-42, though the word specifically qualifying "male" is dropped after the second tribe is numbered – for it is by then taken for granted – and only "war" remains. The word *ben* {bane}, meaning children, is used instead, and while in plural this could mean either males or females it no longer matters as the latter have already been removed from the equation. When the time had come for the Second Census – conducted in Chapter 26 of Numbers – the word *ben* was used from the beginning. This historical account was concentrated on the conquest and propagation of what would become the land of Israel, and such things were considered to be the province of men.

Ritually, women also suffered due to a gift they had received which had not been granted men: the ability to give birth. Passages such as Leviticus 12:2-8, 15:19-30, 18:19, and 20:18 reveal that to give birth or even to menstruate was thought to cause a woman to become *tame'* {taw-may}; "unclean, defiled, or polluted." As with so many of the Biblical laws which may seem strange from a modern perspective, this one was made to protect humanity from foreign elements; in this case germs. People of the ancient world had little to no understanding of bloodborne pathogens or sexually-transmitted diseases, so such precautions inevitably became ritualized. There was some understanding of the significant association between blood and life, however, and indeed Leviticus' *Code of Legal Holiness* begins with the "Sacredness of Blood."[150] The prescription for a woman experiencing normal menstruation was to be left alone for a

---

{kole zaw-kawr gul-go-leth'}, *kol* meaning "every", *zakar* "male" (without any exception besides "child") and *gulgoleth* "head, poll, or skull".

149 The same Hebrew word is here translated both to "war" and to "armies", for it bears both meanings: *tsaba'* {tsaw-baw}, which is used only in its masculine form.

150 Leviticus 17, NAB. The Hebrew word for "blood" is מד *dam* {dawm} ("dal mem"; fittingly enough "ד (the door)/hang/entrance מ blood"); it can also figuratively mean "of wine."

week (specifically "seven days") until her period was most assuredly over (and woe – specifically banishment – betide her and anyone with whom she might have sexual intercourse during this time), yet in the case of irregularly-long menstruation or childbirth she must become purified[151] and in so doing bring for sacrifice two doves (for irregular menstruation or if one cannot afford the normal childbirth sacrifice) or a yearling lamb and a dove (after delivering a child). These rituals eventually culminated in Luke 2:22 & 24, wherein the Blessed Virgin Mother Mary was forced to obey them to purify herself from the 'uncleanness' resulting from the Virgin Birth of Christ. Mary brought doves for a sin offering[152], for she was too poor to provide a lamb.

In spite of this evidence that such superstition was inappropriate, the attitude was difficult to remove, and it remained as a religious concern for many centuries thereafter. In *The Malleus Maleficarum*, it was actually suggested that the sight of an 'impurity' such as a woman during her monthly period could cause the eyes seeing it to contract an 'impurity' themselves.[153]

---

151 The Hebrew words used for this are *taher* {taw-hare} (meaning to be clean of physical disease or morally/ceremonially clean) in Leviticus 12:8 and 15:28 and *tohorah* {toh-or-aw} (purification, cleansing, menstruation) in Leviticus 12:5. These approaches to purification contrast with that underwent by the harem women being prepared for the King in Esther 2:12; *maruwq* {maw-rook} (purification involving bodily rubbings) or *tamruwq* {tam-rook} (things required for such purification) (the characters of which are ובתמרוקי "waw bet taw mem resh waw quph yad": "ו add/secure ב family/house/in ת (the cross in the most Ancient Semitic/Hebrew)/mark/sign מ (water)/blood ר beginning ו secure ק time י worship"; let the reader determine if this has any significant meaning when interpreted logographically).

152 תאטחל *Chatta'th* {khat-tawth'} (purification for sin) ("lam hhet tet El taw": "ל yoke/bind ח outside ט surround/contain א (El)/strong/power/leader ת (the cross)/mark/sign/signal/monument"; see above).

153 Part the First, Question II, by ("of") Heinrich Kramer and James Sprenger, translated with an introduction, bibliography & notes by the Reverend Montague Summers. A Bull of [Pope] Innocent VIII. 1486, 1928, 1948. While it is certainly possible that there is some truth to be found therein, I suspect that there is also no small measure of superstition present in the *Malleus* owing to the limited understanding available at the time of its writing. As a case in point, less than two full pages hereafter the text discusses the case

The concept of ritual uncleanness resulting from shed blood is also not unique to Israel; to draw another example of it, let us examine pre-Christian Benin City, the heart of one of Africa's oldest kingdoms[154] and the first location in Nigeria wherein Christianity was preached.[155] It was (and is) a magnificent place; once possessing a protective circular wall that was the longest manmade object on Earth (even longer than the Great Wall of China) and still producing bronzework which has become legendary throughout the world. At the height of its expansion the Benin Kingdom was known in Europe simply as Grand Benin, and its territory spanned thrice the area of even the Zulu Kingdom of South Africa. According to some, an area near Benin City was even once the home of the Biblical Queen of Sheba[156] (which would give a most impressive interpretation to Jesus Christ's statement that "she came from the uttermost parts of the earth" in Matthew 12:42 (KJV)!), however, under the Obas (god-kings) the Benin Kingdom/Empire itself has never had a female as its supreme ruler...though it almost did.

Princess Edelayo, daughter of Oba Ewuare the Great (who ruled ca. 1440-1473) would not have become Queen in the sense that Esther did and thus received a title that was considered inferior in power to that of its male counterpart on basis of gender-association. Rather she would

---

wherein a man wishes to kill a basilisk [which one may recall from the second *Harry Potter* installment]. He would take with him one or more mirrors, which would cause the beast seeing itself in the mirror to shoot poison towards its reflection, which would then be reflected off the mirror and kill the animal. The *Malleus* then goes on to say that it is not apparent why the man who thus slays the basilisk should not die also, and that the authors can only conclude that this is due to some reason which they don't understand. In reality the basilisk is a moderately-sized sailed lizard from the family *Corytophanidae* and ironically is referred to as "the Jesus Christ lizard", the latter being due to its ability to temporarily run bipedally on the surface of water (a reference to Jesus' actions in Matthew 14:22-34, Mark 6:45-52, and John 6:16-21).

154 Official Website of Edo State Government, Nigeria. http://edostate.gov.ng/omo-noba-nedo-uku-akpolokpolo-erediauwa-cfr-oba-benin-0 Retrieved September 11th of 2012.

155 Edo Nation Online. http://www.edo-nation.net/aisien1.htm Retrieved September 11th of 2012.

156 *Nyame Akuma.* "Sungbo's Eredo, Southern Nigeria." No. 49, June 1998.

have become Oba, which Englishman Captain John Adams described in 1823 as...

> "'...the principal object of adoration...[occupying] a higher post here than the Pope does in Catholic Europe; for he is...a god himself, whose subjects both obey and adore him as such, although I believe their adoration to arise rather from fear than love; as cases of heresy...are followed by prompt decapitation."[157] (Flora Edouwaye S. Kaplan, "Politics in an African Royal Harem," *Servants of the Dynasty: Palace Women in World History*, edited by Anne Walthall, p. 121)

Harem politics have often played a notable part in ancient monarchies, yet in this case the gifts given to (or earned by) royal women extending "unto half the kingdom" would not be entirely inaccurate. According to a Benin oral tradition, Princess Edelayo was nearly as wealthy and powerful as the Oba. But due to a 'feminine indisposition,' she was prohibited from becoming Oba just as she was about to be crowned. Thereafter, it was enacted that women would not be allowed to reign over Benin any more.[158] (Ibid. p. 116). The explanation of this "indisposition" is given that she was unable to ascend to the thrown because she was in her menstrual period.[159] This seemingly insignificant detail apparently produced a profound effect upon the ritualistic and Pagan men of the time.

One may perhaps argue that men's testosterone-fueled "drive and ambition"[160] urged them to keep women subdued, though whatever the

---

157 This was supported partially by a friend of mine from Benin City, however it is suggested that this is no longer the case now that the Benin Kingdom is Christian; capital punishment could be the penalty for impersonation of a member of the royal family (even online), but such punishment appears to have seldom if ever actually been carried out.

158 Flora Edouwaye S. Kaplan, "Politics in an African Royal Harem," *Servants of the Dynasty: Palace Women in World History*, edited by Anne Walthall p. 116.

159 E.N. Mordi and P.O. Opone, "Origins and Migrations of the Enuani People of South Central Nigeria Reconsidered," 2009, p. 49.

160 Eric Dontigney, "What Are the Benefits of Testosterone?" eHow mom, October 26, 2011. http://www.ehow.com/list_6721723_benefits-testosterone_.

cause of their actions God continually was ready to exert His influence to set important precedents toward the cause of sexual equality (and to intervene on behalf of women). A particularly-famous example of property law alteration involved the Daughters of Zelophehad in the Bible's 4th Book:

> "And they stood before Moses, and before Eleazar the priest, and before the princes and all the congregation, by the door of the tabernacle of the congregation, saying,
>
> Our father died in the wilderness, and he was not in the company of them that gathered themselves together against the LORD in the company of Korah; but died in his own sin, and had no sons.
>
> Why should the name of our father be done away from among his family, because he hath no son? Give unto us therefore a possession among the brethren of our father.
>
> And Moses brought their cause before the LORD.
>
> And the LORD spake unto Moses, saying,
>
> The daughters of Zelophehad speak right: thou shalt surely give them a possession of an inheritance among their father's brethren; and thou shalt cause the inheritance of their father to pass unto them." (Numbers 27:2-7, KJV)

I recall when I first begun reading this passage; I had been fed so much slander against the "Old Testament God" that I honestly was not sure of to what decision He would come. Now I feel the hundredfold fool for having ever doubted Him.

God's decree caused some complications in the system that the men already had established, and thus in Numbers 36:1-6 it was determined that the daughters would be able to choose to marry whom they wished so long as their prospective partners were within their own tribe (for their property would pass to their husbands). In Joshua 17:4-6 it was the

---

html Retrieved September 11th 2012.

daughters themselves who received a share of the land given to their tribe of Manasseh. By the time of Job 42:15, this precedent set by the decree of the LORD had led to daughters being given inheritance just as sons were.

An oft-unadmitted fact is that sexual equality is a peculiarity of Christian nations. While that bold statement will always have its naysayers due to unofficiality of legal connections between practices of state and religion (save in Canadian law, which specifically states that it was based upon Christian values) and the intangibility of the advancement of social attitudes, even in countries where the influence of Christian missionaries was limited the cause of women's rights was often advanced.

To provide examples from especially-populous nations, one may note the Zenana Bible and Medical Mission of the late 19th Century in India. As female converts are just as valuable to God as male ones (1 Peter 3:1-7), in involved female missionaries who went to Indian women in their own gender-secluded dwellings ("zenana") and encouraged them to study medicine in their pursuit of conversion (they also provided schooling for girls including the principles of the Christian faith). The Mission thus to some degree helped to break down the male bias against colonial medicine[161].

Still more success was met with in China, where Christian organizations had played key roles in diffusing progressive social ideals. The anti-foot-binding[162] movement, for example, began in 1874 with a

---

161 Julius Richter, Sydney H. Moore, H. Revell Com Fleming H. Revell Company. *A History of Missions in India.* April 6th of 2010 (originally published prior to 1923).

162 Foot-binding was an agonizing procedure which involved the wrapping of young (~7 years of age) girls' deliberately-broken feet in tight bandages so that they would be deformed into the sexually-desirable shape of "three-inch golden lotuses" and thus be permitted as brides for men of the wealthier classes. Historical records from the Song dynasty (960-1279 A.D.) indicate that the practice began during the reign of Li Yu (961-975), when his heart was reportedly captured by concubine Yao Niang, "who bound her feet to suggest the shape of a new moon and performed a 'lotus dance.'" By the 19th century, 40-50% of Chinese women had bound feet. "For the upper classes, the figure was almost 100 percent." Louisa Lim, "Footbinding: From Status

group of sixty Christian women. It was then taken up by the Women's Christian Temperance Movement, which was founded in 1883 and also opposed opium, cigarette smoking, alcohol use, prostitution, and the selling of daughters. A number of male missionaries also advocated for these ideas, such as Timothy Richard and his avid Chinese readers and acquaintances Liang Qichao and Kang Youwei, under the consideration that Christianity would lead to the equality of the sexes.[163]

It is interesting to note that these steps toward sexual equality were made not with any thought of economic gains through women's liberation as in modern times, but simply with the desire to spread Christian morals and ideals. This is another topic, however, that could easily fill a book by itself (as it has already done many times).

Female Submission, Freedom, and Devotion

Classically, femininity has embodied gentle qualities. Should this be a problem? Was not Moses meek? Do not Ephesians 4:1-2 endorse all peoples (both male and female) to be likewise? Does not James 3:17 reveal such as the gift of Divine Wisdom?

> "But the wisdom that is from above is first pure then peaceable, gentle, *and* easy to be intreated,[164] full of mercy and good fruits, without partiality, and without hypocrisy." (KJV)

Permit me now to play the Fool in the Shakespearean sense; that is, to say that of which so many are thinking yet to which none dare give voice: what if women on average – perhaps due to the immense biological responsibility we already possess – really do possess submissive inclinations? What if there is something to that effect

---

Symbol to Subjugation." March 19th, 2007. http://www.npr.org/templates/story/story.php?storyId=8966942 Retrieved September 12th, 2012.

163 Vincent Goossaert; David A. Palmer (15 April 2011). *The Religious Question in Modern China*. University of Chicago Press. pp. 70-71.

164 In Greek *eupeithes*, "easily obeying, compliant." Translated in the NIV as "submission."

responsible for the *Fifty Shades of Grey*[165] phenomenon and all those statistical surveys of dominance/submission prevalence in gender which I have seen and would really rather not reference here?[166] What if such preconceived notions regarding our sex have some often (though by no means universally)-occurring basis in fact? Would that not allow the patriarchal religious extremists of the world to utter a collective cry of "Aha!" (or its equivalent in their respective languages) and oppress us forevermore?

I dare say that if the oft-referenced Baal/Bel/Marduk and the various 'faiths' associated with them are any indication, those who would oppress others will attempt to do so whether their god encourages them to or not (which is why such people try to mold their own religions to support such things). If indeed women are more submissive, that ironically reveals us to be stronger than we have long been imagined to be, for it means that all those millennia of traditional gender roles were at least somewhat consensual, rather than having been forced upon us against our will due to the irresistible strength of men. However, as I of all people should know, it is dangerous to be placed at the mercy of men, for men are often not taught to be merciful. Though as women we may enjoy the reminder that our men are strong, being human we also desire our freedom, and more than that, our freedom is needed by the world.

How then, should women be addressed in a religious capacity? In his article "From the 'Weak Sex' to the 'Devout Sex'", Charles A.

---

165 The title of E.L. James' erotic novel, notable for its explicit scenes involving BDSM. If one enjoyed these works, then one may find parts of the 7th chapter of this book...intriguing. Paul Bentley, "'Mummy porn' Fifty Shades Of Grey outstrips Harry Potter to become fastest selling paperback of all time." *Daily Mail*, 18 June 2012. http://www.dailymail.co.uk/news/article-2160862/Fifty-Shades-Of-Grey-book-outstrips-Harry-Potter-fastest-selling-paperback-time.html#ixzz1y9SHlzQU Retrieved Thursday, October 18th of 2012.

166 However, due to its relationship to the above and its gender discrepancy I will offer this one: "A 1995 study indicates that 89% of heterosexual females who are active in BDSM expressed a preference for a submissive-recipient role in sexual bondage, suggesting also a preference for a dominant male, and 71% of heterosexual males preferred a dominant-initiator role." Ernulf, Kurt E.; Innala, Sune M. (1995). "Sexual bondage: A review and unobtrusive investigation".Archives of Sexual Behavior. Quoted from Wikipedia.

Witschorik recalls how even the most sexist and vitriolic preachers in the early 19th Century offered indication of what would eventually develop as a new strain of church discourses; the celebration of women as the more pious sex specially chosen and ordained by Providence to renew society from within.[167]

Of all the adjectives traditionally placed before the sex of women, "devout" is truly the most flattering, but such a statement has proven to be more than mere rhetoric. Saint Theresa of Lisieux was quite correct in stating that women love God in much greater numbers than men do: a mountain of Gallup survey data attests to her idea that women are more religious than men, hold their beliefs more firmly, practice their faith more consistently, and work more vigorously for their congregations.[168] This has been the case without fail since the earliest book-keeping regarding the subject:

> "In 1660, 'women comprised the majority of communicants in every New England church...'. A century later, women formed a clear majority...in Connecticut. In New London...in 1757 and thirty years later, there were twice as many women as men on the membership rolls...move forward another century...to Muncie, Indiana...[and there again is found a numeric female dominance]"
>
> (Marta Trzebiatowska and Steve Bruce, *Why are Women more Religious Than Men?* Published October 12th of 2012.)

This gender inequality has endured into the present time. A 2007 survey involving interviews with more than 35,000 U.S. adults by the Pew Research Center shows that, compared to men, 7% more women are affiliated with a religion, 12% more women have absolutely certain

---

167 Charles A. Witschorik. "From the 'Weak Sex' to the 'Devout Sex': Women, Gender, and Official Church Discourses in Early Nineteenth-Century Mexico City." University of California, Berkeley, published 04-15-2011. http://escholarship.org/uc/item/1vr9x8zs#page-1 Retrieved October 12th, 2012.

168 George H. Gallup, Jr., quoted in a 28 February 2009 Live Science article entitled "Women More Religious Than Men" by Robert Roy Britt. http://www.livescience.com/7689-women-religious-men.html Retrieved Friday, October 12th of 2012.

belief in a God or universal spirit, 17% more pray at least daily, and 13% more have absolutely certain belief in a personal God.[169] A Harris Interactive survey of 2,306 U.S. adults from approximately five years earlier revealed that women who believed in God outnumbered men by 11%.[170] Another Pew Forum on Religion and Public Life survey, this one released mere days before the time of this writing, shows that 6% fewer women than men are unaffiliated with a religion.[171]

Attempted explanations I have encountered for this gender gap run an extensive and sometimes-sexist gamut. Professor Rodney Stark stated that "studies of biochemistry imply that both male irreligiousness and male lawlessness are rooted in the fact that far more males than females have an underdeveloped ability to inhibit their impulses, especially those involving immediate gratification and thrills."[172] George H. Gallup, Jr. argued that women are more inclined than men toward a basis for faith depending upon empirical evidence rather than rational proof.[173] Evolutionary psychologist Satoshi Kanazawa theorized that "men are more risk-seeking than women, *and*...religion is an evolutionary means to minimize risk..."[174], although this suggestion fails to effectively explain voluntary martyrdom, of which females are just as capable as males. Personal bias can also affect such hypotheses, as evidenced by one embittered suggestion from a commentator on *Atheism+*: "battered

---

169 Ibid.

170 David Gold, 11-02-2003. http://www.goldtalk.com/forum/showthread.php?t=23311 Retrieved Friday, October 12th of 2012.

171 *The London Free Press*. Wednesday, October 10th, 2012. "Rise of the religiously unaffiliated," worldnews, page B2.

172 Rodney Stark, professor of sociology and comparative religion at the University of Washington, arguing in a 2002 paper in the *Journal for the Scientific Study of Religion*. Quoted in the 28 February 2009 *Live Science* article entitled "Women More Religious Than Men" by Robert Roy Britt. http://www.livescience.com/7689-women-religious-men.html Retrieved Friday, October 12th of 2012.

173 George H. Gallup, Jr.. Ibid.

174 *The Scientific Fundamentalist*, "Why Are Women More Religious Than Men? II" by Satoshi Kanazawa. Published on September 19, 2010. http://www.psychologytoday.com/blog/the-scientific-fundamentalist/201009/why-are-women-more-religious-men-ii Retrieved Friday, October 12th of 2012.

wife syndrome, but with religion instead of a husband?"[175] There are however as many specific reasons as to why people are or are not people of faith as there are people themselves, yet the statistics as a whole point to the increasing reliance which Christian churches have on women.[176]

The extolling as feminine those virtues which so benefit the church helps to explain why the relationship of God/Jesus with His church (and the people[177] thereof) are described in Scripture as that of a Bridegroom and Bride. We have seen this relationship alluded to in the Song of Songs/Song of Solomon previously, and it continues to be utilized until the end of Revelation (21:9-10). As pastor Robert L. Deffinbaugh writes, "the bride-groom imagery of the Bible is a wonderful picture of the security of the children of God in their relationship with Him through faith in Jesus Christ."[178]

Femininity has long been associated with submission/obedience; a wonderful virtue, yes, yet one which – as the Marquis de Sade reminded us earlier – is at risk of being easily exploited when placed in the wrong hands. There are verses in the Epistles which have been used as an excuse for some men to exert power over women due to their potential for misinterpretation or the surpassing of their possible extremity. 1 Peter 3 instructs wives to "be in subjection to your own husbands;" with verse six[179] adding, "even as Sara obeyed Abraham, calling him lord:"

---

175 *Atheism+* "Why Are Women More Religious Than Men?" Friday, September 28, 2012. http://atheismplus.com/forums/viewtopic.php?f=17&t=1401 Retrieved Friday, October 12th, 2012.

176 Marta Trzebiatowska and Steve Bruce. *Why are Women more Religious Than Men?* "Chapter I: The Great Divide." Published by Oxford University Press, USA, Friday, October 12th of 2012. p. 2.

177 This is also applied to Jerusalem, as in Isaiah 62:1-5, and the new, heavenly Jerusalem (written of in Hebrews 12:22).

178 "Here Comes the Bridegroom," from the series *I Will Build My Church – A Study of the Church.* http://bible.org/seriespage/here-comes-bridegroom Retrieved Thursday, October 18th of 2012.

179 The following verse reminds us that, according to the NAB footnote on it, the social position of women in both the world and the family matters not, for women are equal recipients of the gift of God's salvation. Paul makes this point very clear (see 1 Cor 11, 11–12; Gal 3, 28). 2003-2004 Edition, p. 1351.

or *kurios* in the original Greek text, which is in itself a difficult thing to deal with as it is a title given to God and the Messiah.

Furthermore, both 1 Corinthians 11:3 and Ephesians 5:23 state that the husband is the head of the wife, as Christ is the head of the church. Though it may be impossible to concretely determine why misogyny developed as it did in so many cultures throughout the world, this demand for female fealty offered an opportunity for even Christian husbands to claim full dominance over their wives, and the practice was not one which men could easily abandon, as seen in the works of Shakespeare and elsewhere wherein females find themselves obliged to address men as "my lord."

The culmination of this was well-expressed in an 1854 poem which is considered to have perfectly captured the essence of the expected role of women in the Victorian era. It was written by Coventry Patmore about his wife Emily, whom he believed was the perfect Victorian wife. Thus he entitled his poem "The Angel in the House", which extolled the saintly qualities believed inherent to women. It was perhaps the first time since the Age of Chivalry that women were widely believed to have great virtues worthy of devotion by default, yet women were expected to focus much of their devotion upon their husbands.

Thus "The Angel in the House" begins with the statement that, while man must be pleased, it is woman's pleasure to please him. Patmore then laments that her self-sacrificing and tireless devotion all-too-often is answered by icy indifference, impatience, or even harsh words. Nevertheless, through it all the ideal woman – like our Lord Jesus Christ – remains too gentle even to speak on her own behalf. Instead she merely awaits her husband's remorse with forgiveness in her eyes, and when he is at last shamed enough to express it, she...

> "...leans and weeps against his breast,
> And seems to think the sin was hers...."[180]

---

180 Department of English – Lilia Melani. William Makepeace Thackeray – Discussion of *Vanity Fair*. "The Angel in the House." March 2, 2011. http://academic.brooklyn.cuny.edu/english/melani/novel_19c/thackeray/angel.html Retrieved Sunday, October 14th, 2012.

Is this not a beautiful display of submissive piety? Is this not truly angelic in nature? Would that everyone upon the Earth paid such loving obedience to God! How wondrous and perfect to have no desire but to do His will; no need save to know His Love...and how distorted and dangerous such devotion becomes when directed instead toward a flawed mortal being (or any being other than God, for that matter)!!

Thus we behold the problem; the immense gentle submission displayed here is not directed toward God, but rather toward man. In the words of Desdemona from *Othello*, "Nay, we must think men are not gods...."[181]

The Father and the Son clearly agree. One recalls Exodus 20:3 ("Thou shalt have no other gods before me") and Matthew 23:10 ("... one is your Master, even Christ."). However, one must still address the Pauline statements regarding the husband being head of the wife even as Christ is the head of the church and how they are to be interpreted. In 1 Corinthians 11:3, Saint Paul stated, "...the head of every man is Christ; and the head of the woman is the man; and the head of Christ is God." Could he have truly been attempting to establish an absolute hierarchy? This seems quite doubtful; especially when one considers that he began the chapter with the statement, "Be ye followers of me, even[182] as I also am of Christ." He could not possibly have been instructing his followers to worship a human en route to worship of the LORD! The Ephesians section dealing with the subjection of wives to their husbands (5:21-33) may remind one of a section from the following chapter (Ephesians 6:7-8), which appears to exhort slaves to be subject to their owners in a rather similar fashion, and this raises additional questions.

To answer them, I defer to the Church Militant, in the form of the Roman Catholic New American [Holy] Bible (2003-2004 Edition) footnote for Ephesians 5, 21-6, 9. This footnote references such verses as Ephesians 5:25 and 6:2 to make it clear that – among mortals – exclusive claims to domination by one party are undermined by the initial principle of subordination to one another *under Christ.* The hierarchy, then, is not absolute, save that all must obey God. Still, the Apostle Paul did not yet

---

181 William Shakespeare. *Othello.* Act III, Scene iv, line 144.

182 Greek *kathos* or simply *hos,* which does translate precisely as it was in the King James Bible.

strive to establish sexual equality in a social sense, and rather affirmed the partriarchal system already established by those societies to which he wrote. 1 Peter 3:1-2 gives an additional reason for female submission to the husband: "...that, if any obey not the word, they also may without the word be won by the conversation of the wives; While they behold your chaste conversation coupled with fear." (KJV)

This reversal of the temptation of Solomon (ie. being corrupted by the heathen influence of wives, of which so many other Israelite men were also afraid) was employed to considerable success by Saint Monica upon her Pagan husband and son (the latter of whom would eventually become Saint Augustine of Hippo), and in this case we cannot expect that the "angel in the house" seemed "to think the sin was hers!"

Verses 3-5 list other feminine virtues and end with mention of how the holy women of old, "who trusted in God," were "in subjection unto their own husbands," reminding the reader that there is indeed precedent for this delegation of power. However, when one thinks of such ancient holy women, another precedent comes to mind: Deborah. This Judge and Prophetess had a husband, and perhaps she was entirely obedient and submissive to him at home (we do not know for certain), but it was nevertheless she who ruled Israel at the calling of God. If she had adhered to decrees of deference, she might have instead merely advised Lapidoth (the meaning of whose name would then recall Romeo's line regarding Juliet, "O, she doth teach the torches to burn bright!"[183]), and it would have been her husband who was "known in the gates, when he sitteth among the elders of the land." (Proverbs 31:23). The fact that God chose a woman for this task instead is a recurring theme we shall see throughout Christian history: women emerging to change a situation in which the masculine heavily outweighs the feminine, even when it requires Divine Intervention to accomplish this change.

Such changes generally do not come swiftly or easily, however. The First Epistle to the Greek Christians in Corinth offers perhaps another example of the Apostle Paul's willingness to accept elements of foreign culture even as he gives new rules by which the faithful among such cultures are to live:

---

183 William Shakespeare. *Romeo and Juliet.* Act I, Scene V, line 41.

> "Let your women keep silence in the churches: for it is not permitted unto them to speak; but they are commanded to be under obedience as also saith the law.
>
> And if they will learn any thing, let them ask their husbands at home: for it is a shame for women to speak in the church." (1 Corinthians 14:34-35, KJV)

I suspect I am not the only woman who finds it difficult to read these verses without pursed lips or clenched teeth. The New American (Holy) Bible I have referenced so much already also provides an insightful footnote here, particularly as its footnotes reflect the position of the world's largest Church. Here the statement is made that it is difficult to harmonize this injunction to silence with Chapter 11 of the same Epistle, as there it is taken for granted the women do pray and prophecy alound in the assembly. 1 Corinthians 14:34-35 are thus often considered an interpolation which reflects the discipline of later churches.[184]

I can by no means speak for women in general, yet I consider myself a tremendously submissive creature (believe it or not) and would gladly "remain silent"[185] if our LORD wished it of us; but I do not believe He does. Instead, I find drawn to my attention the fifth verse preceding that statement of Paul's – "Let the prophets speak two or three, and let the other judge" – and consider Luke 2:36-38:

> "And there was one Anna, a prophetess, the daughter of Phanuel, of the tribe of Aser: she was of great age, and had lived with an husband seven years from her virginity;
>
> And she was a widow of about fourscore and four years, which departed not from the temple, but served God with fastings and prayers night and day.
>
> And she coming in that instant gave thanks likewise unto the Lord, and spake of him to all them that looked for redemption in Jerusalem." (KJV)

---

184 p. 1246.

185 Esther 4:14.

Luke the Evangelist, who wrote in addition to the gospel which bears his name also the Acts of the Apostles, may be considered an ancient male proto-feminist of sorts, for he did all he could to include females in his work whenever possible. Thus it is his gospel which focuses more on the Blessed Virgin Mother Mary than any other, and thus it is he who includes the Prophetess Anna identifying Jesus as the Messiah in the Temple, thus increasing the number of witnesses to His Divine status from one[186] to two. This additional witness is extremely important due to Deuteronomy 19:15....

> "One witness shall not rise up...at the mouth of two witnesses, or at the mouth of three witnesses, shall the matter be established." (KJV)

..and Matthew 18:16, 19 & 20....

> "But if he will not hear thee, then take with thee one or two more, that in the mouth of two or three witnesses every word may be established. ...
>
> Again I say unto you, That if two of you shall agree on earth as touching any thing that they shall ask, it shall be done for them of my Father which is in heaven.
>
> For where two or three are gathered together in my name, there am I in the midst of them." (KJV; to be taken quite literally in the case of Simeon and Anna!)[187]

Anna needed to serve as the second witness to the Child Jesus Christ in the temple, and to do so her testimony needed to be equal

---

186 Simeon; see Luke 2:25-35.

187 Additional Gospel verses which testify to the value of two witnesses are Mark 6:7, wherein Jesus sends His disciples out in pairs to cast out unclean spirits, and John 8:17, in which Jesus reiterates Deuteronomy 19:15 to justify Himself (using the Greek word *anthropos,* which is used primarily to mean humanity in general (whether male or female)). This is also important in the prophecy of the final two witnesses in Revelation 11:3-12.

to that of a man.[188] Discriminatory rules and customs would be ever so much easier to maintain if God did not insist upon constantly and openly defying them!

However, does all this liberation of women not go against the grain of Genesis 3:16, in which God tells Eve that her husband shall rule over her? If one assumes that this statement was not limited to Adam and Eve themselves, it becomes difficult to reconcile with the LORD's selection of Deborah as ruler of Israel. One possible explanation is that this verse contained a combination of direct acts of God (in the statement "I will greatly multiply thy sorrow and thy conception; in sorrow thou shalt bring forth children;") and prediction of events to come (for the vast majority of societies throughout history have been fiercely patriarchal). It is certain that these events were allowed to occur by the permissive will of God and that they were able to exist only through His infinite creative power, but regarding the behaviour of His free-willed children this was perhaps not commandment but portent; not decree but prophecy. Examples of this elsewhere in the Bible include those statements which would otherwise involve God instructing His people to disobey His desires or even His Commandments, such as in the dire circumstances in which the people would eat their own children (including Leviticus 26:29, Deuteronomy 28:53 & 28:57, Isaiah 49:26, Jeremiah 19:9, Ezekiel 5:10, and Zechariah 11:9) and Jesus Christ's declaring that He was come to bring a sword and to set family members against one another in Matthew 10:34-36 and Luke 12:51-53. He knew what must come to pass; yet that does not mean He truly desired it.

Let us now briefly examine another witness of Jesus from the Gospel: Mary of Magdala, whose mysterious relationship with the Saviour is only minimally recorded yet which awarded her an honour received by none of His male followers. She was first to behold His Resurrected form, and was tasked with being the first to spread the Good News that Christ has risen. Thus it could be said that the first test put forth to humanity by the Risen Christ was this: will you listen to – and believe – a woman?

---

188 Another of Luke's writings, The Acts of the Apostles 2:18 also reminds us that God bestows His Prophetic Spirit upon members of both genders and thus that it is wise to heed all who receive it.

In John 4, this question is also answered by (though not expressly asked of) the Samaritan woman who found Jesus at Jacob's well, who believed Him at His word that He was the Messiah and went to tell the people of her city of this. Like Peter and John did the testimony of Mary Magdalene, the people of the city believed her enough to go out and seek Jesus, though they later "...said unto the woman, Now we believe, not because of thy saying: for we have heard him ourselves, and know that this is indeed the Christ, the Saviour of the world." (v. 42)

John also reminds us that female empowerment is not limited to being capable of doing that which is traditionally done by men; for the Scriptures contain a spiritual example of something that was distinctly womanly which only one man was able to accomplish. Saint Theresa of Lisieux established that women were the ones who braved the soldiers to follow Jesus to the very foot of the Cross, but they were not entirely alone in this. There was one man with sufficient bravery to do as the women did.

It was John the Beloved who, after all the other Disciples had fled, possessed the courage to remain with Jesus unto His final moments upon the cross...just like a woman. For after all, Mary Magdalene was one of many women who remained with and followed Jesus to the end... and the new beginning.

The Virgin Mary versus Wonder Woman

No study of the Bible would be complete without reference to the woman who has become most acknowledged: the Blessed Virgin Mother Mary. In a world where women – especially those outside of the aristocracy were historically looked down upon[189] it was she who evinced feminine virtue as the compassionate and loving...

> "...mediator between God and man, and it was she who, with divine authority, took on the devil, rebuking and even punishing him. The cult of Mary paralleled the medieval

189 Ruth Tucker and Dr. Walter L. Liefeld, Ph.D. *Daughters of the Church: Women and Ministry from New Testament Times to the Present.* Zondervan, 1987. p. 168.

> aristocratic concept of chivalry... [and was, in fact, responsible for it]
>
> ...'Mary transformed Catholicism from a religion of terror... into a religion of mercy and love.'"[190]

Indeed, it is her immense significance in Christianity throughout the ages that led the Madonna to become such an icon of femininity.[191] Femininity is a very versatile and complex trait, as we have already seen demonstrated by so many Biblical characters, and the perspective of that which should be valued in a woman has shifted in many directions over the millennia. Mary has endured as a legendary figure throughout all this time, however, and due to her image at times contrasting with that of the "modern woman," there exist a number of people who have had problems with it. Of all these I have encountered, perhaps the most insightful has been John Shelby Spong, retired Episcopal Bishop of Newark, New Jersey, who wrote an intriguing article titled "The Virgin Mary is No Wonder Woman.[192]" In this article, he effectively lists all of the problems with Saint Mary's traditional depiction that interfere with her being seen as an empowering role-model for today's younger females. Spong's complaint is that the Queen of Heaven has been portrayed as too compliant, docile, gentle, passive, sweet, virginal, and unreal to enable the modern young woman to free herself from her stereotypical societal expectations. He states that Mary's call was to obedience rather than to a pro-active existence. According to him:

---

[190] Ibid.

[191] TVTropes.org even refers to her as "the most feminine figure in Christianity." TV Tropes Foundation, LLC http://tvtropes.org/pmwiki/pmwiki.php/Characters/TheFourGospels Retrieved Thursday, October 4th of 2012.

[192] Of course, if one wishes to compare the value as role-model of the Blessed Virgin Mother Mary with that of a comic-book superheroine, one may wonder where upon the spectrum betwixt them would be found the "Warrior Nuns" and Sisters of Battle who were relatively popular during the 1990s.... Indeed, as I recall, the criticism leveled against them by real Nuns was always drawn from the following two arguments: i) that their appearance was sexualized for a male audience, and ii) that they were unnecessarily violent (if only to demons) and thus catered more to typical comic-book content than to the actual values embodied by real Nuns and Sisters of the Church.

> "The Virgin Mary's chief problem was that far from being a woman who could inspire real women to new heights, she was a construct of a male world. She was the kind of woman the defining males of the time, who were overwhelmingly the ordained clergy, wanted women to be."

Forgive me, yet I must confess I am sorely tempted to eviscerate this article with great zeal. However, Mary's call was – and is – also a call to comport oneself as a proper lady, and thus I shall endeavour to retain my composure. The fact is, "the ordained clergy" of Mary's time were prepared to gleefully stone her to death due to her lack of obedience to their teaching.

Here is a little 'proverb' I just came up with (yet one to which I dearly hope people have been adhering for a very long time): If something purportedly related to the Sacred Scriptures feels wrong to you, so that you cannot fathom how it could be the Word of the God who created you in His image, it is time to re-examine that part of said Scripture to see if the truth has been lost in its re-imagining. (It is also wise to consult with others who have entered into the Christian religious life and studied the Scriptures extensively; their enlightened input will be quite useful indeed!)

While I have no doubt that the former Bishop is correct to some degree and that the image of Mary has been misused by men who wish to keep women under control, such attempted disfigurement of what the foremost Saint truly represents requires careful failure to address or acknowledge the full or true meaning revealed in the Scriptures. This technique of control-through-misinformation may be effective for a time, but its success is never permanent.

The virtue of purity embodied by the Blessed Virgin Mary is the virtue for which she is most well-known, and it is true that a life of perpetual virginity may not be for everyone. It is this virtue which makes Mary appear most 'unreal' in a modern world where sexuality is constantly being displayed, appealed to, and discussed, particularly due to the supernatural Heavenly origins of her Son Jesus. However, it must be understood that it is because of our potential to be Heavenly that chastity and monogamy are such important virtues.

In Christianity, chastity and virginity are not simply about ensuring that a woman's reproductive capabilities will be 'possessed' only by one mortal man. This was exemplified by the 3rd - 4th Century maiden Saint Catherine of Alexandria, who answered demands that she take a husband with the statement that she would only marry someone who surpassed her in beauty, intelligence, wealth and dignity. To such an extent did she excel in those qualities that Catherine knew well no mortal man could be found to meet these requirements, and she was soon consecrated to Jesus Christ. This meant that she was not at all ruled by carnal pursuits, nor any feeling of need to bear a son, but could devote her energies to spiritual matters.

Like Saint Catherine, the Blessed Virgin Mother also exemplifies other traits which are very positive for girls and women. Before exploring those of Mary, however, let us first examine those of the superheroine against whom Spong has pitted her.

It is true that fictional characters such as Wonder Woman (a character of whom I myself have always been quite fond) feel more approachable than great historical and religious figures such as Saints. This is because of their being fictional; the artificiality and malleability of such characters allows one to feel more comfortable identifying with them. Thus it feels 'safer' trying to be like Wonder Woman than it does attempting to imitate the dauntingly-perfect Blessed Virgin Mother Mary.

For her part, Wonder Woman, the superheroine Amazon Diana[193], is an inspirational icon in her own way. As she is held in such high esteem, it is useful to examine the character through the eyes of the man responsible for her existence: William Moulton Marston. Marston, an American psychologist/feminist theorist/inventor/comic book writer, described Wonder Woman as "psychological propaganda" for a new kind of woman whom he believed should rule the world, for he had concluded that "there isn't enough love in the male organism to run this planet peacefully." He drew upon the somewhat-dubious scientific understanding that a woman's body contains twice the amount of "love

[193] Wonder Woman was named after the Roman virgin goddess of the hunt and of the moon; called Artemis in Greek. She was associated with mythological goddesses due to their being viewed as images of female empowerment.

generating" organs and endocrinological systems as that of a man, before offering his lament about the female human organism: that she lacks the dominance or self-assertive power to achieve and enforce her loving desires. Thus he gave this dominating force, yet kept her loving, maternal, tender and feminine in all other ways.[194]

(As an aside, it is worthy of note that, 44 years earlier, suffragette Clara B. Neyman made a similar statement in *The Woman's Bible*, albeit with a different inspiration:

> "Like Deborah, woman will forever be the inspired leader, if she will have the courage to assert and maintain her power. Her aspirations must keep pace with the demands of our civilization.
>
> **God never discriminates; it is man who has made the laws and compelled woman to obey him.**"[195])

This image of woman suggests a mass of complexes. It extols the virtues of the female to a point which could even be considered sexist, yet at the same time it states that there is an incompleteness about women that keeps us from realizing our full potential so far as the world is concerned. The required component stated here is aggressive and seems necessary for success because aggression has met with such success in the past, even though the stated mission of Wonder Woman "was to bring the Amazon[?] ideals of love, peace, and sexual equality to 'a world torn by the hatred of men.'"[196] Thus we are left with the potentially self-destructive question of how much gentle femininity needs be sacrificed by a woman to achieve and enforce her loving desires. Marston is brilliant – I might even go so far as to call him a

194 http://www.castlekeys.com/Pages/wonder.html Retrieved Monday, October 8th, 2012.

195 *The Woman's Bible, Part II*, "Commentary on Judges", pp. 22-23, emphasis mine.

196 Crawford, Philip Charles. "The Legacy of Wonder Woman – An enlightening look at the feminist ideals that informed this American icon." *School Library Journal*, 03/01/2007. http://www.schoollibraryjournal.com/article/CA6417196.html Retrieved Monday, October 8th, 2012.

genius, and it pains me to continue – but he is also, perhaps without realizing it, doing precisely what men have been doing for thousands of years: stating that, as a creature, woman is perfect without in fact being quite good enough.

Admittedly, for most people it seems difficult to imagine women ruling the world without employing quite a lot of self-assertive aggression; society has had far too much history of that being the primary means to power and of those possessing insufficient amounts of it being deemed 'weak' and thus unworthy of power. To again use an example from the Benin Kingdom region which could really apply to virtually anywhere in the world:

> "In recent times political scientists have cited sexism as a major obstacle on the way of women's political advancement.... It was in the military regime that women-devaluing attitudes were fostered, in a male dominated, male-oriented military environment. All these obstacles...enhance the invisibility of women in the political centre stage."[197]

Marston was very familiar with the concept of nature versus nurture, which is the ongoing question of how much of a human being stems from biology and how much is a product of social conditioning. He recognized the potential for women to succeed in all walks of life once he beheld how they did precisely that while so many of the men were off fighting in the World Wars (and his having a wife[198] who was among

---

197 Oronsaye-Salami, Irene Isoken (PhD). "Emerging from the Shadows? Changing Patterns in Edo Women's Political Participation." Presented 2-4th of September 2005. http://www.edo-nation.net/salami1.htm Retrieved Monday, October 8th, 2012.

198 Elizabeth Holloway Marston, who in addition to acquiring degrees in both psychology and law, joined her husband investigating the physiological symptoms of deception which led William to the invention of the polygraph/lie detector (precursor to the magic lasso of truth wielded by Wonder Woman, whom she would also help William create). Marguerite Lamb, "Who Was Wonder Woman 1", *Bostonia: The Alumni Quarterly of Boston University*, Fall 2001. http://web.archive.org/web/20071208045132/http://www.bu.edu/alumni/bostonia/2001/fall/wonderwoman/ Retrieved Saturday, October 6th, 2012.

the first women ever to earn a college degree (and also among the first to put off having a child until she had reached her "sexual peak" at 35) likely contributed to his attitude also). Yet women were (and are) trying to find places for themselves in a world filled with war and other forms of conflict, so some degree of competition, aggression, and perhaps even violence seemed acceptable (besides, such would help Wonder Woman comics to be more appealing to the primarily-male audience who read such fare).

The world is a seductively powerful thing, and thus this modern ideal has become dominant, for it seems entirely necessary for success and even for survival.

During World War II, amidst a time when comic books were selling at a clip of fifteen million monthly and accounted for a quarter of all magazines shipped to U.S. servicemen abroad, William Moulton Marston "struck upon an idea for a new kind of superhero, one who would triumph not with fists or firepower, but with love. [His wife Elizabeth immediately replied to this statement with, "Fine...but make her a woman."][199] The result, as is readily apparent, has met with considerable success, however after Marston's passing Wonder Woman herself became subject to the desires of any writer who chose to portray her, and none appear to have known her quite so well as he. From what I have seen of her modern depictions, Wonder Woman seldom uses her magical lariat of truth for any purpose besides that of a super-strong version of the traditional Punjab (or "cowboy's") lasso, and writers more often than not seem to have displayed her as being entirely outmatched by Superman's strength (though in an early 1990s cross-over with Marvel, she was deemed worthy to wield Mjolnir, the Hammer of Thor). Like Storm (with whom she dueled in the aforementioned cross-over)[200] from Marvel's *X-Men* series[201], who

---

199 Lamb, Marguerite. Ibid.

200 *DC vs. Marvel Comics*. 1996. Written by Ron Marz and Peter David. I shan't give you any hints/spoilers as to who was victorious, save to say that she was my favourite of the two superheroines.

201 In one decade-old story arc (that of *X-Treme X-Men #12* (written by Chris Claremont) and its adjoining installments) which comes to mind as an example of how comic books – despite the at times brilliant content found

also begun her career with a code of ethics including literally the phrase "I shall not kill,"[202] Wonder Woman is intimidating to portray because she has become such an iconic example of a minority and is so many things to so many people. Thus it is much easier for authors to write her as if she were "one of the guys" in the established mode for super heroes (particularly if said writers are often not a part of the heroine's aforementioned minority). It is easy to fall into a masculine stereotype when one's goal is simply to compete with men "at their own game." After all, despite the enlightened and positive intentions for her, Wonder Woman remains the work of human beings.

Thus, when we see Wonder Woman gleefully laugh as she thrusts down an energy blade into the eye of alien conquerer Darkseid (pronounced "Dark Side")[203], it is difficult to claim that such a display is a misrepresentation of her character. She, like all fictional characters, may be reimagined in any number of ways, for all she ever was was imagined.

To rewrite a superhero can be legitimate reinventing. To rewrite a Saint can only be slander (or libel).

---

within them – are written specifically to appeal to a target audience, said X-Man found herself captive in the harem of a tyrant named Khan. She first attempted to employ Esther's technique of diplomatic coaxing to keep Khan from his stated goal of conquering the universe, but he failed to acquiesce and thus it was necessary that much butt be kicked by all. (One may take this moment to recall that the source of the film *300*, which featured a...unique... interpretation of the King Xerxes of the Book of Esther as its prime villain, was also originally a comic book.)

202 Marvel Comics Group. *The Uncanny X-Men #159,* "Night Screams!" p. 27. July, 1982. Also written by Chris Claremont. In this issue, Storm faces Count Dracula. I just thought you should know that.

203 *Justice League Issue 6.* 2012. Written by Geoff Johns. In this issue, Wonder Woman did briefly employ the truth coercion feature of her magical lasso (though I'm not quite certain what manner of response she expected as she was at the time also using it to strangle her target). For more information on the issue, one may consult http://www.comicvine.com/news/justice-league-takes-on-darkseid-in-issue-6/144340/ (Retrieved Monday, October 8th of 2012, but I must caution against viewing the related comments, as they involve reader desire to have Green Lantern chain down and abuse "the 'invisable' woman." Such a statement seems unintentionally symbolic.)

Thus it is wise to look beyond the iconography of the Blessed Virgin Mother Mary and examine whom she was prior to what the late-19th Century feminist commentary *The Woman's Bible* inaccurately describes as her "deification."[204]

Luke 2:51 reveals that Mary (perhaps alone among those around her) kept[205] all the teachings of her Son within her understanding, which indicates that she was/is especially wise and intelligent. This intelligence took the form of a quiet, contemplation which suggests far deeper giftedness in these areas than even the more active and aggressive approach taken by so many others.

Additionally, the courage of Mary was the stuff of legends and her faith was unparalleled by any of the other children of God. This becomes readily apparent when one considers how boldly she defied a law of the clergy which would have had her stoned to death for the sake of Christ. In Deuteronomy 22:13-21, we behold the supposedly-immutable Law that almost destroyed her for having become pregnant by means other than that of her earthly husband, for:

> "...if this thing be true, and the tokens of virginity [such as a sheet stained with the blood from the broken hymen] be not found for the damsel: then they shall bring out the damsel to the door of her father's house, and the men of her city shall stone her with stones that she die: because she hath wrought folly in Israel, to play the whore in her father's house: so shalt thou put evil away from among you."[206]

One can only imagine the centuries of suspicion and suffering this wrought, and it is very important to realize that this was the Law which compliant, docile, gentle, passive, sweet, and obedient Mary was up against, and that within the mortal realm she faced it utterly alone.

One cannot imagine just how she felt when the vision faded away and the Blessed Virgin Mother Mary was left with her choice of remaining true to the LORD rather than the world. It was not one to last only the span of a dream or the spark of an inspiration, but rather

---

204 Part II. "Comments on John." Anon. p. 144.

205 In the original Greek *diaterio*; "to keep continually or carefully."

206 Deuteronomy 22:20-21, KJV.

it was a constant choice that likely gnawed at her indomitable resolve continually.

Mary demonstrated the amazingly-immense courage and faith necessary to speak what she knew to be true, despite having no apparent evidence save that which was within her own heart, mind, and soul. In so doing she risked the bitter rejection of everyone she had ever loved in the world, and death at the hands of an angry mob which was convinced that it in its murder would "put evil away from among [it]."[207]

It is not a thing easily done.

Mary risked certain death on the strength of a vision[208], for she had faith as a mustard seed[209] (at least), yet felt no need to toss around trees or mountains to prove her strength. She was not a construct of a male world, and neither was her Child. Sojourner Truth made this very clear when she pointed out that Christ came from God and a woman, and thus:

> "Man had nothing to do with Him."[210]

The Blessed Virgin Mother Mary was and is obedient, yes, yet to God alone.

For I myself, this was the only way in which Mary's call was a call to obedience. My upbringing was far from that of a traditional girl, and thus I am sorry to say that those virtues popularly associated

---

[207] Deuteronomy 22:21 (KJV). The form of death would have been the traditional and readily-available method: to "stone her with stones", Hebrew אבן *'eben* {eh'-ben} (of the letters El bet nun; "א Strong/Power/Leader's ב family/house's ן (seed)/heir", which may be logographically significant when considering John the Baptist's statement in Luke 3:8, "I say unto you, That God is able of these stones to raise up children unto Abraham." (KJV)) The noun itself can mean hailstones, sling stones, stone (in general), or even a perverse, hard heart.

[208] It is also fortunate indeed that Joseph, "being a just man," chose not to 'purge the evil' of the Blessed Virgin, but heeded the dream he received (Matthew 1:19-24).

[209] Matthew 17:20, Luke 17:6.

[210] "Ain't I A Woman?" Speech delivered in December of 1851 at the Women's Convention, Akron, Ohio. Retrieved from Fordham University – The Jesuit University of New York at http://www.fordham.edu/halsall/mod/sojtruth-woman.asp on Thursday, October 11th of 2012.

with the Blessed Virgin were usually disturbingly distant from my mind – and I was reprimanded whenever they were not. I was taught to be tough, unfeeling, ambitious and aggressive, and was successful enough at this that I went fourteen years (from the ages of fifteen to twenty-nine) without weeping...or eventually, having the ability to weep. I *did* feel that Mary was not "a woman who could inspire...me...to new heights," for in addition to her being unimaginably far above me, hers were qualities I was not permitted to even *begin* to imitate; for I was encouraged to defy and challenge everything. Yet I wanted to imitate her; to be possessed of a sweet gentleness that could endure despite all the world's attempts to destroy it, and to understand how such qualities as hers could be of value...that I could receive God's love without having to "challenge" Him. Indeed, though I was forced to keep the fact secret, the Blessed Virgin Mother Mary was and is my hero(ine). Her example was my woman's liberation.

Truly, if the Scripturally-accurate Virgin Mary were taught as a lesson to champion your beliefs and stand up for what you know is right – even if you too have not exhibited "super strength" or the ability to "stop a bullet cold", and even if all the world mounts against you as it did her – then she would be a most powerful feminist message indeed!

Yet in the face of all of this, Saint Mary always exemplified "a meek and quiet spirit, which is in the sight of God of great price."[211] Yes, she was (and is) brilliantly, beautifully submissive, passive, docile and meek, in addition to being unbreakable. Not because of some presumed position as a 'token female' or even due to her role as "Queen Mother" (a prominent position in many cultures, not just Christian ones) is Mary exalted above all other Saints, but because she is the pinnacle of human existence and a perfect exemplar of its relationship with God.

As Roman Catholic Father Chris Pietraszko stated on October 1st of 2012:

> "She is the image of the Church Triumphant[212], because sin did not reign in her, the bearer of God."

---

211 1Peter 3:4, KJV.

212 As opposed to the Church Militant (those Christians living upon the earth, and Christian militia who struggle against sin and those who promote it), the

The Mystery of Joan of Arc

Mary and a number of other saints were instrumental in influencing Saint Joan of Arc in her mission to reunite France and at last bring a conclusion to the Hundred Years' War[213] (a war which wouldn't have happened were it not for a rule against succession to the throne by females preventing a woman named Joan from becoming ruler of France[214], but I digress). However, the nature of her mission also meant calling into question traditional understanding of gender roles and expression. These circumstances together would form a very enigmatic historical figure; one who was abandoned by everyone when she was alive, yet one who has been embraced by nearly everyone long after she was no longer present to speak for herself.

The story of her life is iconic; not only for women, but as the very image of the hero's epic journey. Born a peasant girl in a pastoral setting, Joan Darc led a pious and peaceful life on her family's land, marred occasionally by the ravages of the war of a foreign Empire. Her life changed irrevocably when she came of (teen)age; voices from Heaven (specifically those of Saint Catherine of Alexandria, Saint Margaret of

---

Church Triumphant comprises those who are in Heaven.

213 A series of conflicts waged from 1337 to 1453 between the Kingdom of England (at times aided by Burgundian (Northern French) allies) and the Kingdom of France (at times aided by Scottish allies) for control of the French throne. It is generally divided into three phases which were separated by truces: the Edwardian Era War (1337-1360), the Caroline War (1369-1389), and the Lancastrian War (1415-1453).

214 Joan II of Navarre (28 January 1312 to 6 October 1349) was not permitted to rule France for two reasons. The first was due to her mother Margaret of Burgundy's infidelity; it resulted in Joan's legitimacy being called into question, just like that of Joan of Arc's King Charles VII. This contributed to the second reason: the Capetian (Mediaeval French) rule could thus be more-easily used against her, which prevented succession to the throne by a female. Her father's brother Philip V was crowned at Reims and became ruler of France instead, died without a male heir and was succeeded by his younger brother Charles IV, who also died without a male heir and was succeeded by his cousin Philip VI. However, Charles IV's closest male relative was actually his nephew Edward III...of England. Edward had several disagreements with Philip, and the result was the Hundred Years' War.

Antioch, and Saint Michael the Archangel, not 'Saint Dustin Hoffman' as a certain Turn-of-the-Millennium movie would suggest[215]) spoke to Joan and bestowed unto her the gifts of understanding and of prophecy. They also told her of her destiny to fulfill a seemingly-impossible prophecy: she was to be the legendary Maid from her homeland of Lorraine who would take up arms to drive out the invading English and reunite divided France. With nothing but her faith in her visions, Joan set out to accomplish her God-given mission. Through persistence, diplomacy, and signs, Joan the Maid reached and convinced the *Dauphin* (the French crown prince) and those truly loyal to him to arm her and give her co-command of his army. Being an extremely gifted strategist and charismatic crusader, Joan led this army to liberate Orléans and several smaller towns along the Loire river and clear a safe path for the Dauphin to be consecrated King Charles VII at the city of Reims. However, the freshly-crowned king was more interested in appeasement than in pressing his advantage to take Paris and claim final victory, and thus he ceased to provide Joan with the military support she needed. Forced to rely on mercenaries (with whom she refused to compromise her moral code), Joan of Arc was restricted to coming to the aid of individual small towns until May 23rd of 1430, when she took the place of honour at the rear of her retreating army to hold off their overwhelming pursuers. Locked outside the walls of Compiègne, the city she sought to save, Joan of Arc was captured by the Burgundians and sold to the English for a prince's ransom. She was then tried for heresy by a politically-motivated Bishop and – despite confounding her prosecutors with her brilliant responses to their questions – sentenced to be burned at the stake for the crimes of cross-dressing and remaining true to her visions. In the town of Rouen on May 30th, 1431, Joan of Arc died quite literally in a blaze of glory. She was nineteen.

Primarily because of the detailed records of her trials, the Battle-Saint Joan of Arc is one of the most well-documented people in history and also one of the most confusing. She appears at first to be a mass of contradictions. She was a peasant girl who achieved a knightly and noble rank which noone else of her class (whether male or female) could

215 Specifically *The Messenger: The Story of Joan of Arc*, directed by Luc Besson.

ever have hoped for. She was an overtly-female "chieftan of war" (albeit a title which Joan herself adamantly denied assuming)[216] who dressed as a man and actively discouraged other females from coming near the army. Like Mary, she was a devoutly-religious person chosen by God yet forced to see the fruit of her labour (and herself) condemned by His Church (two new Pontiffs were required before Joan would be considered anything but a heretic, for Pope Nicholas V seemed content to let her condemning Bishop Pierre Cauchon's verdict stand). Divine inspiration is the most satisfactory explanation for her actions in part because they are so difficult to explain.

This difficulty has not prevented people from attempting to explain them in whichever manner most supports the explainer's agenda, however, and thus Joan of Arc has received many often-contradictory titles and roles since her death. French Revolutionaries and their sympathizers were happy to destroy items once belonging to Joan due to her association with Royalism (because she installed a king) while others lifted her up as a champion of the common people (as she was of peasant birth and did indeed champion them). Nationalists praised Joan for removing foreign elements from France while foreigners have praised the saint for her desire to make peace with (and even ally with) her erstwhile enemies outside of France. She is among the only feminist icons to be protested by a feminist group, as FEMEN displayed a banner comparing Joan's conservative supporters to Nazis on the 12th of May 2013, during a celebration around her golden equestrian statue.[217] During the 2012 French presidential election campaign, Socialist candidate and current-President Francois Hollande stated that he would not join in the celebration of Joan of Arc's 600th birthday because he "does not want

---

216 The Condemnation Trial of Joan of Arc. Second Public Examination; conducted Thursday, February 22nd of 1431. The Bishop and 48 Assessors were present. http://www.stjoan-center.com/Trials/sec02.html Retrieved 04/06/2013.

217 This took place at the Place des Pyramides in Paris, where nationalist, royalist, anti-revolutionary, and anti-globalization groups layed wreaths of flowers at the foot of the equestrian statue of Joan of Arc. The feminist group in question, FEMEN, shall be discussed further in the next chapter.

to share an icon with the Far-Right."[218] However, Joan has often been (albeit unofficially) referred to as "the patron saint of queers", and she has helped to inspire homosexuals to return to the Catholic Church, one of whom wrote:

> "It is in her spirit that I preach good news to the queers: You, yes, you too are welcome. Blessed are you whom the Church has heavily laden. God is bigger than the Church, and He aches for your presence."[219]

As with those figures whom I discussed in the previous section, Joan of Arc means many different things to many different people. Just in time for the beginning of the 7th century since her birth, the *New York Times* described her in its article "The Koan of Joan" as "the cross-dressing, teenage virgin-warrior-martyr-saint"[220]. Even the three epochs of the life of Joan of Arc – the humble shepherdess communing with God, the Paladin in shining armour, and the persecuted prisoner who remains true to her faith even when faced with death– each represent a well-known and very Christian archetype. However, it is generally her

---

218 "Sarkozy, rivals fight for the right to claim Joan of Arc" *France 24*. 06/01/2012. http://www.france24.com/en/20120106-sarkozy-far-right-rally-behind-joan-arc-le-pen-600-years-birth-france-election Retrieved November 22nd of 2012. Every May 1st, crowds of the nationalist front rally around a giant golden statue of her in Paris. See also Devorah Lauter, "France's bittersweet birthday party for Joan of Arc" *Los Angeles Times*. January 7th of 2012. http://articles.latimes.com/2012/jan/07/world/la-fg-joan-arc-20120107 Retrieved 22/11/2012.

219 *If I told you. Personal stories that are often difficult to discuss openly within the Church.* "Three: The patron saint of queers" April 22, 2010. http://www.ifitoldyou.org/2010/04/22/three-the-patron-saint-of-queers/ Retrieved April 6, 2013.

220 Sciolino, Elaine. "Lumiere | The Koan of Joan." January 6th, 2012. http://tmagazine.blogs.nytimes.com/2012/01/06/lumiere-the-koan-of-joan/ Retrieved Tuesday, October 9th, 2012, and again on January 18th of 2014. While the article is guilty of some major errors, in its defence it does suggest that "Perhaps a more complex, even more feminine, Joan will emerge." Rest assured that I will later address the "cross-dressing" portion of her 'title' at some length.

role as a military leader for which Joan is most remembered, and thus that shall be the focus of our exploration here.

If "war is the province of men"[221], then in a sense Joan was competing with men at their own game, and as with the young lady who was ready to eat worms with the males, her supposedly self-proclaimed position as "a Chieftan of War" can easily be twisted into a sort of female support and endorsement for such traditionally-masculine activities as warfare. Thus the questions which must be asked are, What did this woman bring to the war? Why did the Maid of Lorraine do what she did and why did God choose her to do it?

Indeed, Saint Joan of Arc was so unabashedly female that even though she wore male garb for her personal protection she, unlike her fabled ~4th Century Chinese predecessor Hua Mulan[222] and other warrior-women, never felt the need to hide the fact that she was a woman. Rather, Joan displayed her femininity as boldly as she did the standard[223] which she waved above her head; reminding all who even heard of her that she was female through her self-given title of *La Pucelle;* "The Maid"[224], and wearing as her helmet a *casque sans masque* which allowed all to see her face. This behaviour contrasted starkly with even modern fictional portrayals of warrior-women; such as Eowyn from *The Lord of the Rings: The Return of the King*, Princess Leia from *Star Wars Episode VI: The Return of the Jedi*, Samus Aran from Nintendo's *Metroid II: The Return of Samus* (and also all other

---

221 *Explosiveweapons.info – Research into the Humanitarian Impacts of Explosive Violence.* Posted on 8 March 2012 by Maya Brehm. http://explosiveweapons.info/2012/03/08/war-is-the-province-of-men/ Retrieved 9 October 2012. (The line itself is spoken by Eomer to discourage Eowyn in the Peter Jackson film *The Lord of the Rings: The Return of the King* (2003).

222 The inspiration for Disney's 1998 movie *Mulan*, Hua Mulan assumed the guise of a man to lead a successful military career as a normal soldier for decades, according to the poem from which she originated.

223 Specifically, a large white banner depicting the Risen Jesus Christ flanked by angels and the words "JHESUS MARIA". It was exceptionally religious even by the standards of the day.

224 The title most often given to Joan of Arc, for it was the one she chose for herself. This reminds one of both her virginity and her position of servitude (to God; see Luke 1:38).

components of the Metroid series), Kitty Softpaws from *Shrek* spinoff *Puss in Boots*, Joan of Arc in the original script for the 1999 Luc Besson film *The Messenger*,[225] etc. The very fact that even now women in traditionally-masculine occupations are encouraged not to draw overmuch attention to their womanliness suggests that Joan of Arc occupied a very unique position indeed.

God was the reason why Joan – unlike so many other female soldiers throughout history who came before and after her – never needed to assume the guise of a man. It is impossible to divorce Joan of Arc from her religion, for the Maid was among the only people ever to be given a military command based entirely upon theological qualifications.

She was trying to fulfill a prophecy: that France, lost by a woman (ie. the Dauphin's mother for denying the legitimacy of her son), would be saved by a maid. This prophecy Joan herself told to both her uncle, Durand Laxart, and to Catherine Royer, the woman with whom she stayed in the town of Vaucouleurs (the first stop on her journey). It was the simplest version of several prophecies which were circulating around France at the time, and some of these specified that the Maiden would be armed and/or would come from the borders of Lorraine. As both of these qualifications were also filled by Joan, the prophecies themselves served to dramatically increase her popularity and following. The rest was accomplished by the endorsement given Joan by courtiers and theologians, and her being a very capable product of the chivalric ideals of the time, which were originally inspired by the Roman Catholic Church through devotion to the Blessed Virgin Mother Mary.

However, while chivalric ideals have suffered considerably in the time since Joan of Arc, nationalism remains as strong as ever. Thus the Maid of Lorraine has been brandished by whatever nationalist force felt it beneficial to appropriate her, even if it meant at times twisting her message. Joan was even held up as a standard for women during World War I, so they might feel more inclined to support the war effort through such things as the purchase of war savings stamps.[226] This becomes rather ironic when one considers Joan's own attitude toward such things.

---

225 http://www.millaj.com/film/joan-script.txt Retrieved Saturday, February 23rd of 2013.

226 "Video – Festivals Begin to Commemorate Saint Joan of Arc" *Nobility*

While on military campaign near the town of Jargeau near the river Loire, Joan of Arc met a woman named Catherine de La Rochelle, who claimed that a voice from God had told her of her destiny to help drive out the English and reunite France. Understandably, Joan found this encounter somewhat awkward. However, the manner in which La Rochelle would supposedly help the war effort was, according to the 'white lady dressed in cloth-of-gold' who purportedly appeared to her nightly, was by going to the friendly towns with heralds and trumpets supplied by the King and collecting treasure with which to pay Joan's men-at-arms. Joan of Arc's initial response was that she should return to her husband, her household and her children. Then, to be certain, the Maid consulted with either Saint Catherine or Saint Margaret (she apparently wasn't quite sure which), who reassured her that La Rochelle's 'mission' was indeed mere folly.

Wanting to avoid making a statement to La Rochelle which could be interpreted as "The Voices in my head say that the voices in your head are lying" and to be absolutely sure of not blaspheming (or at least ignoring) the Holy Spirit, Joan slept with her so that she might see the white lady for herself. The lady did not appear even after two nights, despite Joan's sleeping during the day so as to be awake for the entirety of the second. Additionally, La Rochelle advised Joan against assaulting the town of La Charite sur Loire, saying that it was too cold and she would not go and would rather make peace with the Duke of Burgundy. *La Pucelle* was less than impressed by La Rochelle's 'divine calling'.[227]

---

and Analogous Traditional Elites In the Allocutions of Pius XII. January 5, 2012. http://nobility.org/2012/01/05/orleans/ Retrieved 22/11/2012. Here one finds a scan of the original poster depicting Saint Joan in a triumphant pose (though she would not actually be canonized by the Roman Catholic Church Militant until two years after the war (Jim Eagles, "Joan of Arc, Daughter of France." *New Zealand Herald.* Friday, August 31, 2012. http://www.nzherald.co.nz/travel/news/article.cfm?c_id=7&objectid=10829831)) accompanied by the message: "Joan of Arc Saved France....Women of America, Save Your Country: Buy War Savings Stamps" This poster is also used as the image for her at Saints.SQPN.com (http://saints.sqpn.com/saint-joan-of-arc/ Retrieved Saturday, October 20th of 2012).

227 It was here that Joan issued her (in)famous statement that it seemed to her that they would find no peace save at the end of the lance. Ironically, however,

Joan cared nothing for money-making, especially if it employed such deceptive means, and she even told King Charles VII that La Rochelle was all madness and should not be heeded. However, Joan's adherence to the truth displeased both La Rochelle and the Maid's companion, Brother Richard; the latter of whom believed that Catherine could be useful and should be put to work.[228]

In much the same way, Saint Joan of Arc has been used to sell people on concepts of female empowerment through battle and bloodshed, or even empowerment through masculinization(!). The appropriate term here is "used", however. Joan gained great prestige as a military symbol of French nationalism because of what she did, but she endures as a saintly hero to the world because of how she did it.

To understand this, we must dispense with the cultural baggage of the 21st Century and try to understand Joan's own perspective as a devoutly-Christian woman from several centuries earlier. This is easier said than done.

So we see Joan of Arc depicted in artful digital painting standing menacingly over a fallen soldier with a bloodstained blade, whilst the latter feebly lifts his hand in a manner which looks, in the words of one commentator, "as if her enemy was begging for mercy."[229] So we see Joan of Arc as the poster child for an article entitled "Guns don't kill people, women do" (an article which also suggests that women 'served

---

La Rochelle's advice proved sound in this case; the assault on La Charite sur Loire (which was NOT recommended by the Saints who spoke with Joan) would fail. Joan would find it necessary to lift the siege and withdraw on or around December 25th of 1429 and return to King Charles VII's court for the winter. Her last military victory would come at the age of 18 in April of 1430, when Joan of Arc would vanquish freebooting warlord Franquet d'Arras and his Burgundian contingent on the open field near the town of Lagny with approximately 200 soldiers.

228 The Condemnation Trial of Joan of Arc. Sixth Public Examination; conducted Saturday, March 3rd of 1431. The Bishop and 41 Assessors were present. http://www.stjoan-center.com/Trials/sec06.html Retrieved 04/06/2013.

229 Hideyoshi. *Jeanne D'Arc or Joan of Arc* (for CHOW, 1.5 hours' work, **no reference.**) http://hideyoshi.deviantart.com/art/Jeanne-D-Arc-120883629 Retrieved 08/10/2012. Emphasis mine.

their country' by being army-accompanying prostitutes).[230] So we see Joan of Arc impale people on *The Deadliest Warrior* and the like[231] (even when played by 8-year-old Lisa on *The Simpsons*!), and listen to the words which William Shakespeare supposedly placed into her mouth:

> "Joan la Pucelle: ...One drop of blood drawn from thy country's bosom
> Should grieve thee more than streams of foreign gore:"[232]
> (*Henry VI Part i*, Act III, Scene III (3.7), lines 54-55)

When we see the Maid divorced from her own ethics, she becomes merely an example of military success whose worthiness is measured only by that sphere, restricting Joan of Arc to the realm of militant nationalism. The limitations of such an approach become excruciatingly clear when viewing such things as the Shakespearean play mentioned above. Though it should be noted that *Henry VI* is believed to have authors other than Shakespeare alone, they were all apparently English writing for English, and thus one might expect them to be biased in favour of the English. This "patriotism" provides a sort of counterpoint to the use of Saint Joan as a nationalistic figure, and reflects the kind

---

230 Gayle, Damien. "Guns don't kill people, women do: Historical analysis finds fairer sex just as likely as men to fight in wars" November 2nd of 2012. http://www.dailymail.co.uk/sciencetech/article-2226867/Guns-dont-kill-people-women-Historical-analysis-finds-fairer-sex-just-likely-men-fight-wars.html Retrieved Saturday, November 17th of 2012. The picture in question is a screen capture from *The Messenger*, naturally.

231 The 2003 documentary miniseries *Warrior Women with Lucy Lawless* (of *Xena: Warrior Princess* fame (who also has voiced Wonder Woman at least once)) actually does go against the flow of the mainstream by pointing out that Joan of Arc never killed anyone, though unfortunately the episode devoted to her is very skeptical of the veracity of her visions. In mainstream depictions of Joan there is often clear bias in favour of the secular (which was also the case at her condemnation trial....)

232 This is spoken to the Duke of Burgundy, as the Burgundians were people of France fighting upon the side of the English. Also, if you think this is bad, just wait until Act V, Scene III (5.3) in which a thunderstorm is invoked while Joan la Pucelle is depicted summoning demons so that she might entreat their aid!

of attitude which prompted her examiners to ask the Maid at her condemnation trial, "Does God hate the English?"[233]

(Given the title of this book, I feel somewhat compelled to give an answer to this 582-year-old question to the best of my own meager ability: No, I do not believe God hates (or hated) the English, but I also believe that He is not (nor ever was) fond of invasion and harrassment of any people who love Him.)

To dispel the limitations and inaccuracies placed upon Joan of Arc, we find it necessary to examine the actual historical records regarding the Saint. She herself stated that her purpose for bearing her standard was to avoid killing anyone, for she has never killed anyone.[234]

It has been argued that the above statement must have been a bold-faced lie; that "in the middle of the battlefield, [her] sword in [her] hand, waving it above [her] head, charging against the enemy, screaming and yelling, fighting for [her] life" one could not be expected to believe that, "in the middle of all this excitement," she never killed anyone.[235] The Saint spoke true, however, and the fact that that has recently been called into question reflects modern sensibilities more than any difficulty in avoiding killing if one does not wish to kill. There is no evidence to indicate that Joan of Arc used anything but the flat of her sword, and she probably seldom drew it in mounted combat. Even when she did, she had better things to do than finish off the wounded or try (unsuccessfully, as the young Maid would certainly have found) to decapitate her foes as though she were in a Peter Jackson Middle Earth movie.[236] The modern imagination of Mediaeval combat is one which has been heavily filtered through the lens of modern media. Even miniature strategy games such as England's *Warhammer*, which have at their core an approximation

---

233 Specifically Commissary Jean Delafontaine, Nicolas Midi, and Gerard Feuillet at the Eighth Private Examination; conducted Saturday, March 17th of 1431. http://www.stjoan-center.com/Trials/sec12.html.

234 Fourth Public Examination; Tuesday, February 27th of 1431. http://www.stjoan-center.com/Trials/sec04.html.

235 *The Messenger: The Story of Joan of Arc.* Directed by Luc Besson, starring Milla Jovovich in the titular role, released in 1999.

236 Such would include any of the *Hobbit* or *Lord of the Rings* films released this past decade or so.

of how battles of the Middle Ages were actually fought, are inclined to embellish for the sake of drama:

> "Although the standard bearer has to carry a banner as well as fight, he is chosen from the meanest and most determined individuals in the unit, and this more than makes up for any disadvantage suffered because of the weight and inconvenience of the standard."
> – *Warhammer Rulebook,* published in 1992 by Games Workshop, Ltd. in Nottingham, England, p. 82

The Maid of Lorraine was not the meanest individual, nor was she the most determined, at least when it came to murder. She was known to have at times charged in with her battle lance, which is considerably more dangerous than a jousting-lance, but it still could quite reasonably have been used for an attempted dismount in the same manner (for Joan was naturally gifted in horsewomanship). In most cases, however, Joan went through battle with her banner in one hand and the reigns of her steed in the other (she did not even use a shield). Mediaeval melee (close-quarter) combat was a somewhat-chaotic, very visceral and at times even personal affair vastly unlike modern warfare. The standard was a very important component for thousands of years until its use was at last proven impractical by World War I. Indeed, the entire national anthem of the United States of America is fundamentally about the psychological effect of a banner when it is in a strategically-valuable location. Here Joan of Arc really was the most determined individual, not simply in her unit, but also in the entire French army. Even if one's familiarity with her tactics were limited to the victory flags atop the little castles in *Super Mario Bros.*, one can imagine the effect of Joan's similarly-coloured flag among the crenellations[237] atop the *Tourelles*[238]

---

[237] From the ancient French word *cren,* which means a notch, mortice, or other gap which has been cut out, often to receive another element of fixing. Crenellations are thus the gaps occurring in the parapets which comprise the battlements of a castle or fortress.

[238] Meaning literally "The Turrets" in French, *Les Tourelles* was a powerful fortress on the south side of the river Loire directly opposite Orléans and linked to it via a bridge. Originally constructed to make Orléans less

outside of Orléans; the fortress would appear to be already in the hands of the French. This is why Joan was always at the front of her army, trying to scale castle walls without having to cut down anyone who stood in her way.

Thus we must realize that we have erred in our previous assumption. As I have at times stated in a manner which doubtless the humble spinner/shepherdess could have phrased better: it requires far more courage to stand up for what one believes in when one does not have the option of "kicking butt."[239]

Joan of Arc's adherence to standards difficult for fictional superheroes (such as Storm or Wonder Woman) to maintain – let alone someone operating under extremely trying real-life conditions as she was – came not through censorship or adherence to the "comics code", but from a code infinitely higher. This code was not merely the nobility-favouring classist system of her day's chivalry, but rather embodied the romantic ideals associated with chivalry centuries later.[240] Despite leading forces from the front through all the mire and misery of very real Mediaeval combat, Joan of Arc's loyalty was to "Jesus [and] Maria," and she stayed true to the teachings of God. Saint Joan of Arc can only be fictionalized through deception, and likewise she must not be transformed into mere propaganda.

---

vulnerable to attack, this design backfired when the *Tourelles* was taken by the English, thus preventing friendly frontal access to the city.

239 Inspired after hearing a quote from Miranda Otto regarding her portrayal of Eowyn in The Lord of the Rings, in which she noted how it is always nice "when girls get to kick butt."

240 In a play review I wrote for my Dramatic Arts class at the age of 19 and during one of my more brooding moments, I actually compared the idealism of Joan of Arc with that of the far-more-comical Man of La Mancha, writing, "...by choosing this particular fantasy, the 'Knight Errant' Don Quixote (James Robert Woods) displays a heroic inner nature, a soul seeking to help a world that has no room for heroes. It has been written that Quixote sets out on his quest '300 years too late', but this is simply not true. There was never any time, never any place in which Quixote's dreams would have been realistic." <u>THE QUEST CONTINUES</u>, 11/12/1998 by Sir Ted Pesando (my masculine identity; by the end of high school, even the faculty called me "the Paladin").

In fact, it is rather amazing just how easily the Maid's Christian nature can be parted from her military career; especially when it is in the interest of causing Joan of Arc to appear more warlike. This became disturbingly evident recently, when I found myself in an argument with a militant French nationalist who closely identified with the 'fiery-eyed Maid of War'. After a short discussion on Mediaeval tactics and what the militant called Joan's "instinctive accordance to the eternal laws of warfare" which bled into my needing to argue that the United Nations was favourable to the Age of Empires, the conversation took a disconcerting turn. The militant suggested that Joan would have been better off serving the gods of the Romans, saying...

> "...the age of the Roman Empire was quite nice, though the Romans failed to crush Christendom and so warlike Jeanne [Joan's French name] had to invoke the Prince of Peace, and Baby Jesus is really no good in warfare, unlike Mars or Athena."

This statement would doubtless be somewhat disconcerting to Joan herself, for it was always her desire that the Prince of Peace must increase whilst the 'chieftan of war' must decrease.[241] It is because of her adherence to the teachings of the Prince of Peace that Joan of Arc can never be properly viewed as the archetypical warrior or archetypical military leader; her code of morality and honour meant that she must both defy and surpass such understanding.

Joan intuitively held true to St. Augustine's rules of "just war" and always gave her enemies every opportunity to peacefully withdraw. She also refused to allow her troops to pillage anything – even food – from liberated towns and became greatly angered whenever she was disobeyed in this.[242] However, due to the nature of chivalry, these policies cannot be considered specifically feminine.

Joan's womanliness came out in many other aspects of her military career, however. This included what we consider traditional femininity,

---

241 John 3:30.

242 Richey, Stephen W. *Joan of Arc – The Warrior Saint.* Praeger Publishers, 2003. Chapter 5 – Joan's Achievement in Raising French Morale: The First Part of "What", pp. 39-40.

such as Joan's showing great compassion for friend and foe alike[243] and weeping often. However it also revealed itself in the manner in which she chose to wage war.

On May 8th of 1429, the final day of the Siege of Orléans, Joan of Arc completed her most prominent military victory in a most unusual manner. After being driven from their forts, the English present had gathered their full army together for a climactic battle in the open field. They had set up pointed forward-facing stakes in the ground to receive the charge of the French cavalry, fully expecting to slaughter them with the longbowmen positioned behind the stakes as they had at the Battle of Agincourt in 1415. This was a tactic for which the French heavy cavalry had fallen many a time – after all, not to charge into battle would have been unmanly – and until Joan of Arc it had worked successfully against them for 83 years. It was, however, Sunday – the Sabbath day of rest – and thus Joan saw an opportunity for religion to save lives. As it was a Holy Day, the Maid determined that the soldiers should not attack aggressively but rather only defend themselves if attacked. The French Knights could instead set up their own sharpened cabers and position their bowmen behind them, leaving the English to perhaps grumble about how it was no fair playing fair. Driving her point home, Joan had an altar brought forth and back-to-back Masses performed for the French until the English became so demoralized that they left Orléans, never to return. By piously defying traditions of aggressive manliness, Joan of Arc achieved a bloodless military victory.[244]

Nor was the Saint herself so aggressive that she lacked the skill in discourse so recommended by her contemporary, French court writer and sage of chivalry Christine de Pisan. Though Joan of Arc may have been a woman of few words, she employed them expertly to avert conflict where possible. A perfect example of this occurred at Beaugency on June 16th of 1429, where Joan diplomatically forged an alliance between the mutually-hostile Duke of Alençon and the great Breton nobleman Arthur de Richemont, disobeying the order of the

243 Ibid. Chapter 6 – Joan's Achievement as a Military Commander: The Second Part of "What", p. 57.

244 Ibid. pp. 63-64.

Dauphin Charles and risking royal disgrace so that she might increase her own fighting force and prevent another French civil war.[245]

Nevertheless, despite whatever femininity Joan *la Pucelle* possessed, she was still a war hero. As such, she could be used as propaganda whenever needed. In the case of Joan, the worse the situation became for France, the more warrior images such as hers became useful. This was especially true during the World Wars, which have been used to justify virtually every war that has occurred since. As Sister Mary Therese lamented in response to her brother's death during the World War II naval battle at Corregidor:

> "To rout the bitter pagan horde,
> O God of peace, give Joan a sword!"[246])

Yet the warrior woman Joan would still not have slain anyone with the sword given her. Her sword was unlike Durendal (from the French *dur* ("hard") or *durer* ("last, endure")), the sword of the Paladin of Charlemagne Roland, with which he according to legend slew many of the hundred-thousand-strong army of Saracens at the Battle of Roncevaux Pass and which tore out a breach in the Pyrenees forty metres across rather than yield to destruction. Instead, Joan's sword of Saint Catherine of Fierbois – located by Joan in a vision yet which she valued "forty times" less than her standard – was merely a device of authority to her. Her sword was also believed to be connected to Charlemagne (specifically to his grandfather Charles Martel[247] ("Charles the Hammer")), yet while it is thought to have then been used to kill Muslims, its blade tasted no blood in the hands of the Maid. Instead, her weapon did indeed break; due to her only striking nonfatally with the flat of its blade.[248] Saint Joan of Arc would want a sword far less than a

245 Ibid. p. 74. The French Wikipedia article *Bataille de Beaugency* served as a secondary source.

246 "Give Joan a Sword" http://www.stjoan-center.com/topics/poems.html Retrieved Thursday, October 18th of 2012.

247 "Joan of Arc: Her Sword." http://saint-joan-of-arc.com/sword.htm Retrieved 31/10/2012.

248 This is according to the retrial testimony of d'Alençon and the chronicle of Jean Chartier (and according to the latter the newly-crowned King Charles

standard to bear once more, to remind all who looked upon it of the love of Jesus (and Maria) at a time when all hope seems lost.[249]

Saint Theresa of Lisieux in the titular role of her play *Joan of Arc Accomplishes Her Mission,* the second of two 'pious recreations' written by the Saint; small theatrical pieces performed by a few nuns for the rest of the community, on the occasion of certain feast days. Performed at the Carmel on January 21, 1895, the play focuses more heavily upon Joan's interaction with her visions than most other pieces written about her. Despite the sword in her hand, Theresa was not a woman of nationalism or militancy, and during World War I requests for her intercession were directed to her from even the German side.

VII was so dismayed when he heard of this that he scolded Joan for not using a stick instead; while endeavouring to chase away a prostitute, the Maid had broken the blade upon her backside!) Richey, Stephen W. *Joan of Arc – The Warrior Saint.* Praeger Publishers, 2003. Chapter 7 – Joan's Leadership Qualities: The First Part of "How", p. 105-106.

249 To those who would suggest that Joan of Arc's unwillingness to break the Fifth Commandment relegated her military role to "nothing more than that of a 'cheerleader'" I must place emphasis upon the root word **leader**. (http://www.stjoan-center.com/military/stephenr.html Retrieved October 22nd, 2012 (which also adds that in any case she was one of "superb tenacity and fortitude."))

So then let us consult another Sister Thérèse; one who also offered herself as holocaust to the consuming Fire of Merciful Love and wrote that like Joan of Arc, her "dear sister," she would whisper at the stake the Name of Jesus.[250] Saint Theresa of Lisieux was always of kindred spirit with Joan, and in her zeal to please God she also found herself called to many things, some of which defied traditional gender roles. In her autobiography "she wrote that she passionately desired to be a warrior, priest, apostle, doctor of the Church, martyr, crusader, and papal guard as well as Carmelite, spouse, and mother of souls!"[251] However, she was of course limited in her options. Thus, in the life she led as a Bourgeoisie Victorian girl-turned-Carmelite nun she found another way; a "Little Way" which eventually resulted in her becoming co-patroness of France (along with St. Joan of Arc), Doctor of the Church, and perhaps the most important Saint of the last century.[252] Likewise she was able to find another way of understanding Joan of Arc, for she too was quite aware that our God is a God of peace.[253] She thus was able to see past all of the militant nationalism that had so fervently inspired the cult of Joan since France's humiliating defeat in the Franco-Prussian war in 1871 and the loss of Joan's birthplace to Germany.[254] In fact, despite leading an extremely-traditional feminine "protected and childlike life"[255] which seemed to be quite different from that of Joan, Saint Theresa somehow possessed deeper insight into the Maid than anyone before or since. Perhaps the secret behind this was revealed in the fact that she did exactly as she said she would; after a long and agonizing time being

---

250 *L'Histoire d'un Ame,* Manuscript B. Chapter IX – My Vocation Is Love (1896) p. 193.

251 *St. Therese of Lisieux – Essential Writings.* Institute of Carmelite Studies. Orbis Books, Maryknoll, NY. 2003. "Introduction" p. 14.

252 This is a perfect example of Jesus' teaching in Matthew 23:12 and Luke 14:11; "For whosoever exalteth himself shall be abased; and he that humbleth himself shall be exalted."

253 *L'Histoire d'un Ame.* Manuscript A. Chapter VIII – Profession and Offering to Merciful Love (1890-1895). p. 169, referencing 1 Corinthians 14:33.

254 *St. Therese of Lisieux – Essential Writings.* Institute of Carmelite Studies. Orbis Books, Maryknoll, NY. 2003. "Introduction"; subheading "The Night of Nothingness" p.26.

255 Ibid. "Introduction" p. 15.

burned from within by tuberculosis, Theresa died with her love for Jesus upon her lips.

The Little Flower could even be said to be the woman who knows Joan best. She wrote numerous pieces about the Maid from Lorraine, including two plays in which she played the role of Joan of Arc herself (a Saint in the role of a Saint, if you will). In the second of these, titled *Joan of Arc Accomplishes Her Mission*, the Little Flower of Jesus made it clear that the Maid of Orléans did not wish to be a warrior first and foremost. When in prison in the second Act, Joan admits to Inquisitor Jean Massieu that, to bear a greater resemblance to her Beloved Saviour, she does not want to enter into martyrdom as a warrior[256]. In the final Act, Joan states to France herself that if she is honoured in Heaven, it is not for having been a warrior but because she has united virginity to martyrdom![257]

However, neither Theresa of Lisieux nor Joan of Arc had been declared Saints by that point in earthly history. Thus the Little Flower had also written the *Canticle to Obtain the Canonization of the Venerable Joan of Arc.* In it, she further clarified that it was not Joan's desire to be a conqueror for "guilty France" and that all heroes matter less than a martyr. Though it was by fighting that Joan saved France, her true virtues needed to be marked with suffering; the divine seal of her Spouse, Jesus Christ. Thus...

> "It is not Joan's victories
> We wish to celebrate this day.
> My God, we know her true glories
> Are her virtues, her love."
> (May 8th of 1894)[258]

Saint Theresa has given us our answer. War is a dark tool of a primitive time. By itself it can never truly be the stuff of saints, but

---

256 *Joan of Arc Accomplishes Her Mission*, Part II: The Captivity. The Martyrdom. Scène 10. January 1895. Translated from the original French by myself.

257 *Joan of Arc Accomplishes Her Mission*, Part III: The Triumphs in Heaven. Scène 2. January 1895. Translated from the original French by myself.

258 "St. Therese and St. Joan of Arc." *Maid of Heaven.* http://www.maidofheaven.com/joanofarc_st_therese.asp Retrieved Monday, November 26th of 2012.

merely filth to soil the hems of their baptismal robes. As with so many of the deeds of Christendom, a desirable end was reached using less-than-desirable means. However, the ends never justify the means, and thus it was very important that Joan go about accomplishing them as she did. Yet why was it so necessary that they be accomplished by a woman?

Marina Warner wrote in her book *Joan of Arc: The Image of Female Heroism* that, "Ironically, Joan's life, probably one of the most heroic a woman has ever led, is a tribute to the male principle, a homage to the male sphere of action."[259] However, the true irony here is that Joan's most masculine trait – her aggressive strategy of striking first, fast, and hard – stemmed from her most feminine one.

To understand this, it helps to have been raised as a man. Societies have historically overwhelmingly promoted the concept of preparing their males for conflict. Even today, when there is far less segregation between male and female roles than ever before, boys are especially inundated with influences promoting competition and/or violence, including media such as toys, films, and video games. What this environment provides is, more than an effective form of mind control, the reinforcement of a societal framework of obligation. This glamourised sense of duty can effect people even on a subconscious level, as evidenced by the statement made by a soldier just before he was sent off to Iraq in 2003:

"I always wanted to be in a war, but now that I might die I'm not so sure."

In each generation, those of us who are brought up in such an environment are pressured to answer the call of duty whenever it is heard, thus proving our worthiness to our country and to our own family line. Thus it was that the Hundred Years' War was self-perpetuating.

To quote another of William Shakespeare's plays, in the most-famous scene of *Henry V*[260] the titular character exhorts his men to proceed "Once more unto the breach" or else betray the memories of those English dead who gave their lives to re-establish his control over

---

[259] Marina Warner, *Joan of Arc: The Image of Female Heroism* (London: Weidenfeld and Nicolson), 1981. "The Life and Death of Jeanne la Pucelle, Chapter 7 – Ideal Androgyne," p. 155.

[260] Act 3, Scene 1, lines 1-8 (additional quotes from lines 18 and 22, respectively).

France. He reminds them that in times of peace "modest stillness and humility" are most becoming to a man...

> "But when the blast of war blows in our ears,
> Then imitate the action of the tiger.
> Stiffen the sinews, conjure up the blood,
> Disguise fair nature with hard-favoured rage. ..."

...and it goes on, as the king insists that those who are descended "from fathers of war-proof" "dishonour not [their] mothers" and continue the war on foreign soil. The English did not have the resources necessary to effectively conquer and hold France, but France was in such a situation of political disarray that they could certainly make a jolly good show of it. Additionally, the method by which war was waged was fundamentally a futile system. It involved a strategy of attack/retreat (rinse/repeat) which was concerned as much with acquiring ransom for captured lords as with claiming and reclaiming territory. Under these circumstances, it was disturbingly easy for the defenders to become demoralized amidst prolonged sieges and changing fortunes.

Enter Joan of Arc. To her foes she was announced as a chieftan of war, yet to her close friend Jean de Novelemport – called Jean de Metz, Joan's first knightly advocate – she confided that, while their was no succor to be expected for France save from her, and that it was God's will that she go forth...

> "...nevertheless, I would rather spin with my mother – poor woman – for this is not my proper estate...."[261]

Joan of Arc's accordance to the 'eternal laws of warfare' was tempered by the fact that she did not want war to be eternal. As a woman, she was not indoctrinated into and not affected by the glory-lust

---

261 *St. Joan of Arc's Trial of Nullification: Vaucouleurs and Journey to Chinon.* http://www.stjoan-center.com/Trials/null04.html Retrieved Tuesday, October 2nd of 2012 and ***Procès de rehabilitation.*** *V-2 Deposition de Jean de Nouillompont dit 'de Metz'* http://www.stejeannedarc.net/rehabilitation/dep_jean_de_metz.php. Added Sunday, August 21st of 2011. Retrieved Wednesday, December 6th of 2012.

that perpetuated the Hundred Years' War; she just wanted it to end. As opposed to participating in "the gentlemanly sport of continuous warfare, which had cost so many lives, military and civilian"[262] that merely perpetuated bloodshed, Joan's entire career was characterized by an intense sense of urgency. When she spoke to the *Dauphin* Charles and told him of the components of her mission, Joan of Arc also added:

> "I shall last a year, and but little longer; we must think to do good work in that year."[263]

Joan's motivation kept her focus upon the overarching strategy necessary to complete her mission. Her's was not about conquest but about liberation; not a call to war but an end to war.

God raised Joan of Arc up to her calling not because *even* a girl could accomplish the tasks He set for her, but because *only* a girl could; such was the value of femininity. She approached the Hundred Years' War with the attitude of one who had no desire to partake of it for its own sake, but rather to simply resolve it swiftly, decisively, and permanently. Thus she was able to bring about what Shakespeare's interpretation of Richard the Duke of York called "effeminate peace."[264]

Joan of Arc embodied resolution rather than aggression, determination rather than ambition, a gentle love that extended even to her enemies, and a courage dauntless even to the point of utter self-sacrifice. In her deeds and in her soul, Joan of Arc provides us with an early glimpse into the ultimate answer to a very bold question.

---

262 Beaudry, Irene. "The Military Genius of Jeanne d'Arc, and the Concept of Victory." May, 2000. *The Schiller Institute.* http://www.schillerinstitute.org/educ/joan_ib.html Retrieved October 23rd, 2012.

263 Willard Ropes Trask, Joan of Arc: In Her Own Words, *p. 27,* Retrieved from http://saint-joan-of-arc.com/prophecies.htm on June 11th of 2013.

264 *1 Henry VI*, 5.6, line 107.

Why Be a Woman?

God clearly understands and values the versatility of the female. He has raised them up to bear His prophets and to *be* His prophets; and due to Him females have shown themselves able to rule nations with great wisdom, restore nations through many victories, save an entire race through gentle allure and clever strategy, and possess unheard-of levels of courage, loyalty, and faith. All told, women are pretty amazing, but what are we meant to be and do as a whole? The simple answer to this question is: whatever we wish; such is freedom. However, humans are such social creatures that it is very difficult indeed not to want to be and do that which is valued by one's society, and sadly human society does not have a history of placing a terribly high value on femininity.

This is especially the case regarding traditional ideals of femininity, and it calls into question the idea of what it means to be female. In her book *What Our Mothers Didn't Tell Us: Why Happiness Eludes the Modern Woman*, neo-feminist Danielle Crittenden gives voice to a shocking understanding which most modern women are trepidatious to even mention: the idea that, since the coming of second-wave feminism, "women have been taught to deceive themselves about what it is they want." After being obligated back into the kitchen and disparaged for having done so in the 1950s, women reacted by initiating a second wave of feminism in the early 1960s, which unfortunately resulted in a sacrifice of fundamental female roles so that those normally filled only by males could be more easily accessed. This was done in the name of independence and equality, and Crittenden laments that we have thus been told by our elders to deny our natural feelings. We have been advised not to become too emotionally invested in the men with whom we have sexual relations in our youth, to suppress our desire for commitment, to delay any desire to have children (and "when we do have children, we are encouraged to sacrifice them to our jobs"), and "to not trust or depend upon the men to whom we finally pledge our hearts."[265] The end result is that, despite women now having more

---

265 *What Our Mothers Didn't Tell Us: Why Happiness Eludes the Modern Woman*, "epilogue: What We Tell Our Daughters," Simon and Schuster.

legal rights than ever before, the value placed upon actual womanhood is at one of its lowest in history. The attitude is that femininity could never have been terribly valuable if females themselves were so swift to abandon it.

Having been brought up as a man in an environment which apparently did not want me to be anything else, I found myself forced to answer a strange question: disregarding any physical qualities or capabilities, what is so special about being a woman that it could be worth abandoning even the option of being a man?

This question might have been easily answered if not for – ironically enough – what feminism has already achieved for womankind, as it has not yet reached full fruition. It has become quite apparent that women are more than capable of performing those tasks traditionally thought to be in the realm of men. However, the traditional realm of women has not been kept so well, in the sense of those qualities which are especially feminine being considered equally desirable as those which are masculine. It is not even considered appropriate to suggest that certain qualities are manly while others are womanly, as the former have been idealized and the latter disparaged by so many civilizations throughout history. Perhaps if we could present a quality of pure womanliness that has, clearly and singularly, *saved the world* in a manner which continues to keep the aforementioned world from destruction each and every day, our shared self-confidence would be improved. Yet how and when did womanliness ever save the world?

For the answer one may begin by consulting – intriguingly enough – the Book of Esther, though we shall not end there. Here we have a heroine who, despite being in one of the most repressive, suppressive, and oppressive environments imaginable for a woman, nevertheless managed to save all of God's people. Impressive.

To compare a more masculine perspective/approach, we need look no further than King Ahasuerus himself. He is generally believed to be Xerxes I[266] (*Ahasweros* being Xerxes' name in Tiberian Hebrew), who

---

[266] According to the footnote in the NAB. Other possibilities include his son, Artaxerxes (as he is referred to in the Greek version (Septuagint) or even Artaxerxes II, the son of Artaxerxes' son (Xerxes II)'s murderous brother (Sogdianus)'s murderer (Ochus), whom he was identified as being

was an epitome of a man of war. His numerous military campaigns are the stuff of legend, and he is said to have controlled 40% of the world's population. He even thought nothing of risking rebellion among his own subjects; as evidenced by his purloining of the statue of Marduk and even killing the priest of Marduk who tried to stop him.[267] The concerns of a small fraction of the populace such as the Jews would be but a mere easily-forgotten footnote in the records of the vast empire. Yet he and his lieutenants were defied.

The open defiance of Vashti – a woman – in refusing to come when King Ahasuerus called her[268] resulted in severe retributive measures of a nature which was not fully revealed. The open defiance of Mordecai – a man – in refusing to bow down before Ahasuerus' vizier Haman[269] resulted in the attempted annihilation of the Jewish people. This is not to suggest that these two were wrong in taking their chosen paths of courage, but something more than courage[270] was needed here. Esther was to intercede with and entreat a mortal king, as opposed to Mary, who intercedes with and entreats the King of Heaven...yet so too did Esther, before seeing the earthly king:

> "**Prayer of Esther.**
> Queen Esther, seized with mortal anguish, likewise had recourse to the LORD. Taking off her splendid garments, she put on garments of distress and mourning. In place of her precious ointments she covered her head with dirt and ashes. She afflicted her body severely; all her festive adornments were put aside, and her hair was wholly disheveled.

---

by 6th Century Church leader John of Ephesus. However, http://www.jewishencyclopedia.com/articles/967-ahasuerus also supports the theory that Ahasuerus was Xerxes I. (Retrieved October 19th of 2012.)

267 Of course, this is not to say that he was so bad as his counterpart in the blockbuster movie *300*, in which he even has himself called by such blasphemous titles as 'King of kings' and 'Lord of hosts'....

268 Esther 1:10-19.

269 Esther 3:2-6.

270 Certainly courage was not a quality lacking in Esther, either (see Esther 4:15-16).

> Then she prayed to the LORD, the God of Israel, saying: "My LORD, our King, you alone are God. Help me, who am alone and have no help but you, for I am taking my life in my hand. As a child I was wont to hear from the people of the land of my fore-fathers that you, O LORD, chose Israel from among all peoples, and our fathers from among all their ancestors, as a lasting heritage, and that you fulfilled all your promises to them. But now we have sinned in your sight, and you have delivered us into the hands of our enemies, because we worshipped their gods. You are just, O LORD. But now they are not satisfied with our bitter servitude, but have undertaken to do away with the decree you have pronounced, and to destroy your heritage; to close the mouths of those who praise you, and to extinguish the glory of your temple and your altar; to open the mouths of the heathen to acclaim their false gods, and to extol an earthly king forever.
>
> "O LORD, do not relinquish your scepter to those who are nought. Let them not gloat over our ruin, but turn their own counsel against them and make an example of our chief enemy. Be mindful of us, O LORD. Manifest yourself in the time of our distress and give me courage, King of gods and Ruler of every power. Put in my mouth persuasive words in the presence of the lion and turn his heart to hatred for our enemy, so that he and those who are in league with him may perish. Save us by your power, and help me, who am alone and have no one but you, O LORD." (Esther Chapter C, Verses 12 to 25, NAB.)

Esther's tearful entreaties directed at both God and man may not be the standard methods employed by Biblical heroes, but her skill in negotiation accomplished a feat no less great, and if not for the stubbornly irrevocable character of the laws of the Medes and Persians[271] she would have accomplished it in an entirely peaceful manner[272]. One of the great messages of the book is that – through faith in the LORD – diplomacy can succeed where other methods fail.

---

271 Esther 1:19 and Daniel 6:9.

272 Esther 8:3-11.

> "Skill in discourse should be a part of every woman's moral repertoire..."
> (Christine de Pizan, proto-feminist author of *The Book of Deeds of Arms and of Chivalry*[273] *and professional writer at the court of Charles VI of France, in The Treasure of the City of Ladies*, circa 1405.)

This skill is also exemplified by Saint Catherine of Alexandria, the very-early 4th Century princess who was given in marriage by the Blessed Virgin Mother Mary to Jesus Christ in a vision and who remained true to her vows even on pain of death. After protesting the Roman Emperor Maxentius'[274] persecution of Christians for not worshipping idols, Saint Catherine vanquished all of his best Pagan philosophers and orators in debate (and according to legend, they all even converted to Christianity themselves!). This is probably one of the reasons why, in addition to being a virgin martyr, this aptly-titled Holy Helper was one of the Saints who often appeared to Joan of Arc (especially during the period of the Maid's imprisonment and trial, when she too needed to defend herself against overwhelming numbers of hostile theologians).

However, even as a teenager Saint Catherine was extremely intelligent and greatly learned. Thus one may still ask what indication we have that diplomacy and discourse are strengths of the general feminine population.

When seeking an example of such female achievement, the present day seems a very logical place to turn. Women in the First-World nations enjoy more rights and freedoms and are more active in the workforce than ever before, and thanks to the United Nations these rights and freedoms are gradually extending to other nations as well. While people

---

273 "The foremost piece of military theory written in Western Europe during the Middle Ages..." Richey, Stephen W. *Joan of Arc – The Warrior Saint.* Praeger Publishers, 2003. Chapter 7 – Joan's Leadership Qualities: The First Part of "How", p. 96.

274 The 58th Emperor of Rome, Maxentius drowned in the aftermath of the October 28th, 312 Battle of the Milvian Bridge against Constantine the Great; the first Christian Roman Emperor.

may often think that whatever society in which they exist at the time is the pinnacle of human existence, the present time does much to showcase the success of women's diplomatic/communication skills. In her *TED* talk providing new data on the increased success of women in (that which is financially acknowledged to be) the working world, Hanna Rosin noted that the economy's requirements have changed, and that these changes better facilitate the evidenced strengths of women. The world today needs intelligence, an ability to sit still and concentrate, open communication and listening skills, and the ability to operate in an ever-more-fluid workplace. These are all things that women have been shown to do extremely well.[275]

Rosin is the author of *The End of Men: and the Rise of Women,* which argues that men have suffered most from the economic recession that has gripped the world these past several years (due to their not fully adapting to the decline in manufacturing industries and to the challenges of post-modernity[276]). As a result, (American) women now outnumber men in the workforce (dominating 12 of the 15 most-expanding job categories there) and outnumber men on post-secondary degree courses by a ratio of three to two. The somewhat antagonistic-sounding title of the book suggests a competitive attitude which may seem necessary in the modern environment but which can also be counter-intuitive. There is much noble instinct and many noble deeds to be found among men, and the fact that they are blamed for so much of the world's woe stems largely from the fact that they have held so much power for so very long (in that sense, they are not without parallel to Christians in general).

Yet it cannot be denied that some men have long ravaged women's rights, freedoms, and self-esteem, and thus one might expect to find women learning of the recent developments inclined to "gloat over [their (highly arguable, as among other things men still average a 20% higher

---

275 "Hanna Rosin: New data on the rise of women" Posted December 2010. http://www.ted.com/taks/hanna_rosin_new_data_on_the_rise_of_women.html Retrieved 20/10/2012.

276 Mary Beard. "The End of Men: And the Rise of Women by Hanna Rosin – review (Women have taken over, apparently. If only, argues Mary Beard" Wednesday 3 October 2012. http://www.guardian.co.uk/books/2012/oct/03/end-of-men-hanna-rosin-review Retrieved Saturday, October 20th of 2012.

income than women)] ruin[277]". Fortunately, this does not seem to be the case: women readers of the book have found it both fascinating and frightening. To quote one female volunteer on (perhaps appropriately) Amazon.ca in a review she entitled "Disturbing Portrait of the Rise of Women -- Role Reversal, Not Equality:"

> "We wanted equality for women, not to make women the dominant sex."

Perhaps what we see now is the beginning of the time when "the meek...shall inherit the earth."[278] This might perhaps be the case, if not for the fact that as she also notes levels of physical fighting, crime, and violence are on the rise among young women. This fact keeps this feminine achievement from being truly satisfying, although another observation made by Rosin is strangely promising: that women "carry psychological baggage into the workplace: a lingering ambivalence about their ambition, a queasiness about self-promotion, a duty to family that they can't or won't offload on to their husbands, etc etc.[279]" The fact that this is still the case actually reveals a weakness on the part of society and a strength on the part of women; by holding true to humility and love, the devout sex is maintaining her Christian virtue, even in the midst of the intense self-absorption of the world.

In seeking equality with men in a society whose jobs and means of gain have largely been designed with men in mind, women often find it necessary to prove themselves in what has traditionally been regarded as solely the province of men. Thus there exists the temptation to abandon two things which some portions of men have constantly attempted to wield against women: the Sacred Scriptures and our own femininity.

---

277 Esther C:22, NAB.

278 Matthew 5:5, KJV.

279 Mary Beard. "The End of Men: And the Rise of Women by Hanna Rosin – review (Women have taken over, apparently. If only, argues Mary Beard" Wednesday 3 October 2012. http://www.guardian.co.uk/books/2012/oct/03/end-of-men-hanna-rosin-review Retrieved Saturday, October 20th of 2012.

Antonio Ciseri, *Ecce Homo!* Painted in 1871 on commission on behalf of the Italian Government.

There exists a stunning painting which tacitly displays ignorance of the true value of both. In this 1871 piece by Antonio Ciseri, the Lord Jesus Christ has been handed over by the Sanhedrin[280] clergy to the secular Roman authority, Pontius Pilate. After having had Him scourged, Pilate positions our Saviour near a pillar to his left. It is a crowded scene, and thus it is easy to miss one woman in the palatial estate who is turning sadly away from the proceedings (and is thus ironically the only figure whose face the viewer can clearly see): the unnamed wife of Pontius Pilate; for...

> "When he was set down on the judgment seat, his wife sent unto him, saying, Have thou nothing to do with that just man [the term used for Jesus in the prophecy of the Book of

---

280 ויתקנס "Sin (an Hebrew character originally representing a thorn) nun hey dal resh yad waw". Sanhedrin means "sitting together", and while Napoleon Bonaparte convened a Jewish Grand Sanhedrin (mostly from the Alsace and Lorraine regions) in 1806, the word is generally used in reference to the council of Biblical times. Its constituent characters can be read logographically as "ס Grab/hate the נ Son Who ה Reveals (or Breathes) the ד Entrance to the ר First/Top/Beginning, the י Hand and the ו Nail." Wow.

> Wisdom[281] (circa ~100 B.C.)]: for I have suffered many things this day in a dream because of him." (Matthew 27:19, KJV)

However, she was of course unheeded, and thus the title of the painting: *Ecce Homo;* "Behold the Man!"[282] takes on an additional meaning in light of this, as it is not Jesus but Pilate, his cloak and stooped posture suggesting some ghostly reaper, who is positioned front and center. The events depicted here reveal that, just as it was the first question asked after His resurrection, the last question silently asked by God/Christ before Christ's death was "will you listen to a woman?"

However, if noone will listen to a meek and gentle woman, has there ever been any way for women to not embrace ambition or aggression and yet still achieve their goals in a patriarchal society?

So it is that the devout sex finds itself obliged to abandon qualities precious to God because they are undervalued by man.

Now that I think upon it, there is one rhetorical question asked by Jesus between the time of the warning of the wife of Pilate and that of the Lord's departure from this world:

> "But Jesus turning unto them said, Daughters of Jerusalem, weep not for me, but weep for yourselves, and for your children.
>
> For, behold, the days are coming, in the which they shall say, Blessed are the barren, and the wombs that never bare, and the paps which never gave suck.
>
> Then shall they begin to say to the mountains, Fall on us; and to the hills, Cover us.
>
> For if they do these things in a green tree [lush summer], what shall be done in the dry?" (Luke 23:28-31, KJV)

It must truly be a dark and desiccated time when the masses not only obsess but also worry about the end of the world. World War II, however, provided one such time. Olive Byrne, writer for *Family*

---

[281] 2:12-23.

[282] John 19:5, KJV.

Circle magazine and polyamorous second partner to William Moulton Marston, described the resulting sensations of worry and depression from women's perspective in a 1942 article for said magazine titled, "Our Women Are Our Future." In it she detailed her awareness of the danger and her exhaustive effort to contribute to the war effort from home, having paid her income taxes, **bought war stamps**[283] and bonds, volunteered for every defense project she could find, cut out sugar and all pleasure trips with the car, and made the decision that she "would look awful but patriotic" in her old clothes. This was immediately followed by still more war-news' dismal prediction of much worse disasters than any which had yet been suffered and the demand that women must do many difficult things while remaining perpetually charming. Byrne found this sense of powerlessness, both personal and associated with her sex, overwhelming.

As such, the heroic image of Wonder Woman caught her eye and seemed very appealing. She thus visited the superheroine's creator Marston and asked him a very pointed question:

> "Will war ever end in this world; will men ever stop fighting?"

Marston's response was that it would, yet "not until women control men." He continued to suggest that men wanted to be dominated by exciting-yet-loving women who were stronger than they were and that "the Wonder Woman formula" proved this, for "by their comics tastes ye shall know them![284]"

This is an...interesting theory, but here once again female achievement was being measured by how much it could affect the males. Furthermore, because the standards of success for a female were being set by a man, they were viewed in terms of masculine qualities such as physical strength. There was still insufficient respect for the distinctly womanly, and thus there was more to be understood.

---

283 Olive Byrne (under the pseudonym "Olive Richards"). "Our Women Are Our Future." *Family Circle,* August 14, 1942. Emphasis mine.

284 A...modified...version of Matthew 7:20 (KJV). Article retrieved from http://www.castlekeys.com/Pages/wonder.html Sunday, October 21st of 2012.

As Marston himself stated in an issue of *The American Scholar* the following year:

> "Not even girls want to be girls so long as our feminine archetype lacks force, strength, and power. Not wanting to be girls, they don't want to be tender, submissive, peace-loving as good women are. Women's strong qualities have become despised because of their weakness."

This was a necessary attitude in the midst of World War II; after all, Adolf Hitler was by his own admission a Haman rather than an Ahasuerus. Unlike World War I, in which the majority of people in each of the warring countries believed themselves to be fighting not as aggressors but rather in self-defence,[285] World War II featured clearly belligerent attackers, and this was certainly a case in which, to quote Joan of Arc, "we would find no peace, if it was not by the end of the lance.[286]"

Yet what if the war had been averted in the first place? I entreat you to indulge me as we continue on our quest for answers....

How Women Invented the United Nations

> "Preachers likewise continued to highlight women's virtues. [Sermonizers praised women's devotion to the Virgin Mary through their shared gender and], with an increasingly feminized tone, emphasized the importance of promoting the 'sweetness,' 'tenderness,' and 'affection' of religion, bolstering the cult of a Savior no longer associated with war but with 'perpetual peace.'"

---

285 "Final Resolution." Moved by Rosika Schwimmer, Seconded by Mme Daugaard. *INTERNATIONAL CONGRESS OF WOMEN. Report of Business Sessions.* Third Day, Friday, April 30th. (Morning Session). President: Jane Addams. p. 131.

286 Sixth Public Examination; Saturday, March 3rd, 1431. http://www.stjoan-center.com/Trials/sec06.html. See also Robo, Etienne. "The Holiness of Saint Joan of Arc." http://www.ewtn.com/library/mary/joan1.htm I have translated the phrase somewhat more directly from the original French. Retrieved Monday, October 22nd of 2012.

(Charles A. Witschorik. "From the 'Weak Sex' to the 'Devout Sex'")[287]

Women would indeed do such a thing; and to a level unknown even now to most people on Earth, and previously unimagined by all thereon.

The Victorian Era was a time of brutal disparity between classes, and many minds were inspired to rise up against them. While Karl Marx (who, like the Marquis de Sade believed religion to be the "opium of the people"[288]) responded to the gross iniquities of the class system by writing *The Communist Manifesto*[289] and Charles Dickens addressed them with such stories as *A Christmas Carol,* the women of the era were still encouraged to be passive helpers to their husbands, yet they too would soon challenge the iniquities of their society in a unique way. One intriguing side-effect of the "Angel in the House" attitude was that, like the traditions of chivalry, it effectively neutralized the tradition "that portrayed women as vice-ridden, fickle, vicious, foul, and disgusting, and which urged men not to marry"[290] that had been maintained for many centuries in many cultures. Women's now-acknowledged Christian virtues gave them a new moral authority[291], and with it the confidence

---

287 Subtitled "Women, Gender, and Official Church Discourses in Early Nineteenth-Century Mexico City." http://escholarship.org/uc/item/1vr9x8zs#page-1 Retrieved November 28th of 2012.

288 Marx, *Contribution to the Critique of Hegel's Philosophy of Right,* Introduction..., p. 1 (1843). He also stated, in a letter dated 28 December 1846 on the *Rue d'Orléans*, that "to do away with slavery would be to wipe America off the map." *Letters of Marx and Engels 1846.* http://www.marxists.org/archive/marx/works/1846/letters/46_12_28.htm Retrieved 29/11/2012.

289 In 1937 Pope Pius XI wrote an encyclical letter entitled *Divini Redemptoris* which condemned communism and pointed out its errors. "The Pope concluded that Catholics may not become associated with communism under any pretext without committing sin." NAB 2003-2004 Edition "Encyclopedic Dictionary", p. 36.

290 *Joan of Arc: Documents* (prepared for the web by Prof. Leah Shopkow). http://www.indiana.edu/~dmdhist/joan.htm Retrieved 29/11/2012.

291 Again, true feminism seeks equality rather than replacement. Hanna Rosin also mentions that the loss of sense of traditional masculine identity came firstly (listed just before ceasing to be needed for emotional support and not really being the provider anymore) from the appearance that "they no longer

to criticize the many injustices they beheld around them. Being legally unable to affect change yet now possessing the belief that they had the right to affect it, women unitedly sought the suffrage that would open these options to them.

Thus we now come to it at last: what clearly and traditionally feminine contribution would women give to the world? The acid test was to come just after the turn of the 20th Century. The first wave of feminism – the suffragette movement – had been in operation for decades, but it was still in a state of relative infancy by then, and 1914 was to give it a baptism of fire.

In one forgotten moment of history all the negative illusions about feminism would be seared away, for it began not with some belligerent desire of woman to enforce her will, but rather with her answer to man's desperate call for help.

Jane Addams' tale was heart-wrenching. She described wounded young soldiers lying in helpless pain, waiting too long for the field ambulance, and how they would constantly call out for their mothers, impotently beseeching them for help. She and her fellow suffragettes had been told of wounded men who said to their hospital nurses that they could do nothing for themselves; they could only repeatedly return to the trenches so long as they were able. These men of ceaseless battle had all asked the nurses:

> **"'Cannot the women do something about this war? Are you kind to us only when we are wounded?'"**
> – Jane Addams, Presidential Address to *The International Congress of Women*[292]

The past century has in a sense been a hundred years of war, and it has also been the bloodiest in all history. It began with an act of

had any moral authority..." *TED: Ideas worth spreading.* "Hanna Rosin: New data on the rise of women" December 2010. http://www.ted.com/talks/hanna_rosin_new_data_on_the_rise_of_women.html Retrieved Thursday, November 29th of 2012.

292 *INTERNATIONAL CONGRESS OF WOMEN.* p. 21 (English), 27 (German), 32 (French).

terrorism[293] which set in motion a destructive chain of events, just as it ended with one which has done the same thing. The September 11th of 2001 terrorist attacks on the World Trade Center and the Pentagon were blamed on religious "Islamic" extremism, and then-U.S. President George W. Bush's "crusade" rhetoric made the far-right Christianity which followed appear to be simply the other side of the same coin. It is as Joan of Arc stated in her letter to the rogue group known as the Hussites, who had split from the Roman Catholic Church and taken to destroying their churches, monasteries, and villages: when Christians embrace doctrine which causes them to commit acts of barbarism, they are no better than the Islamic extremists.[294]

To quote a 2002 article of American political newsletter *counterpunch*:

> "Islamic fanatics flew those planes a year ago and here we are with a terrifying alliance of Judaeo-Christian fanatics....War on Terror? It's back to the late thirteenth century, picking up where Prince Edward left off with his ninth crusade after St Louis had died in Tunis with the word Jerusalem...."[295]

---

293 The assassination of the Archduke Ferdinand by an organization calling itself "The Black Hand" fomented the international strife which would eventually become World War I.

294 Literally "Saracens", which were what Islamists were called during the Crusades. Written on March 23rd of 1430 during a brief truce between the Kingdom of France and that of England. Joan of Arc did not trust this truce, but she was so infuriated by the actions of the Hussites that she wrote to them stating that if she didn't find that they had reformed themselves, she might leave the English behind and go against them [Joan's visions were not advising her at this point, and thus she was something of a free agent]. She added that thus, by the sword – if she couldn't do it any other way – she would eliminate their false and vile supersitions and relieve them of either their heresy or their lives. Such brutal threats may have been necessary to drive home Joan's point, but this pinch of foreshadowing into Joan's own life reminds one of the fate of those who live by the sword. (Matthew 26:52, Revelation 13:10) http://archive.joan-of-arc.org/joanofarc_letter_march_23_1430.html Originally dictated to Friar Jean Pasquerel, Joan's scribe and confessor. Retrieved this Day of the Epiphany, Sunday, January 5th of 2014.

295 This reference actually draws from both the Eighth Crusade (1270 A.D.) and the Ninth Crusade (1271-1272 A.D.). St. Louis was Louis IX , King of France, who was along with his army devastated by disease in Tunisia in North

(Alexander Cockburn, "The Tenth Crusade," September 7-9, 2002)[296]

Yet it was not 9/11 that actually marked the point at which Christianity begun to decline; the point at which people's faith began to burn out and they were prompted to shop around elsewhere in effort to rekindle their spirituality: it was World War I, a tragic and despair-inducing conflict on a scale then unheard-of, one hundred years ago.[297]

Though women would continue to outnumber men among the religious faithful, their roles elsewhere in society changed dramatically. After the first World War, women emerged from what William Moulton Marston described as a false and haremlike protection and began taking work normally done by men. While haremlike protection may be nice if one can get it, as said it was false, for as Mordecai noted it was not always 100% safe[298] and it was also a luxury generally limited to the wealthy. To quote Sojourner Truth:

> "Nobody ever helps me into carriages, or over mud puddles, or gives me any best place! And ain't I a woman?"[299]

Africa, and thus the last major attempt to take the Holy Land was ended. The future Edward I of England, who had accompanied him on this Crusade, then undertook an unsuccessful expedition against the Egyptian Sultan Baibars the following year. In the aftermath, Christians in the region were expunged from settlements in the realm, including Tripoli, Acre, and the island of Ruad occupied by the Knights Templar (who, believe it or not, a Freemason former pool manager of mine attempted to convince me to apply to. Not knowing at the time the enmity between them and Roman Catholics, I refused simply because the Knights did not permit women in their ranks).

296 http://www.counterpunch.org/2002/09/07/the-tenth-crusade/ Retrieved December 19th, 2012.

297 Marta Trzebiatowska and Steve Bruce. *Why are Women more Religious Than Men?* Published by Oxford University Press, USA, Friday, October 12th of 2012. p. 2. Emphasis mine.

298 Esther 4:12-14.

299 *History of Woman Suffrage, 2nd ed. Vol.1. Rochester, NY: Charles Mann, 1889.*, edited by Elizabeth Cady Stanton, Susan B. Anthony, and Matilda Joslyn Gage.

Still, the alternative remained a difficult prospect. With the possible exception of mythological figures such as the amazons, there are virtually no records of any concerted female efforts on such a large scale having ever been attempted before. Thus there was considerable confusion and disagreement as to the path women's liberation should take (such confusion even persists to some degree today, which is why we can be told that almost anything is "liberating" or "empowering" and some of us shall believe it, even if it involves slowly slaying oneself by smoking cigarettes[300] (a practice which the suffragettes staunchly *opposed!*)).

Some women wanted to focus on proving themselves to men by helping them win the war, as this seemed immediately necessary and they had become accustomed to the view that traditionally-male roles were ideal. God had showed that women are capable of performing quite well in the role of military commanders (as exemplified by the Prophetess Deborah and Saint Joan of Arc), however restricting their aspirations to such competitive careers served to perpetuate desire (and need) for such things.

The Boer War[301] had made British militarists shocked that their army had been so ill-equipped and created a sense of crisis in Britain.

---

300 Once called "torches of freedom" in an effort to market them to women. A perfect example of such deception is found in the cigarette advertisement campaigns of Eve (yes, *Eve*) and Virginia Slims. The latter actually juxtaposed images of Edwardian suffragettes with glamourous modern smoking women to suggest that the freedom to smoke was something for which our sisters from a century ago fought...though of course they never did anything of the sort!

301 Known in Afrikaans as *Vryheidsoorloe* (lit. "Freedom wars"), the Boer War(s) actually consisted of two wars (1880-1881 and 1899-1902) fought by the British Empire against the two independent Boer republics of South Africa: the Oranje Vrijstaat (Orange Free State) and the Republiek van Transvaal (Transvaal Republic). The first broke out after republic unrest following the British defeat of the Zulu kingdom (which had cost the British immense losses), whilst the second did so because of the finding of lucrative mineral deposits. Emily Hobhouse, herself a delegate of the South African Women and Children's Distress Fund, visited some of the British-operated concentration camps in the Oranje Vrijstaat and, appalled by the horrific conditions therein, helped to alter public opinion and to force the government

The necessity that Britain and her Empire be better defended in future demanded greater defence expenditure, and the looming outbreak of the First World War encouraged everyone – including women – to throw themselves headlong into the war effort. 50,000 women flocked to become Voluntary Aid Detachment members, and women in general were urged to help with fund-raising. Like more genuine modern answers to the 15th-Century Catherine de La Rochelle, a great number of women were thrilled at the thought of playing an important role in this manly art which was so enshrined in history.

The war offered to women a seemingly-irresistible chance for excitement and travel, coupled with the reassurance that they were dedicating themselves to partriotic service. How could they do any less? The nature of warfare was about to change dramatically, and this deepened the complex debate about what women's role should be. Intellectuals such as Bertha von Suttner had predicted a time when entire nations would fight, possibly including regiments of women, and modern weaponry would horrifically increase the numbers of dead and wounded. (A 1912 pamphlet titled *Barbarity in the Skies*, written by von Suttner herself, warned of the use of aeroplanes in war.)[302] Those women whose views were anti-militarist were far fewer and thought to be far less organized, though they asked the question:

> "Was this – the reproduction of fodder for gun and cannon and aerial attack – really the end to which women's lives should be dedicated?"
>
> (Jill Liddington, *The Road to Greenham Common: Feminism and Anti-Militarism in Britain Since 1820*, pp. 59-65)

Warfare, so glorified over so many millennia, proved very difficult for women to resist, despite its being so detrimental to their way of life. As stated by Dutchwoman Amy Lillingston of the International Congress of Women, for every hundred women that were willing to

---

to improve conditions in the camps.

302 Jill Liddington, *The Road to Greenham Common: Feminism and Anti-Militarism in Britain Since 1820*, pp. 59-65.

come to their Congress of peace, there were a thousand women ready to go to France and fight.[303]

There existed much confusion as to what women's role was to be in the brave new world of suffrage, and the mysterious groundbreaking image of Joan of Arc was often used as inspiration. Appropriately enough, as with Joan, God did not want women to support war so much as He wanted them to end it for all time.
(British poster circa 1914-1918 by Bert Thomas, American poster circa 1914-1918 by Haskell Coffin, and *The Suffragette* cover circa 1912 by Hilda Dallas. The initials on Joan's new banner stand for "Women's Social and Political Union".)

There were especially wise women, however, who decided that there were gifts womankind could offer the world which had nothing to do with childbirth yet which were still distinctly feminine, and they ensured that these would be – in every sense of the term – Christmas gifts.

Thus in 1914, in the same season as the Christmas Truce (in which members of warring sides simply refused to fight one another after the mutual singing of carols reminded them that they were all Christian) came about the Open Christmas Letter with which I began the second chapter of this book, under the heading "On Earth Peace, Goodwill towards Men."[304] Written by welfare campaigner Emily Hobhouse and

---

303 *INTERNATIONAL CONGRESS OF WOMEN. Report of Business Sessions.* THIRD DAY, FRIDAY, APRIL 30th. "Woman Suffrage Resolution." p. 128.

304 Luke 2:14, KJV. The New American (Holy) Bible (2003-2004 Edition) notes that this is the Byzantine text tradition, however, and instead reads "on earth peace to those on whom his favour rests." This is because, according to the footnote found therein, that reading is the one found in the oldest Western

signed by 101 British women, it was written in response to a German letter received earlier that year entitled "To the International Woman Suffrage Alliance, through its president, Mrs. [Carrie] Chapman Catt." Beginning with the greeting, "To the women of all nations warm and hearty greetings in these wretched and bloody times," this letter conveyed the deep disgust at the war possessed by the peace-loving women of Germany, one of whom wrote:

> "True humanity knows no national hatred, no national contempt. Women are nearer to true humanity than men."

Fortunately, most of the women contacted in such correspondences did not share the bitter sexism displayed by that statement[305], and all agreed that war was an atrocity against which they must rise. Thus was born a mutual understanding between women of opposing nations that the best way for this war to end was through peace of a nature that granted equality to all sides. The women believed also that the best way to accomplish this end was through the gift of discourse and diplomacy, using neutral nations such as the United States of America as mediators.

Thus was born the International Congress of Women, and "born" was most definitely the operative term here. In her "Foreword" to the Congress, Emily Hobhouse stated that though the declaration of War had had a stunning and paralytic effect upon the minds of the world, an idea now in its embryonic stage had been silently and spontaneously conceived within the hearts of women; the idea that the women of

---

and Alexandrian texts and is the preferred one. It seems rather fitting that the lines of angels were selected, considering what Sir Arthur Conan Doyle referred to as "the angelic nature of women" in his 1890 Sherlock Holmes novel *The Sign of Four.*

305 On the fourth day of the International Congress of Women, Mme De Jong Van Beek en Donk, while noting that the Congress was placing emphasis upon the duty of women to protest against war, proposed the motion that *peace is best served by cooperation between men and women.* It was immediately carried by the Congress. *INTERNATIONAL CONGRESS OF WOMEN. Report of Business Sessions.* FOURTH DAY, SATURDAY, MAY 1th. (MORNING SESSION). "Women's Voice in the Peace Settlement." p. 162.

the world must come to the aid of the world.[306] Perhaps, then, this contribution of women *did* have something to do with childbirth, yet only in the form of the feminine imagery used here.

The daughter of the first (Anglican) Archdeacon of Bodmin (Cornwall, England), Emily Hobhouse also employed a great deal of Christian imagery in her writing upon this subject, as is evident upon the pages of the report which immediately follow. Her Foreword likened the ardent yearning of the women of all countries for peace and justice to a spirit of light, which Aletta Jacobs[307] discerned as it moved upon the face of what Hobhouse described as the world's dark waters (a reference to Genesis 1:2). She then described Jacobs as being gifted with both wisdom and practical power, allowing her to both seize the psychological moment – pregnant with living desire – and also concentrate and organize the deep, scattered forces at her command (a reference to Genesis 1:6-10). This epoch-making week (Genesis 2:2) stirred the world in spite of itself.

Hobhouse then immediately began to compare the International Congress of Women in the Dutch town of the Hague to the shepherds around Bethlehem in Luke 2:8. Representing both the Heavenly Host and the Infant Jesus was Peace, who again appeared and became a living force upon the Earth (Luke 2:11, 14). Like Jesus, Peace was nurtured by womanly love and wisdom, and she burst her swaddling bands (Luke 2:7), swept the world in her wings and wrought a miraculous change in the universal attitude (Luke 2:10 and 13:34, Matthew 23:37). Peace is still amongst us, and now wrestles with war, and those of every race and tongue rally to her standard, as Hobhouse put it. Men's eyes now turn with relief to this new, bloodless battleground where Peace wrestles and will prevail (Genesis 32:24-28), for hers is the vital principle of Love.

---

306 Emily Hobhouse, "Foreword" to *INTERNATIONAL CONGRESS OF WOMEN, THE HAGUE – APRIL 28TH TO MAY 1ST 1915, BERICH – RAPPORT – REPORT,* p. IX. http://archive.org/details/berichtrapportre45wome Retrieved Tuesday, October 23rd of 2012.

307 Aletta Jacobs, one of the most noted members of the International Suffrage Alliance, who was credited with the concentrating and shaping of the ardent yearning in question. (Ibid.)

Women, who have always been the chief sufferers from war's curse, must vow to never again let it usurp control.[308]

The Judeo-Christian symbolism was not lost upon the women of faith involved with the International Congress. In speaking sense to the rulers of nations, they were taking a page from Esther's book[309], as was strongly suggested by the Congress Platform's Italian representative Signora Rosa Genoni. She described the members of this convention as the "queens" who would implore both parliaments and kings on behalf of the people who were at war.[310] Thus it was that women delegates went forth to present the message expressed in their Congress' resolutions before the rulers of both the belligerent and neutral nations of Europe as well as to the President of the United States. Given that they were clearly neutral non-combatants, these women received very frank information from these rulers regarding the war, finding in it much atrocity and no necessity. Congress speaker Louise Keilhau, the Platform's Norwegian representative, even suggested that there was something present in the international politics of the day, which were managed only by men, which caused war.[311]

Thousands of peace-seeking women met at the Congress, representing twelve countries (with expressions of sympathy from an additional ten[312]) to further their cause. There they discussed proposals and democratically confirmed resolutions regarding the future of the

---

308 Emily Hobhouse, "Foreword" to *INTERNATIONAL CONGRESS OF WOMEN, THE HAGUE – APRIL 28TH TO MAY 1ST 1915, BERICH – RAPPORT – REPORT*, pp. X-XI

309 Specifically, this would have been the fifth page of the Book of Esther, according to my little King James Bible from 1868, for it includes Chapter VIII verses 3-17.

310 Translated from the original French. *INTERNATIONAL CONGRESS OF WOMEN. Report of Business Sessions.* FOURTH DAY, SATURDAY, MAY 1st. (MORNING SESSION). p. 171.

311 Ibid. FIRST DAY, WEDNESDAY, APRIL 28th. Protest. p. 78.

312 Those countries represented were Austria, Belgium, Canada, Denmark, Germany, Great-Britain, Hungary, Italy, the Netherlands, Norway, Sweden and the United States. Expressions of sympathy were received also from the Argentine, British India, Bulgaria, Finland, France, Portugal, Romania, Russia, Switzerland and South Africa. Ibid. p. XLIII.

world, interrupted only by brief discussion on the sending of flowers to the wounded to act as messengers of peace, sympathy and goodwill[313] reminiscent of St. Theresa of Lisieux's promise to send a shower of roses upon the earth. These proposals determined the manner in which nations should agree to treat and attend to one another in a just manner. Such proposals included international arbitration and federation, foreign policy being controlled by public discussion and parliaments, principles to determine which territory should or should not be transferred, reduction of armaments, **international levies to provide for the reinstatement of devastated territories**, etc. The Congress also made it clear with their delegates from Women's Societies that **all discussion as to who was responsible for the present war should be ruled out of order.**[314]

These concepts discussed were refined by the women into cohesive points which should be quite familiar to those with knowledge of the United Nations, including that:

1. No territory should be transferred without the consent of the men and women living in that territory, and that there should be no recognition of 'the right of conquest.'
2. Autonomy and a democratic parliament should be granted to any people who desire it.
3. The governments of all nations should agree to refer all future international disputes to arbitration and conciliation and to place social, moral and economic pressure upon any country which resorts to arms.
4. Foreign politics must be subject to democratic control.
5. Women should be granted equal political rights as men.[315]

---

313 Ibid. p 236.

314 Ibid., p. XXXVIII. Emphasized text shall prove of particular note.

315 This was elaborated upon on the following page, forming a strong justification for women's rights. The Congress demanded that, due to the combined influence of the women of all countries being among the strongest forces for the prevention of war, and due to the fact that women can only have full responsibility and effective influence when they have political rights equal to those of men, women must be politically enfranchised. "**III. PRINCIPLES OF A PERMANENT PEACE.**"Ibid. "PREAMBLE AND RESOLUTIONS

Among those rulers with whom the women delegates conferred were American President Woodrow Wilson, whose unofficial support for the Congress of Women was noted in its documents, and many of the women's proposals were incorporated into his famous Fourteen Points. These Points became the basis for the German Surrender as negotiated at the Paris Peace Conference and were documented in the Treaty of Versailles at the end of World War I. While the Fourteen Points included such specific and immediate concerns as that of the Eighth (that all French territory should be freed and those portions which were invaded restored), they also contained goals which were far-reaching in both space and time. Examples of these included the First, which demanded transparency of international action and open covenants of peace, the Second, which demanded absolute freedom of navigation upon the seas except when necessary for the enforcement of international covenants, and the Fourteenth, which called for a community of nations to mutually ensure political independence and territorial integrity for all countries regardless of size. All of these Points were addressed by the International Congress of Women, and some of them are nearly word-for-word appropriations from it.

So influential was the women's work that it was instrumental in the creation of two non-partisan international organizations. These were the League of Nations (founded in 1920) and its replacement: **the United Nations** (founded in 1945).[316]

It is a sad thing that the latter was necessary at all. However, like Mary Magdalene and the wife of Pontius Pilate before them, those of the International Congress of Women were not properly heeded, and the consequences were dire indeed. Grace Abbott of the U.S.A. stressed that, to bring together mankind in the building up of humanity's common civilization, they must do all in their power to promote mutual

---

ADOPTED. II. ACTION TOWARDS PEACE. 3. The Peace Settlement." pp. 36-37.

316 "How Did Women Activists Promote Peace in Their 1915 Tour of Warring European Capitals?" Documents selected and interpreted by Kathryn Kish Sklar and Kari Amidon; State University of New York at Binghamton, May 1998. http://womhist.alexanderstreet.com/hague/intro.htm Retrieved Tuesday, October 23rd of 2012.

good will and understanding and resist any tendency toward hatred and revenge.[317]

Like Saint Theresa of Lisieux, the women of the International Congress foresaw the danger of the French nationalistic movement following their loss in the Franco-Prussian war, and the resulting desire for vengeance. Unfortunately, blaming the defeated Central Powers as being the cause of the War was disturbingly central to the Paris Peace Conference and the resulting Treaty of Versailles. The victorious French and British paid little acknowledgement to Wilson's Fourteen Points. The French Prime Minister, George Clemenceau, was determined to weaken Germany so that it might never again attack France. He stated that Mr. Wilson bored him with the Fourteen Points, commenting that even God Almighty has only ten. British Prime Minister David Lloyd George joked that, situated betwixt the ideals put forth by Wilson and the retributive desires of Clemenceau, he was seated between Jesus Christ and Napoleon Bonaparte.

Napoleonesque or not, the stance taken by Clemenceau was understandable; it was France upon which so much of the fighting had taken place, and it was France which saw so many of its children fall to the bloody ravages of the conflict. Additionally, though it was by far the more important, this Treaty was in fact the *second* Treaty of Versailles. The first was written in 1871, at the end of the Franco-Prussian war, in which the defeated France had lost its precious Alsace and Lorraine regions, which were of not merely symbolic but also strategic significance. These regions, which stretched all the way to the Rhine, were to exchange hands between France and Germany four times in the course of 75 years, and the Rhineland would intentionally become Adolf Hitler's staging grounds for the beginning of World War II. Likewise, the choice of Versailles for the signing of the Treaty

---

317 Moved by GRACE ABBOTT (U.S.A.) and seconded by Mme. KULKA. Dr. Aletta H. Jacobs, President of the Netherlands Executive Committee. *INTERNATIONAL CONGRESS OF WOMEN. Report of Business Sessions.* FIRST DAY, WEDNESDAY, APRIL 28TH. I. Opening of the Congress. "Promotion of Good Feeling between Nations." p. 82.

marked for France the opportunity to symbolically erase the humiliation of the defeat in the war of 1870.[318]

However, this stance resulted in the demand for full, immediate, and severely-broad restitution from Germany. This was a blatant rejection of the International Congress of Women's recommendation that international levies be made to provide for all devastated countries, and it paid heed to neither the fact that hundreds of thousands of Germany's civilian populace had already starved to death nor the nigh-unimaginably devastating effect this would have upon its economy. The resulting inflation caused the German *mark* to dip so low in value (to eventually approximately one trillionth of a U.S. dollar) that workers took their wages home in wheelbarrows and the nigh-worthless paper money was burned as fireplace kindling.

The Pontiff at the time, Pope Benedict XV, was disgusted at all of the suffering, devastation, and loss of human life brought about by the massive international conflict and reportedly described the war as a "useless massacre". The Vatican believed the conditions inflicted upon Germany were too harsh – it was even suggested that the European economic stability as a whole was threatened and that the humiliated Germany would start another war as soon as it was militarily able – and focused its efforts upon overcoming the famine and misery there and elsewhere in Europe.

Yet what of the heroic women of the Congress, who rose up in effort to save the world in its time of need? What became of them when the image of the "modern woman" morphed into that of the boyish, short-haired, short-skirted, hard-drinking, and cigarette-smoking "flapper" of the 1920s? The American delegates, who had received particular recognition for their efforts (the President of the Congress Jane Addams being one of them who would even win a Nobel Peace Prize), were targeted by government authorities individually. They were accused of being everything from 'Communists' to 'German sympathizers' so that these women might never again interfere in such a way upon the world stage. The International Congress of Women's influence appeared lost. Hearts were hardened...lest the women's message of peace and

---

318 *Traite de Versailles.* http://fr.wikipedia.org/wiki/Trait%C3%A9_de_Versailles Translated from the original French by the author. Retrieved 15/06/2013.

love – the message of Christ – be heard, and hearkened to, and heal them.[319] Pity came too late for Germany; the Weimar Republic was horribly discredited by the depression and – as is so often the case in desperate times – the nation was forced to embrace a tyrant who suddenly emerged, promised the world...and almost delivered.[320]

Yet the only hope of preventing such deeds as those wrought by Adolf Hitler was given by the Victorian/Edwardian-era members of the International Congress of Women; these docile and delicate creatures raised in the "haremlike protection" so summoning the image of Esther, with their petticoats and their perfume, their kid gloves and corsets and collars and their willingness to leave warfare to the menfolk...save when it was wisest to stop it.

TOP, Reading from left to right: Dr. ALETTA H. JACOBS, President of the Dutch Executive Committee; EMILY HOBHOUSE, delegate of the South African Women and Children's Distress Fund and writer of the Foreword to the Congress; JANE ADDAMS, President of the International Congress of Women.
BOTTOM: **PHOTOGRAPH OF THE PLATFORM.** Reading from left to right: Mme. THOUMAIAN, Armenia; LEOPOLDINA KULKA, Austria; Miss HUGHES, Canada; ROSIKA SCHWIMMER, Hungary; Dr. ANITA AUGSPURG, Germany; JANE ADDAMS, U.S.A., President of the Congress;

---

319 John 12:40.

320 Matthew 4:8-9, Luke 4:5-7. This is of course not to imply that Adolf Hitler was Satan, even if Michel de Notre Dame (a.k.a. Nostradamus) did reportedly describe him as "the Second Anti-Christ" (Emperor Napoleon Bonaparte is said to have been the First).

EUGÉNIE HAMER, Belgium; Dr. ALETTA H. JACOBS, President of the Dutch Executive Committee; CHRYSTAL MACMILLAN, Great Britain; ROSA GENONI, Italy; ANNA KLEMAN, Sweden; THORA DAUGAARD, Denmark; LOUISE KEILHAU, Norway. The banner borne by Mme. THOUMAIAN translates from French to "One for all, all for one," but due to its being in all-capitals it provides unintentional foreshadowing: "*UN* for all, all for *UN*."

Whenever there is perception of difference – be it sexual or anything else humanity can find – there is discrimination. As such, to prove their worthiness to the men of the world, feminists would take an increasingly masculinized approach over the past hundred years. However, is it truly a sexist thing to suggest that the female has something uniquely hers to contribute, and that this necessitates her being permitted a leadership role?

The International Congress of Women did not believe so, even if some of its statements might be accused of being such. In her Address of Welcome to the Congress, Dr. Aletta H. Jacobs stated that women judge war in a different manner than men. She suggested that men primarily consider its economic costs or gains; in money, commerce, industry, the extension of power, and so forth. This material loss is not so important to women; not when compared to the number of fathers, brothers, husbands, and sons marching out to war never to return. Women know far too well that whatever may be gained by war, it is not worth the bloodshed, tears, cruel sufferings, wasted lives, agony, and despair it has caused. However important the economic interests of a country may be, the interests of the human race are more vital. Thus, as "by virtue of our womanhood" these interests are of greater sanctity and value to women, we are justified in demanding a voice in the governments of all countries.[321] How accurate this may or may not be I cannot say with full reliability, but it should be noted that Dr. Jacobs was viewing things from the feminine perspective of a Victorian background, and that it was necessary to the world that her views be heeded.

Truly the Second World War, and all its warping of the world: the expulsion of Christians from Japan and the nation's military's horrors

321 *INTERNATIONAL CONGRESS OF WOMEN*. "Address of Welcome *by* Dr. ALETTA H. JACOBS", p. 6.

in China and elsewhere as it was encouraged to emulate Nazi-like arch-nationalism, the Cold War (and with it the quagmire of the Vietnam War and the rise of the Taliban in Afghanistan (and thus 9/11)), the faulty aid model which has empowered countless tyrants and caused immense poverty in Africa, every atomic- or nuclear-related disaster, and yes, as in the Book of Esther, the attempted annihilation of the Jewish people in the Holocaust, would not have happened had men listened to women...

....Christian women. Not only was there much use of Christian imagery and mention of spiritual/apostolic components in the International Congress of Women, but it was also specifically and vocally based upon Christian values. In fact, on the first day of the Congress, Anna Lindhagen of Sweden summed up the women's collective feeling of purpose quite bluntly with the statement:

> "It is that we are all a Christian world and it is the soul of Christianity to give peace to all peoples."[322]

One may, it appears, remove the angel from the house without removing the angel from the woman, and her contribution to the world will not be limited to the purchase of war savings stamps!

> "Aha!! What honor for the female sex!
> God shows how he loves it, ...
> No men could do this deed, but more:...
> No one would credit this before."
> ("The Song of Joan of Arc," the final work of Christine de Pisan, Stanza XXXIV[323])

---

322 *INTERNATIONAL CONGRESS OF WOMEN.* **"Transference of Territory."** The International Congress of women affirmed that there should be no transference of territory without the consent of the men and women residing therein. p. 109. Translated from the original French by the author. Retrieved Sunday, December 9th of 2012.

323 Translated from the French text in *Christine de Pisan, Diti de Jeanne d'Arc*, ed. Angus J. Kennedy and Kenneth Varty (Oxford: Society for the Study of Medieval Languages and Literature, 1977), trans. L. Shopkow. Prepared for the web by Prof. Leah Shopkow. http://www.indiana.edu/~dmdhist/joan.htm Retrieved Monday, October 22nd of 2012. The original French version may be found in http://www.scribd.com/doc/70815123/Poems-in-Honor-of-Jeanne-D

As one raised in a purely masculine environment, I can state from experience that we are encouraged to undervalue anything which is traditionally feminine, especially when thinking in terms of achievement. Even now in some mostly-non-Christian nations (despite women being a prominent part of the workforce) baby girls are aborted or murdered in infancy simply because of their sex. However, despite all the disparagement and degradation which we have endured, it is difficult to argue against a known feminine achievement that produced the potential for peace on earth!

Indeed, Christianity began to decline at that pivotal moment in history that was World War I; once called "The War to End All Wars." This war showed just how much warfare had been transformed by the industrial age into a filthy, disease-ridden, blood-soaked and highly-impersonal mire which would no longer even abide any illusion of honour or chivalry. Truly, the continued and large-scale practice of the evils I have attempted to address in this book have always been the greatest bane of Christianity.

Thus is revealed what has been femininity's unappreciated gift throughout history; the all-too-often thankless task of desperately trying to change through peace a world which was not yet capable of such things.

> "Jerusalem, Jerusalem, who kills the prophets and stones those who are sent to her! How often I wanted to gather your children together, the way a hen gathers her chicks under her wings, and you were unwilling!"
>
> – Jesus (Matthew 23:37, Luke 13:34,
> New American Standard Bible)

Still, as I also noted earlier, the women's mission was not truly a failure. In 1945 the world quietly acknowledged its grave mistake and dusted off these ideas of woman born. This time – perhaps because of the even more immense price paid in this Second World War so soon after the First – they were heeded, and the result was the United Nations. So it was that humanity's newly-acquired ability to end the world in fire

---

Retrieved Friday, November 9th of 2012.

at any moment has been stayed for nearly seven decades, and we have thusfar managed to avoid a Third World War. I submit this as further evidence that women can indeed do anything with God on their side, and that God truly is on our side; for ours is no war.

> "Blessed *are* the peacemakers: for they shall be called the children of God."
>
> – Jesus Christ, Matthew 5:9 (KJV)

If there is any folly in feminism, it is in the assumption that it was inherently and necessarily selfish; that it was and is merely a case of women looking after and seeking to advance their own interests through competition. However, once the unique contributions women have offered and are still capable of offering are understood, it becomes quite apparent that feminism is not truly "self-interest" (as it has been called by both its supporters and its detractors). True feminism is not like Eve, eating of the forbidden fruit so that she could be "empowered". Rather, feminism is more like Mary, defying social conventions and even the Law so that she could, through her faith in God, save the world.

Yes, the United Nations were originally controlled by men, and even now only 6% of UN diplomats are women.[324] This needs to change if the necessary balance is to be achieved. However this also shows, due to the fact that the United Nations have generally still been maintained to a reasonable degree, that the male gender is capable of "feminine" virtues just as the female is capable of "masculine" ones, and the organization would be among the first to note that a nation may be measured by the treatment of its women. As the International Congress of Women so often noted, if suppression or deception are used effectively against us, then we cannot fulfill our role necessary in saving the world.

In time, it may not even be necessary to extol the "feminine" virtues. Only so long as there is inequality shall there be any need for feminism. Feminism, too, shall be fulfilled once final justice is done.

---

324 Guest Author. "Celebrating the Rise of Women in Diplomacy". *The Next Women Business Magazine.* 07 March 2012. http://www.thenextwomen.com/2012/03/07/celebrating-rise-women-diplomacy Retrieved Monday, April 22nd of 2013.

Jesus Christ: The Ultimate Feminist

Even those women who were acknowledged by the Biblical writers were still written about by men, and (save for such things as the prayers attributed to Judith, Esther, and Mary) thus the women of the Bible are known for their deeds more than their words, while their hearts and inner feelings remain largely unknown.

What a mystery is a woman to the men who write of her! How can they know the deep struggles of femininity in their masculine society? Imagine being a loving creature of peace in a world which worships the Man of War, one who longs to nurture rebellious children yet is given no honour from them, one whose every spiritual insight is met with suspicion and the threat of death by horrible means, and one who still does not take up the sword even when they are at last faced with death.

Is it any wonder, then, that approximately 85% of all the original followers of the Ascended Jesus Christ were women?

> "...where abode both Peter, and James, and John, and Andrew, Philip, and Thomas, Bartholomew, and Matthew, James the son of Alphaeus, and Simon Zelotes, and Judas the brother of James.
>
> These all continued with one accord in prayer and supplication, **with the women**, and Mary the mother of Jesus, and with his brethren.
>
> And in those days Peter stood up in the midst of the disciples, and said, (the number of names together were about **an hundred and twenty**,)"
>
> (Acts of the Apostles 1:13-15, KJV, emphasis mine)

Here Luke the Evangelist subtly used the traditional style of ancient writing to paint a fascinating picture of the first post-Ascension Christian congregation. Jesus' "brethren" (believed to be His cousins or half-brothers) were only four in number (James the Just, Joses, Simon and Jude), and thus there were fifteen men mentioned in this passage among the one hundred and twenty people. One may assume that there were at least a couple more men present, as this was the event at which Matthias was selected as the replacement for Judas the Iscariot. Nevertheless, we cannot safely assume based upon this chronicle that there were more than twenty men present in the congregation, meaning that their numbers were dwarfed by those of the *one hundred women* there also (who had, after all, been following and helping Jesus in great numbers for some time according to Luke 8:1-3)! This provides some of the earliest evidence that women are especially religious, and in Christianity we have especial reason to be religious.

Jesus Christ is the greatest feminist ever to take the form of a man. This is due to His acceptance and defence of women as well as to His (in His gentleness and submission to the will of God) exemplification of feminine virtues.

To lead into another example of this, earlier in this chapter we discussed the concept of women holding property. Due to the precedent set with the daughters of Zelophehad it is apparent that God is certainly in favour of it, yet other writings of Ancient Israel indicate that it would have been beneficial if He had been consulted directly more often....

> "The man is a slave, in disgrace and shame,
> when a wife supports her husband.
> (Sirach 25:21, NAB)

The last fourteen verses of Sirach 25 are controversial for feminists, for they contain no small measure of misogyny. Beginning with a bitter expression of emotional betrayal in v. 12 ("Worst of all wounds is that of the heart, worst of all evils is that of a woman" (NAB)), the author goes on to note the virulency of a woman's venom (v. 14) and further describes his position thusly:

> "With a dragon or a lion I would rather dwell
> than live with an evil woman." (v. 15, NAB)

He does not elaborate on the details of these proposed living arrangements (though picturing them has provided a fair amount of amusement over the centuries), but rather continues to assault the female gender for the various ills that befall man and recommends that one "be not indulgent to an erring wife."[325] Thankfully no mention is made of actually physically harming one's wife, but as the chapter's grand finale, the following advice is given:

> "If she walks not by your side,
> cut her away from you [divorce her]." (v. 25, NAB)

Oh dear, deeply-wise Jesus, son of Eleazar, son of Sirach (whom I shall henceforth refer to simply as Sirach to avoid obvious confusion), lover of the law, the priesthood, the temple, and divine worship, why must you have written such things to appear in the Bible so that we women must deal with them? Once such things are (Deutero-) Canonized, not even a king can counter them....

However, the King of kings can.

> "And he saith unto them, Whosoever shall put away his wife,
> and marry another, committeth adultery against her."
> (Mark 10:11, KJV; see also Matthew 5:32 and Luke 16:18)

The beginning of *The Imitation of Christ* states that the teaching of Christ surpasses all the advice of the saints[326], and I must say that it is immensely wonderful indeed to know that there is One who will never abandon us!

In the modern world there appears to be a popular attitude that to consider divorce wrong is anti-feminist. It is true that to disallow divorce runs the risk of keeping one in an abusive relationship, such as that which Saint Monica was forced to endure from her violent-tempered Pagan husband and dissolute son (who would later become Saint Augustine of Hippo). However, it also appears to have been largely forgotten that in the time of Christ (and Sirach) a man could divorce a

---

[325] Sirach 25:24, NAB.

[326] The First Chapter, "Imitating Christ and Despising All Vanities on Earth". This is very useful to remember when testing the spirit (as Pope Francis advises) in those cases when it appears that one is contacted by one or more saints; they must be in agreement with the Faith in and teachings of Jesus Christ.

woman freely and thus rob her of her social security, while a woman could never divorce a man for any reason[327].

> "They say unto him, Why did Moses then command to give a writing of divorcement, and to put her away? [Deuteronomy 24:1]
>
> He saith unto them, Moses because of the hardness of your hearts suffered you to put away your wives: but from the beginning it was not so." (Matthew 19:7-8, KJV)

In repudiating the Mosaic Law, Jesus further affirmed His Divine Authority and in so doing took quite a risk. However, this would not stop Him; Jesus' desire was to protect women.

So too it was even during the crucifixion; His holy head pierced and bloodied by His crown of thorns[328] and the beating He had received from the very rod He had been given by the Romans[329], His raw whip-wounds[330] scraping against the splintering wood of His cross, His hands and feet issuing His Sacred Blood and radiating pain under unnatural pressure from which there was no relief, His own body's weight slowly and excruciatingly forcing the life out of His lungs, His agony unimaginable, His concern was for the security of His mother as He seared His chest by drawing the breath necessary to utter,

> "...Woman, behold thy son!
> Then saith he to the disciple, Behold thy mother! And from that hour the disciple took her unto his own home." (John 19:26-27, KJV)

---

327 New American (Holy) Bible, 2003-2004 Edition footnote for Matthew 19, 9. It notes that this was the case in Palestine, unlike in the places where Roman and Greek law prevailed, and addresses the previous verse with the statement that Moses' concession to humanity due to its sinfulness (*the hardness of your hearts,* 8) is repudiated by Jesus, and thus the Creator's original will is reaffirmed. p. 1040.

328 Matthew 27:29, Mark 15:17, John 19:2.

329 Matthew 27:30, Mark 15:19.

330 John 19:1.

His mother, as we have noted previously, has received much exaltation. However, John Shelby Spong's article "The Virgin Mary is No Wonder Woman" states that Mary's power was never direct, but always secondary. Spong goes on to clarify that this was a reflection of what girls were supposed to be in a patriarchal society; her power was at best intercessional. Such is the nature of saintly power and duty; and Mary is so pure and gentle as to be able to move with her requests the Father God or the judging Son Jesus. However, Spong refers to this as 'divine pillow talk' and points out the problem with her as the highest-ranking female: the Father and Son are still the ones with the real power.

• • •

Hrm. John of Patmos did note that "before the throne [of God] there was a sea of glass like unto crystal" (Revelation 4:6), yet I do not believe that this was ever intended to be interpreted as a "***glass ceiling***"[331]! I think I shall also assume that Spong's article does not there include a complaint about the power structure of the Divine 'regime'. I will note, however, that the Bishop's statement invites an examination of gender-representation within the Holy Trinity.

The Divine Feminine

Though I must disagree with the writers of *The Woman's Bible*[332] on a number of points (as it commits the classic error of encouraging disregard for Scripture; such as in the dismissal of Biblical miracles such as the Virgin Birth of Jesus) it is still quite a profound work which contains some intriguing ideas. One of these involves co-author Frances Ellen Burr's realisation that the translators of the Bible have taken care to smother up every reference to the fact that the Deity is both masculine

---

331 My belief is supported by Revelation 15:2, as many who have resisted the Beast are present upon this sea of glass.

332 It should be noted that author Elizabeth Cady Stanton did specify that 'The Woman's Bible' was intended for readers who neither cared for nor would be convinced by a learned, technical work of 'higher criticism.' *The Woman's Bible,* "Preface to Part II", January 1898, p. 8.

and feminine. Another is Burr's belief that the Holy Spirit, though usually represented as masculine, is in fact feminine.[333]

Neither of these statements is entirely accurate, but both offer much food for thought. Though it is referred to in the masculine, it is clear that the Holy Spirit operates independently of sexual traits. When one considers its nonhuman, transcendant, immortal and usually quite-invisible nature, its gender assignment ceases to matter, unless it is for some reason considered terribly important whether it was a male or female dove which the Holy Spirit descended like unto upon Jesus.[334]

However, there is a more personified aspect of the Divine which is distinctly feminine. In Hebrew She is know as תומכה *Chokmah* or *Chockmoth*; Her name is pronounced "Khok-moth" and read logographically as "*Hey Kaph Mem Waw Taw*" ("ה Behold the כ Open Palm, the מ Blood, the ו Nail, and the ת Cross"). In Greek She is known as *Sophia* (or *Pistis* ("Faith") *Sophia*), and in English She is known as Wisdom. The New American Bible describes Her as being God's external revelation of Himself. Wisdom is sometimes divine, sometimes a synonym for God's law, and sometimes human. However, it is properly understood that, even when Wisdom is human, She comes from God.[335]

Due to Her versatility, etherealness, and potential omnipresence, Wisdom appears to bear much in common with the Holy Spirit. Indeed, there does exist a definite connection, as is shown in the very first chapter of the Deuterocanonical book named for Her:

> "For the holy spirit of discipline flees deceit
> and withdraws from senseless counsels...
> For wisdom is a kindly spirit,
> yet she acquits not the blasphemer of his
> guilty lips;
> Because God is the witness of his inmost
> self
> and the sure observer of his heart

---

333 Frances Ellen Burr, The Woman's Bible, Part II, "Comments on the Kabbalah", p.107.

334 Matthew 3:16, Luke 3:22, John 1:32.

335 *The New American [Holy] Bible, 2003-2004 Edition,* Sirach 1:1 footnote, p. 700.

> and the listener to his tongue.
> For the spirit of the LORD fills the world,
> is all-embracing, and knows what man
> says." (Wisdom 1:5-7, NAB)

Wisdom is, however, given far more personification than is the Holy Spirit. She is depicted as an entity taking action in such verses as Sirach 1:17, when She showers down knowledge and full understanding and "heightens the glory of those who possess her."[336] Wisdom is also depicted as a mysterious entity who is Herself capable of deep thought in Sirach 24:26-27, where She is described as being forever unfathomable to man, with thoughts "deeper than the sea" and counsels deeper "than the great abyss."[337]

Additionally, Wisdom is even revealed to be capable of independent emotion. The Proverbs 1:20-25 depict Her as though She were present in the physical form of a woman, calling out in the street, asking why noone will listen to Her. As has been previously evidenced, this is an all-too-common pastime for women, and thus verses 26-27 provide proof that even the "sweet, docile, passive, compliant" female can be pushed too far. Thus the entire passage paints a fascinating picture of this mysterious entity:

> "Wisdom crieth without; she uttereth her voice in the streets:[338]
> She crieth in the chief place of concourse, in the openings of the gates: in the city she uttereth her words, saying,
> How long, ye simple ones, will ye love simplicity? and the scorners delight in their scorning, and fools hate knowledge?
> Turn you at my reproof: behold, I will pour out my spirit unto you, I will make known my words unto you.
> Because I have called, and ye refused; I have stretched out my hand, and no man regarded;

336 NAB.

337 Ibid.

338 Contrast Isaiah 42:2 and Matthew 12:19.

> But ye have set at nought all my counsel, and would none of my reproof: I also will laugh at your calamity; I will mock when your fear cometh;
> When your fear cometh as desolation, and your destruction cometh as a whirlwind..."
> (Proverbs 1:20-27, KJV)

This may seem somewhat vengeful, but Wisdom has had to endure much; more indeed than we can imagine (though I am now getting ahead of myself). The Proverbs chapter 8 depicts Her in a similar situation: "She crieth at the gates, at the entry of the city..." and Her "voice is to the sons of man." (Verses 3-4.) However, as the chapter progresses, She tells us of Her origins...which is to say, She has no origins, for:

> "The LORD possessed me in the beginning of his way, before his works of old.
> I was set up from everlasting, from the beginning, or ever the earth was.
> When there were no depths[339], I was brought forth....
> Then I was by him, as one brought up with him; and I was daily his delight, rejoicing always before him;" (Proverbs 8:22-24 & 30, KJV)

The Deuterocanonical book bearing Her name presents further evidence of Her eternity and a hint as to Her relationship to the Holy Spirit:

> "Now with you is Wisdom, who knows your works
> and was present when you made the world....
> Or who ever knew your counsel, except you had given Wisdom and sent your holy spirit from on high?" (Wisdom 9:9 & 17, NAB)

---

[339] The Hebrew word used here is מוהת *tehowm* (pronounced "teh-hoime"; read logographically as "Taw hey waw mem": "ת The Cross/Sign ה Reveals/Breath the ו Nail(s) and מ Water/Blood"), just as it is to describe "the deep" in Genesis 1:2, further revealing how Wisdom was present even before the beginning. It is the Hebrew equivalent of the Sumerian/Babylonian "Tiamat".

This latter verse invites comparison with John 14:26, in which Jesus reveals that the Holy Spirit will be sent by the Father in His name to teach and remind His disciples of all that He has said to them. However, the former verses quoted here, both from the Proverbs and from Wisdom itself (a book which predicts Jesus Christ's Passion) invite comparison with John 17:5 and 17:24:

> "And now, O Father, glorify thou me with thine own self with the glory which I had with thee before the world was. ... Father, I will that they also, whom thou hast given me, be with me where I am; that they may behold my glory, which thou has given me: for thou lovedst me before the foundation of the world." (KJV)

Indeed, the Gospels are very important to the understanding of Wisdom, and not only because of Her association with the Holy Spirit. Wisdom is personified as female, even by the Son Jesus Christ in Matthew 11:19 and Luke 7:35. In both of these Gospel verses Jesus states that Wisdom is justified; [340] yet in Luke She is said to be justified by Her children while in some Matthean transcripts She is said to be justified by Her works. The first interpretation is easily understood: as Wisdom is an aspect of God, Her children are therefore His children. The second interpretation is explained in the New American Bible's footnote regarding Matthew 11:16-19; that here it is made apparent that the works of Jesus the Messiah are those of divine Wisdom, for He is the embodiment of Her.[341] Both of these suggest a mysterious connection between Wisdom and Jesus which is most certainly worthy of exploration.

Is our Saviour Wisdom? Is Jesus Christ Pistis Sophia? Is the Son, in a sense, also the Daughter? Difficult complications can arise from this question, but then Jesus did challenge human perceptions of Heavenly things, and they are still vastly preferable to the suggestion that there is a *fourth* member of the Trinity![342] To address them efficiently and

---

340 See also 1 Timothy 3:16, which describes Jesus as having been "justified in the Spirit." (KJV)

341 2003-2004 Edition, p. 1025.

342 "Sophian Heresy." http://ecumenizm.tripod.com/ECUMENIZM/id17.html

effectively, it must be noted that Jesus as Man was most assuredly physically male (as evidenced by His circumcision in Luke 2:21 and the fact that His manliness was never questioned by anyone who knew Him while He walked the earth), but as God He is beyond gender, and 1 Corinthians 1:24 specifically refers to Him as "the wisdom of God."

The association of Wisdom with Christ, and therefore Her position in the Holy Trinity, is stated succinctly in this passage from the Seventh Ecumenical Council, also known as the Second Council of Nicea:

> "The Wisdom which is truly according to the nature of God and the Father--our Lord Jesus Christ, our true God-- who... by taking on him our nature, hath renewed the same by co-operation of the Spirit, which is of the same nature with himself..." (*Acts of the Seventh Ecumenical Council.* "The Imperial Sacra. Read at the First Session." Circa 787 A.D.)[343]

Still, the assignment of a gender carries with it a number of social expectations. This is the case regarding Wisdom as well, for even as a Divine entity, She is viewed by men in the traditionally-female sense.

As God is Most Worthy of all manners of pure and true love, He can also be viewed as a Spouse, particularly to those who have chosen lives of chastity. Roman Catholic Sisters, for example, are considered brides of Christ (hence the veil which is generally part of the sister or nun's habit). In a similar manner, St. Augustine of Hippo is said to have experienced "at last the gradual calming of his passions and the great resolution to choose wisdom for his only spouse (Soliloquies, I, x)."[344] This provides a versatility wherein one may find it easier to devote oneself utterly to Him regardless of one's attitude toward any

---

Retrieved Monday, December 31st of 2012.

343 *Fordham University: The Jesuit University of New York.* "Medieval Sourcebook: The Second Council of Nicea, 787" (c)Paul Halsall Feb 1996. http://www.fordham.edu/halsall/basis/nicea2.asp Retrieved Monday, December 31st of 2012.

344 *New Advent Catholic Encyclopedia.* "St. Augustine of Hippo." http://www.newadvent.org/cathen/02084a.htm Retrieved Monday, December 31st of 2012.

given gender, yet it is important to understand that such a relationship is utterly beyond any that could exist between the sexes.

This does not prevent the metaphor of human lovers from being employed in Scripture, however. Such is the case, for example, with the Song of Solomon/Song of Songs and also with some sections of Sirach. Though this may seem ironic when one considers Sirach's willingness to see a wife divorced according to Ch. 25 v. 25, Sirach writes of Wisdom:

> "How irksome she is to the unruly!
> The fool cannot abide her.
> She will be like a burdensome stone to test him,
> and he will not delay in casting her aside."
> (Sirach 6:21-22, NAB)

How important is gender to any of this? Is there any indication that God would be treated differently if He were instead thought of as a She? Would, for instance, a man of the ancient world be more aggressive, domineering, or possessive toward a Female Divine? Knowing what we do about Sirach, let us examine his attitude toward Wisdom in more detail....

> "Happy the man who meditates on wisdom,
> and reflects on knowledge;
> Who ponders her ways in his heart,
> and understands her paths;
> Who pursues her like a scout,
> and lies in wait at her entry way;
> Who peeps through her windows,
> and listens at her doors;
> Who encamps near her house,
> and fastens his tent pegs next to her walls;
> Who pitches his tent beside her,
> and lives as her welcome neighbor;
> Who builds his nest in her leafage,
> Who takes shelter with her from the heat,
> and dwells in her home." (Sirach 14:20-27, NAB)

This relationship is intriguing in its mixed metaphors and might even be somewhat frightening if one were unaware of its utter consensuality. In the author's romantic courtship with Wisdom, Sirach offers fascinating insight into intimate relationships with females in the ancient world. In Sirach 15:2-8, Wisdom is described as meeting a man who seeks Her like a mother and embracing him "like a young bride", nourishing him with "the bread of understanding" and "the water of learning." The author of Sirach, who at times seems bitter regarding females, notes that this seeking man can safely trust Wisdom, and that "She will exalt him above his fellows; in the assembly she will make him eloquent." This last quality is also mentioned as a trait of the Ideal Wife in Proverbs 31:23, whose "husband is known in the gates, when he sitteth among the elders of the land." The rest of the passage[345] also paints a picture of Wisdom as the perfect wife in accordance with Proverbs 31:26: "She openeth her mouth with wisdom; and in her tongue is the law of kindness." (KJV) Sirach deepens this romantic allegory to a personal level as he describes his own relationship with Wisdom:

> "When I was young and innocent,
> I sought wisdom.
> She came to me in her beauty,
> and until the end I will cultivate her. ...
> I became resolutely devoted to her –
> the good I persistently strove for.
> I burned with desire for her,
> never turning back.
> I became preoccupied with her,
> never weary of extolling her.
> My hand opened her gate
> and I came to know her secrets.
> For her I purified my hands;
> in cleanness I attained to her.
> At first acquaintance with her, I gained understanding
> such that I will never forsake her.

345 The passage ends by stating that Wisdom is far from the impious and "not to be spoken of by liars." Even this calls to mind the falsely-accused, virtuous Susanna in Daniel 13; specifically verses 44-49.

My whole being was stirred as I learned about her;
Therefore I have made her my prize possession. ...
I open my mouth and speak of her:
gain, at no cost, wisdom for yourselves."
(Sirach 51:13-14, 18-21, 25, NAB)

Sirach here reveals that his attitude toward the female is retained even when the female in question is an essence of the Supreme Being. He approaches Her like a passionate bridegroom longing to make Her his "prize possession," and even the final verse conjures the image of a "bridal price." [346] Their ancient attitude toward women encouraged men to think of them as at best equal partners even if they were higher powers. One is invited to compare 2 Maccabees 1:14, "On the pretext of marrying the goddess, [Nanea, an oriental goddess similar to Artemis of the Greeks[347]] Antiochus with his Friends had come to the place to get its great treasures by way of dowry."

However, this does not preclude man's submission to Wisdom, for in the same breath Sirach advises the reader to "Submit your neck to her yoke, that your mind may accept her teaching." (51:26). Much earlier in the book, Sirach employs similar imagery when he advises the reader to...

"Put your feet into her fetters,
and your neck under her yoke.
Stoop your shoulders and carry her
and be not irked at her bonds.
With all your soul draw close to her
and with all your strength keep her ways."
(Sirach 6:25-27)

Truly Sirach has an intriguing relationship with Wisdom. Yet, being both well aware of this overly-sexualized modern world in which we

---

[346] As mentioned in Genesis 34:12 and elsewhere. This custom, which is in essence the gender-reversal of dowry payment, is still practiced in Africa today.

[347] New American Bible, Footnote for 2 Maccabees 1,13. p. 498.

live[348] and that even Wisdom Herself has purportedly been subject to what has been called "spiritual delusion and somewhat sinister metaphysical 'romance'"[349], I shall note with distaste that some may find that this imagery recalls a modern female icon, considering William Moulton Marston's fascination with submission and bondage....

Yes, as though it were not enough to compare Wonder Woman to the Blessed Virgin Mother Mary, her underlying concept shall now be compared with some of the images given to Divine Wisdom Herself. The problem is that with the superheroine there is a clear component of sexualization. Marston stated that the one truly great moral contribution of his Wonder Woman strip was to encourage mutual submission in a stable, peaceful environment, yet he also stated that submission cannot possibly be enjoyable without the presence of a strong erotic element.[350] This may be congruous with the Freudian concept which suggests that subconscious motivations are largely sexual in nature, yet it does not allow us to grow sufficiently far beyond the animalistic.

One may notice that I have until now remained oddly silent regarding the sexualization of Wonder Woman; even when comparing her to the Blessed Virgin Mary, in whose presence no impure thought can abide. This would otherwise seem an obvious point to address, especially in a time when people are beginning to realize that a very thin line indeed exists between sexual liberation and sexual exploitation. However, as no impure thought can abide the presence of Wisdom either, sexual interpretations simply fail to apply to this relationship.

Lest one think Marston (as opposed to Sirach)'s approach simply is that of a sexually-submissive male, Marston also spoke of the additional component of his vision. He stated that the one reason women are exciting; that, in fact, "it is the secret to women's allure – [is that]

---

348 As a consecrated maiden studying to become a Carmelite sister, I have even been asked by a member of a *Roman Catholic congregation* if I "have spiritual sex with Jesus."

349 "Sophian Heresy." http://ecumenizm.tripod.com/ECUMENIZM/id17.html Retrieved Monday, December 31st of 2012.

350 http://www.castlekeys.com/Pages/wonder.html Retrieved Monday, October 8th, 2012.

women enjoy submission, being bound."[351] Once again Marston may provide an excellent male perspective, but it is of course limited to a male perspective, and for his desires of world peace to be truly achieved, qualities associated with femininity must be respected through more than just the male gaze.

Sirach 6:28-31 suggests simultaneously possessing and being possessed, while also blurring the line between Wisdom's metaphorical representation as a physical woman and that of a mental/spiritual essence:

> "Search her out, discover her; seek her and
> you will find her.
>
> [This verse was of course referenced by Jesus Christ in Matthew 7:7, "Ask, and it shall be given you; seek, and ye shall find; knock, and it shall be opened unto you:" (KJV)]
>
> Then when you have her, do not let her go;
> Thus will you afterward find rest in her,
> and she will become your joy.
> Her fetters will be your throne of majesty;
> her bonds, your purple cord.
> You will wear her as your robe of glory,
> bear her as your splendid crown." (NAB)

Despite the Wisdom imagery being approached by Sirach as a man would approach a woman, in the case with Wisdom Herself there is no erotic element whatsoever, because the relationship is purely spiritual; to seek Her is to seek the Kingdom of Heaven.

Thus we are left with the true nature of Wisdom, and another of the manners in which Jesus Christ associates Himself with Her:

> "Take my yoke upon you, and learn of me; for I am meek and lowly in heart: and ye shall find rest unto your souls.
>
> For my yoke *is* easy, and my burden is light." (Matthew 11:29-30 (KJV))

---

351 Ibid.

Jesus/Wisdom is also identified as Logos, a Greek term for the Word of God. This association was employed by 1st–Century philosopher Julius Philo of Alexandria, who (like St. Augustine of Hippo) endeavoured to harmonise Hellenistic/Platonic philosophy and Jewish scripture, and it was a concept adapted by the author of the Gospel of John. The 2nd–Century Christian apologist Justin Martyr identified the Logos with several emanations of God found throughout the Bible which have their unity in Jesus Christ, and used this as a way of arguing Christianity to both Jews (who would embrace the Scriptures) and (Greek) non-Jews (who would embrace the concept of the Logos):

> "I shall give you another testimony...from the Scriptures, that God begot before all creatures a Beginning, [who was] a certain rational power [proceeding] from Himself, who is called by the Holy Spirit, now the Glory of the Lord, now the Son, again Wisdom, again an Angel, then God, and then Lord and Logos...."
>
> (*Justin Martyr: Dialogue with Trypho.* Chapter 61. Wisdom is begotten of the Father, as fire from fire.)

One may be by this point noticing something of a trend here: each aspect of the Trinity contains both male and female elements (if having elements associated with either gender has any relevance). For as among humans the two shall become one flesh, neither gender should be a cancer for the other.

As difficult as it may be for one with my personal "gender-based gifts" to admit, one's gender marker/affiliation really does not matter; it is but the trappings of this mortal world which provide the illusion that this is otherwise, and which force the need to act upon that illusion. Instead:

> "Wisdom instructs her children
> and admonishes those who seek her.
> He who loves her loves life; [John 6:47-58, 14:6]
> those who seek her out win her favor.
> He who holds her fast inherits glory; [John 5:24]
> wherever he dwells, the LORD bestows

blessings.
Those who serve her serve the Holy One; [Mark 9:37, Luke 9:48]
those who love her the LORD loves.
He who obeys her judges nations;
he who hearkens to her dwells in her
inmost chambers. [Luke 22:28-30]
If one trusts her, he will possess her;
his descendents too will inherit her.
She walks with him as a stranger,

[This quite literally happened in what is known as "The Appearance on the Road to Emmaus" (Mark 16:12, Luke 24:15-16), when the newly-Resurrected Jesus Christ appeared to His disciples and walked with them in a form which they did not recognize.]

and at first she puts him to the test;
Fear and dread she brings upon him
and tries him with her discipline;
With her precepts she puts him to the proof,
until his heart is fully with her.
[Matthew 10:22, 16:24, 24:9, 13, Mark 14:27, Luke 21:12-19]

Then she comes back to bring him happiness
and reveals her secrets to him.
[Matthew 10:26, 24:30-31, Mark 4:22, 13:26-27; Luke 12:2 see also the Resurrection narratives.]

But if he fails her, she will abandon him [Luke 9:26, 12:8-9, John 8:24]
and deliver him into the hands of
despoilers." (Sirach 4:11-19, NAB)

This passage may sound a wee bit familiar to those who are familiar with the Gospels. The walk with Wisdom parallels the journey with Jesus.

As established by the Seventh Ecumenical Council/Second Council of Nicaea, Jesus Christ is considered to be a manifestation of Logos, or the female-personified Divine Wisdom. Thus the question is raised:

did She/He take a masculine form so that the people of the patriarchal society of the time would "Listen to Him" (Matthew 17:5, Mark 9:7, Luke 9:35)? I assumed this ever since I was a child, and while one may only assume it to be the case, it is supported by a decision which occurred shortly after His ascension. When determining who was to replace Judas the Iscariot as the Twelfth Apostle, Mary Magdalene, an obvious choice based on her loyally following Jesus all the way to the tomb and also being the first to witness and proclaim His resurrection, was overlooked in favour of a heretofor-unmentioned male possibility (Matthias, chosen by the casting of lots in Acts 1:26). Paul's earlier-noted Epistle to the Corinthians supports this with the statement that the law states that women must remain silent in places of worship, and further evidence is provided by how surprised the disciples were earlier to see Jesus speaking with the woman at the well.[352] In any case, although Jesus Himself was most assuredly male in form, He did refer to Wisdom as female, as noted at the very beginning of this chapter.

All this discussion of feminist theory and deep theology might have been very confusing, and it would be much easier if only there were some simple, unassailable statement regarding the relationship of Wisdom and Logos and Jesus Christ and God the Father. However, sometimes the truth just isn't simple....

> "In the beginning was the Word, and the Word was with God, and the Word was God." (John 1:1, KJV)
>
> ...and sometimes it is.

Still one may attempt to argue that this is, if not Apocrypha, then at least apology, and that whether or not it is evidenced by Jesus' physical masculinity the LORD Himself is an entirely male Deity. After all, is this not confirmed by the choice of pronouns used in the words from His mouth, which we heed in hope that He will not turn His back but rather His face to us and save us with His strong hand and His mighty, outstretched arm?

What other parts of the body does God, by His word, refer to Himself as having?

---

352 John 4:4-42; especially v. 27.

"Out of whose **womb** came the ice?
and the hoary frost of heaven, who hath gendered it?"
(Job 38:29, KJV, emphasis mine.)

God is a Spirit (John 4:24) and thus all of these body parts mentioned are to be presumed metaphorical. Still, it is intriguing that despite the commonly-held belief that the *massebah* of the Ba'als are phallic representations of the false gods' masculine sexual possession, God never asks His people to erect equivalent objects for Him, nor does He ever refer to Himself as having any male reproductive organs (rather, He encourages the destruction of these 'sacred poles' throughout the Bible). This is probably due to the fact that, like the breasts, the womb has significance that goes beyond the purely carnal or sexual.

This is not to suggest that the LORD is much more female than I am male, however it does help considerably in explaining expressions of feminine perspective. Jesus Christ's description of the time of tribulation as "the beginning of the labor pains"[353] indicates that the womb is a very important image in God's message. When taken to its full extreme, the Womb analogy further reveals God's absolute power over us and how everything we have – indeed everything we *are* – is utterly derived from and dependent upon Him: our entire world is, in a sense, within His Womb!

In Genesis 3:16, God increased woman's pain of childbirth (and scientifically speaking, most of the pain of deliverance comes from the emergence of the infant's oversized head, for it contains a very large brain which will be necessary to receive and process that which she or he will gain over the course of his or her entire life: knowledge). How much more did Adam and Eve's actions increase the pain of His!

> "We know that all creation is groaning in labour pains even until now..." (Romans 8:22, NAB)

---

[353] Matthew 24:8, Mark 13:8, NAB. The Greek word is *odin*; pronounced "o-deen", it literally means "the pain of childbirth" or "birth pangs", but due to a lack of understanding it was translated simply as "sorrows" in the King James Version of the Bible.

The Abrahamic religions' patriarchs, priests, scribes, Pharisees, etc. did not focus on a spiritual duality of masculine/feminine attributes (and thus lack the common philosophical side effect of suggesting that one side is good/superior whilst the other is evil/inferior; instead they directed the occasional attack at women themselves). Rather, they found it very important to concentrate on God's masculine qualities. Thus the only Biblical references to the Father's feminine attributes come from the Father Himself (Job 38:29, (via the Prophet) Isaiah 46:3-4) and the Son (Matthew 24:8, Mark 13:8).

This might seem strange, when one considers the duality of gender in all of the People of the Trinity. However, there is wisdom in understanding the Being who created both sexes to be beyond either of them. One does not need to seek a Divine Feminine, for God is the Divine Feminine (as well as the Divine Masculine).

God is neither man nor woman; God is God, and thus trying to understand in mortal terms a Being beyond all mortal understanding will only limit one's own understanding. Thus there remains one question: why then are any spiritual aspects of God given gender-specific labels?

For the answer to this, I invite one to recall Marduk in the Babylonian *Enuma Elish;* unable to create without Tiamat's body. This gender-assignment was all necessary to fit the understanding of the ancient world; to be seen as a Ruler, God needed to be viewed as masculine, yet to be seen as a Creator, God needed to have a womb....

...and His Wisdom needed to be feminine.

Chapter the 6th

More Precious Have I held Love for you than Love for Women

Issues of Biblical Homosexuality

Homophobia is the only moral grounds upon which NOT to be a Christian. It is the supposed chink in the Armour of God[354], through which the burning arrow of hatred may pierce and perhaps transform the best of humanity into the enemy.

The Christian doctrine of universal love has been gradually seeping into Christian society over the course of history, eroding policies of injustice as Christians collectively became less and less afraid. With homosexuality, however, though Christianity is thus passively part of the solution, it appears to be actively part of the problem.

Christianity and the LGBT (Lesbian, Gay, Bisexual, and/or Transgender) community thus seem to find themselves at an impasse. At best, we Christians accept and even embrace homosexuals, even when it seems to mean ignoring the passages of Scripture which might otherwise condemn them, because our God is a God of Love. At worst, Christians use these same passages to not only condemn but also make scapegoats of the entire LGBT community, and end up unintentionally taking sides with some of the most oppressive governments in the world.

At best, we of the LGBT community cling desperately to God, taking it on pure faith that being LGBT is the way we were made for His glory and His delight, for as was phrased so powerfully by an anonymous Catholic lesbian:

---

354 Ephesians 6:11.

"...[we] have no other ground on which to stand."[355]

At worst, members of the LGBT community abandon this ground, and not only turn away from Christ but even sometimes actively desire the destruction of His Faith. They do this for a depressingly-understandable reason: because they believe that the religion which is supposedly of acceptance and love has betrayed them, and that though they still believe in such Christian virtues, they must now search for them elsewhere.

After all, Christian condemnation of homosexuality has caused an immense amount of suffering for those within the LGBT community. Anyone who has spent sufficient time with this community is aware of the difference between those who are simply experimenting with homosexuality for a thrill or to defy established social norms, and those true homosexuals who were, in fact, born this way. The question then, is: Why did the Holy Bible – the text given to us by the All-Knowing Creator – fail to acknowledge this difference...or did the Bible secretly, unbeknownst perhaps even to its publishers, succeed in acknowledging this difference and thus validate all forms of true love?

Why There Were Biblical Laws Against Homosexual Practices

The attention-grabbing title of this chapter (2 Samuel 1:26) is a quotation from King David, yet it is of course not an attempt to suggest that he himself was homo- or bisexual (he could not possibly have been the former as he was tempted by the beauty of Bathsheba, the wife of Uriah[356]). I have encountered those who have suggested the possible homo- or bisexuality of Biblical characters, but even if these allegations were true they would not serve as justification due to the fact that human Biblical characters are not necessarily infallible, unlike God.

---

[355] *If I told you. Personal stories that are often difficult to discuss openly within the Church.* "Three: The patron saint of queers" April 22, 2010. http://www.ifitoldyou.org/2010/04/22/three-the-patron-saint-of-queers/ Retrieved April 6, 2013.

[356] 2 Samuel 11:2-5.

As intriguing as the question "were any of our Biblical heroes bi- or homosexual" might be, a better question is "does homosexuality need such justification?" Thus the goal here is rather to expose slander as slander, libel as libel, and truth as truth.

The truth is that homosexuality *is* rather maligned in the Scriptures. As one goes backwards through the Bible one will find homosexuality considered an abomination (which is, ironically, a word which Roman historian Tacitus used to describe the practices of Christianity[357]). Homosexuality is associated with prostitution, adultery, Pagan worship, and rape. However, it is always treated as a symptom rather than a cause.

Let us begin with Sodom. In Biblical times the destruction of this city was so well-known that it became immediately associated with divine wrath on a massive scale[358], yet in modern times it has become so associated with homosexuality that the act of gay intercourse is also known as "sodomy." This is due to Genesis 19, in which two angels who had taken the form of human males were sexually harassed by the entirety of Sodom's male population. Lot clearly recognized the men of the city's wicked intentions, and in an act of desperation offered them the use of his two virgin daughters instead (this lawless and hideous practice was apparently disturbingly-common in the Ancient World, for precisely the same thing occurred even within the lands of Israel in Judges 19:22-30). In this case the men insisted upon their original targets to the extent that they threatened to "deal worse with [Lot], than with them" (Genesis 19:9). Truly these Sodomites were monstrous, yet one should ask oneself what was their truly immoral and retribution-worthy quality: homosexuality, or the intention to gang-rape a pair of God's messengers?!

Is it at all unreasonable to assume the latter? To assume the crime of the Sodomites to be merely homosexuality is to avoid the actual sinfulness of the city, which went beyond even the aforementioned attempted rape. God explained the city's sins quite clearly to the Prophet Ezekiel, so that we have no excuse to confuse the matter:

---

357 Wampler, Dee. *The Trial of Christ.* Winepress Publishing, 2000. p. 39.

358 As in Matthew 10:15, 11:24, and Luke 10:12, for example.

> "Behold, this was the iniquity of thy sister Sodom, pride, fulness of bread, and abundance of idleness was in her and in her daughters, neither did she strengthen the hand of the poor and needy." (16:49, King James Version).

It was apparently this abundance of idleness, luxury, and pride which caused the men of Sodom to feel entitled to indulge in the pleasures of the flesh with whomever was attractive, whether male or female, whether consensually or by rape. This is the key to understanding the real reason – of which religious condemnation is a symptom more than a cause – why homosexuality is hated and feared; why even those who are openly welcoming of homosexuals may be nevertheless terrified by the possibility of being thought to be homosexual themselves.

When I was a student at Cardinal Newman High School[359] during the Pontificate of Pope John Paul II, the approach taken toward the LGBT community was one of more open debate, and it was considered far more important to love and protect homosexuals than to condemn them for whatever actions they might take. As such, the openly-homophobic were visible as the bigots they were. One such homophobe, whom I shall call Sean, was actually called out by one mildly-exasperated girl in our class who asked him:

> "Why do you hate gays? They just like other men!"

Sean answered honestly: "I'm afraid that they will like *me*."

Why would this be a problem? Why would it be so frightening to be the one chased rather than the one chasing? What could be so horrible about being a strong man's object of affection?

To understand this, it helps to be a woman. As one encounters in such work as that of meso-feminist Simone de Beauvoir[360], it has become understood that a primeval possessive association exists between the passive, receptive partner and the active, insertive partner. In short, the sexual act is believed to involve the former being 'possessed' by

---

[359] The specific event to which I refer occurred in the autumn of 1994, during the 16th year of his Pontificate. I myself was fifteen years old.

[360] Her 1949 work *The Second Sex* is particularly informative in a modern context.

the latter. This stemmed from a male-oriented perspective; whereby copulation would promise that the female was impregnated by a certain male's particular genetic material, which he had taken so much effort to distribute.

Clearly homosexual males cannot (with society's current level of genetic engineering) become pregnant, but the principle has become so subconsciously ingrained within the human animal that it applies to them also. This means that, in the presence of powerful homosexual males, other males find themselves in the same position that most females have known all their lives. To homophobes, the acceptance of gays means that males are no longer sexually 'safe'; they too are at risk of unwanted attention, harassment, or even rape.

> DISCO/DISCUS STU: "Discus Stu has ouzo for twozo!"
>
> BART/TELEMACHUS *(to MARGE/PENELOPE)*: "I'll leave you guys alone."
>
> DISCO/DISCUS STU: "Discus Stu was talkin' to *you*!"
>
> (*The Simpsons* Episode 283 (March 17th of 2002): "Tales from the Public Domain")

In Ancient Greek civilization, with which Saint Paul the Apostle often had to deal, both males and females were at risk of sexual predation all of their lives. There even existed the practice of grown men having boys in whom they were interested abducted, sometimes by the boys' own friends, so that they could serve the homosexual as sex slaves. The parents would then be paid off for the services of their son.

This was such a proliferate custom that it was written into Greek mythology, in much the same way that more traditional forms of slavery were written into Babylonian mythology. The story of Ganymede[361] offers excellent assistance in understanding this widespread and socially-acceptable Grecian custom of pedophilia. Ganymede's name in

---

[361] After whom is named the planet Jupiter's third moon. The largest moon in the Solar System, it is an orb of ice and rock likely containing a saltwater ocean ~200 km below its surface.

Latin is *Catamitus*, source of the word catamite, which means a boy who has a sexual relationship with a man[362]. His story takes the traditional approach of the interested man capturing and paying compensation for the desired boy to that boy's parents. In this case, the interested party was Zeus, the king of the Greek gods, who for this purpose took the form of a giant eagle (just as he did a swan to impregnate Leda, the queen of Sparta). The desired boy was the handsome prince Ganymede (whom Homer described as the most beautiful of mortals), and the payment was a number of horses of the kind that carried the immortals (according to the *Iliad*).

Whether from the Old or New Testament, passages of the Bible which refer to Sodom's carnal lusts tend to be quite vague and thus may logically be interpreted as relating to rape or other exploitative sexual acts. For instance, when Jude 1:7 refers to the people of Sodom "going after strange flesh" in the King James Version of the Bible, which is often also translated simply as "perversion" and assumed to be synonymous with homosexuality, it is (ironically enough) in the original Greek written "*heteros sarx*" ("strange flesh") which by the very definition of "heteros" would seem difficult to apply to homosexuality!

Nevertheless, Saint Paul is quite clear in his terminology when addressing those in societies influenced by Ancient Greek culture. In his letters to such peoples as the Romans and Corinthians, who had been known to practice homosexual acts, and in his First Epistle to Timothy (1:10), which warns of the dangers of homosexual acts, the Apostle is swift to condemn such acts as abominations. Why? Because the acts he describes *are* abominable (note: if one happens to be a natural homosexual seeking acceptance and is now tempted to close this book in disgust, please read on; if one will pardon the expression, it gets better).

Homosexuality as condemned by the Bible **always** appears in monstrously aberrant forms. Gang rape was mentioned previously in Genesis and Judges. Adultery was suggested in Romans 1:27, when Saint Paul accused homosexuals of "leaving the natural use of the woman" because they "burned in lust one toward the other". Prostitution is a particularly intriguing accusation leveled against homosexuals, as

---

362 http://education.yahoo.com/reference/dictionary/entry/catamite

it was associated with the widespread negotiated pedophilia described earlier. In addition to "them that defile themselves with mankind" ("*arsenokoites*"), 1 Timothy 1:10 also contains "*pornos*", the Greek word generally translated as "whoremonger". *Pornos*, however has the especial meaning of "male prostitute" (so that's where the word came from!). 1 Corinthians 6:9 refers to the victims of those who defile themselves with boy prostitutes, who were described simply as "effeminate" by the somewhat-confused translators of the King James Bible's version of this Epistle[363]). If you happen to be a homosexual and are now thinking to yourself, "I would never do any of those things," then there is good news for you (in every sense of the term)....

Biblical Proof That God Does NOT Condemn Homosexual Christians

Homosexuals have been seen as frightening in many cultures, for they complicate understandings of the gender dynamic; women preferring women to men, and men finding themselves at risk of being viewed as prey by other men who might easily overpower them. Christianity appears to view lesbians and gays in precisely the same light, yet only because we have formerly seen "through a glass, darkly".[364] The true light given to us by God is far brighter.

When homophobic people try to use the Bible to support their hatred, they usually quote Leviticus 18:22, which reads: "Thou shalt not lie with mankind, as with womankind: it is abomination." (KJV) At first glance, this law of Moses seems simple, irrefutable, and eternal. It thus appears to be excellent ammunition for the homophobic. However, to dupe others into believing this to be a blanket condemnation of homosexuality, they must take the verse entirely out of context and thus corrupt its intention. This intention is clearly stated at the beginning of that very chapter of Leviticus:

---

363 This shall be elaborated upon further in the following chapter, as it is in modern times wielded especially against the transgender community.

364 1 Corinthians 13:12, KJV.

> "After the doings of the land of Egypt, wherein ye dwelt, shall ye not do: and after the doings of the land of Canaan, whither I bring you, shall ye not do: neither shall ye walk in their ordinances." (Leviticus 18:3, KJV)

This order relates to the very First Commandment, "Thou shalt have no other gods before me." (Exodus 20:3, KJV) It is very important that God's people keep His ways undiluted by Pagan religious customs so that they shall not fall to worshipping false gods. As such, this Levitical verse also relates to the Second Commandment, which states that one shall not make any sort of idol or any sort of likeness of any heavenly, earthly, or aquatic thing, and that one shall not bow down or serve any such idol (Exodus 20:4-6). This is the beginning of the answer to the question of homosexuality.

Keeping this in mind, one may view with a light of wisdom what follows, which is a chapter consisting of a long list of criminal acts of widely-varying levels of severity. If one takes a closer look at the contents of this chapter, one finds laws whose moral motivations are either self-explanatory or given an explanation within Leviticus itself. These include such things as not stripping one's relatives naked/having intercourse with them (Leviticus 18:7-17), not marrying one's wife's sister as her rival (v. 18), not having intercourse with a woman during her period (v. 19), not committing adultery (v. 20; though this was of course covered earlier as the Sixth Commandment in Exodus 20:14), and not burning one's babies in sacrifice to the Ammonite/Phoenician god Molek/Moloch (Leviticus 18:21; also covered earlier in the Fifth Commandment in Exodus 20:13). Immediately thereafter we have the declaration that gay intercourse is an "abomination" to be avoided. This obviously does not mean that homosexual acts are worse than ritualistic infanticide, but what exactly *does* it mean?

Why, for instance, does the very next verse state that the crime with which it deals – bestiality – is not "abomination" but rather "confusion"? The Hebrew word translated "confusion" in the King James Bible is לבת *tebel*, and it means specifically a violation of nature or divine order or a perversion (as in a sexual sin). This is very noteworthy indeed, especially for those who may be afraid that homosexuality is a sort of "gateway" to truly heinous sexual offences.

The Ancient Hebrew word הבעות *tow'ebah*, generally translated as "abomination", has a number of meanings. Its general meaning is that of a disgusting thing, which is an abomination, or abominable, either in the ethical sense (of wickedness, etc.; see the story of Sodom) or in the ritual sense (of unclean foods, idols, or mixed marriages). Now Jesus Christ (whose Matthean genealogy includes the mixed marriages of both Ruth and possibly Rahab of the Book of Joshua[365]) has fulfilled these Ancient Laws, as was revealed in Saint Peter's vision[366] wherein formerly-unclean foods were declared acceptable (as were the Gentiles acceptable to receive the Holy Spirit, as the rest of that story reveals). This leaves only one of the above possibilities to be considered as a possible cause for the condemnation of homosexuality: idol worship!

Saint Paul offered this very explanation as his understanding of the root of the homosexual "abomination" in his Epistle to the Romans, chapter 1, verses 22-27:

> "Professing themselves to be wise, they became fools, and changed the glory of the incorruptible God into an image made like to corruptible man, and to birds, and fourfooted beasts, and creeping things.
>
> Wherefore God also gave them up to uncleanness through the lusts of their own hearts, to dishonour their own bodies between themselves: who changed the truth of God into a lie, and worshipped and served the creature more than the Creator, who is blessed for ever. Amen.
>
> For this cause God gave them up unto vile affections: for even their women did change the natural use into that which is against nature: and likewise also the men, leaving the natural use of the woman, burned in their lust one toward another; men with men working that which is unseemly, and receiving in themselves that recompense of their error which was meet." (KJV)

365 Joshua 2:1-21, 6:22-25.

366 Acts (of the Apostles) 10:9-35

This rather harsh passage follows what is implicit in Leviticus 18's 22nd verse due to its clear reference to idol worship, and it is itself followed by a reminiscent ream of reprobate sins which have nothing to do with homosexuality. Included are "covetousness, maliciousness; [being] full of envy, murder, debate, deceit, malignity; whisperers [Gr. *psithuristes*; secret slanderers, detractors], backbiters, haters of God, despiteful, proud, boasters, inventors of evil things, disobedient to parents...without natural affection...etc." (Romans 1:29-31, KJV). These evils are clearly considered by the Saint to be self-evident, yet as we have seen Paul has devoted a number of verses to explaining the presence of the condemned homosexuality. Thus it is heavily implied that any evils associated with homosexuality do in fact originate with the worship of idols as Saint Paul suggests, though it is not openly and unquestionably stated as such in Canonical Scripture.

The question then becomes twofold: from what source did this additional assumption originate, and is this source truly Sacred Scripture, that it may be taken as absolute proof? It is only implied in Leviticus due to homosexuality's association with foreign cultures, yet the Apostle Paul was quite certain that homosexuality stems from Pagan religious practices. What clarifying source did the learned scholar formerly known as the Pharisee Saul of Tarsus have access to to connect the book of Leviticus with his own Epistle to the Romans? What is the missing link?

The Book of Wisdom[367], which was written approximately one century before the coming of Christ and directly prophesies the Passion

[367] It is quite clear that Paul was familiar with the Book of Wisdom; the 2003-2004 Edition of the NAB even contains a footnote on Ephesians 6:10–20 (the famous "Battle Against Evil" allegory, which exhorts Christians to "Put on the whole armour of God...the breastplate of righteousness; And your feet shod with the preparation of the gospel of peace; Above all, taking the shield of faith, wherewith ye shall be able to quench all the fiery darts of the wicked....the helmet of salvation, and the sword of the Spirit, which is the word of God:..." (KJV)) which even refers to Paul as having drawn upon the imagery and ideas of Isaiah 11, 5; 59, 16-17; and Wisdom 5, 17-23, the latter of which includes: "He shall take his zeal for armor and he shall arm creation to requite the enemy; He shall don justice for a breastplate and shall wear sure judgment for a helmet; He shall take invincible rectitude as a shield and whet

of our Lord[368], is Deuterocanonical (and thus a Canonical text of the Roman Catholic Church (and one which is also greatly respected among others)). It also provides – beyond the shadow of a doubt – proof of the connection between forbidden sexual practices and the worship of idols:

> "For the idea of making idols was the beginning of fornication, and the invention of them was the corruption of life..." (Wisdom 14:12, Revised Standard Version)

That piece of clarification is all well and good, but it still leaves us further to journey in our quest for understanding. Now we can be certain that the association of homosexuality with sin was due to an association of homosexuality with idol worship, but can we be so sure that that is the *only* sin attached to homosexuality in and of itself?

> "For the worship of idols not to be named is the beginning and cause **and end** of every evil." (Wisdom 14:27, RSV, emphasis mine)

As excruciatingly-tempting as it might be to charge forth with this as our standard, we must first be aware of what precisely it means. While it would be foolhardy to assume that this verse freely gives Christians an excuse to commit truly evil deeds, it does effectively eliminate the sinfulness of things which are strictly *tow'ebah*; specifically, of things which are condemnable only through a connection to Pagan ritual.

Why then, one asks, do homosexuals continue to be condemned? The answer is revealed throughout the Bible, but particularly in the passage previously quoted from Saint Paul's Epistle to the Romans: surrounded by Pagan cultures, both Jews and Christians alike placed their focus upon the elimination of any foreign practices that seemed destructive or unnatural. In their effort to put an end to such things as adultery, rape, and child prostitution, they never dared consider that homosexuality might not only be entirely distinct from these things, but also in itself quite natural. Homosexuality as a quality with which one

---

his sudden anger for a sword...and as from his sling, wrathful hailstones shall be hurled...." (NAB) p. 1283.

368 Wisdom 2:12-20.

is born and which thus can be possessed by entirely-moral Christians was not considered, for it is not condemned.

In fact, I would go so far as to state that the plight of homosexual Christians *was* considered – thousands of years before it would become a major issue – but by God alone. Though many have largely ignored Wisdom, Jesus Himself did reference it when He spoke with Nicodemus about the difference between the belief in and understanding of earthly things and that of heavenly things.[369] Likewise the Book of Wisdom has been retained by the Roman Catholic Church (in fact, the 2003-2004 Edition of the Church's New American Bible even indicates at Romans Ch. 1 v. 24 a direct and overt reference to the source from which it was drawn: Wisdom 14:22-31 (p. 1211)). It was necessary that Wisdom be preserved throughout the ages, and one of the reasons for this – however inconspicuous – was to defend homosexuals.

> "He that believeth on him is not condemned: but he that believeth not is condemned already, because he hath not believed in the name of the only begotten Son of God." (John 3:18, KJV)

If homosexuality is something with which a person is born and thus exists from even a state of pure innocence, and if a given homosexual lives a good, God-revering and loving life even within their sexual inclination, then they are not an abomination at all.

Christianity and the 'Gay Marriage' Issue

> "[Almighty God] vouchsafe unto these, Thy servants [N and N], the grace to love one another and to abide without hate... all the days of their lives, with the help of the Holy Mother of God, and all Thy saints...And they shall kiss the Holy

---

369 The NAB (2003-2004 Edition) references John 3:12 ("If I tell you about earthly things and you do not believe, how will you believe if I tell you about heavenly things?" (NAB)) at Wisdom 9:16 ("And scarce do we guess the things on earth, and what is within our grasp we find with difficulty; but when things are in heaven, who can search them out?" (NAB)) and vice-versa. pp. 687 & 1141.

> Gospel and each other, and it shall be concluded." – Order for Solemn Same-Sex Union", 13th Century A.D.[370]

If one visits Saint Catherine's monastery on Mount Sinai in Israel, one will find an intriguing icon. It depicts two robed male Christian saints – Roman soldiers *Primicerius* (commander) Sergius and *Secundarius* (subaltern officer) Bacchus – being joined in what appears to be holy matrimony. Between and above them is a traditional Roman '*pronubus*' (a best man) overseeing the union: He is Jesus Christ.

The union of Saint Sergius and Saint Bacchus at the monastery of Saint Catherine. The oldest record of their martyrdom describes the men as *erastai* (Greek for "lovers"); they were apparently openly gay, but secretly Christian. Once they were "outed" as the latter, the two men were arrested, chained and paraded through the streets in women's clothing in an effort to humiliate them. It was unsuccessful; Sergius and Bacchus reportedly responded that they were dressed as "brides of Christ", and that as women's dress never stopped women from worshipping Christ it would not stop them either. They were separated and beaten until Bacchus died... only to appear to Sergius in an angelic form and promise that they would soon be reunited in Heaven.

---

370 "When Same-Sex Marriage Was a Christian Rite" Reproduced by Gwinna in the blog "anthropologist" on December 11th, 2009. http://anthropologist.livejournal.com/1314574.html Retrieved June 18th of 2013.

Recent decades have brought forth evidence that same-sex unions have been performed by Christians for centuries, and that the last of these occurred as recently as six hundred years ago. Professor John Eastburn Boswell, the late chairman of Yale University's history department and controversial Roman Catholic author, argued that the *adelphopoiia* (Greek for "brother-making") liturgy which Saints Bacchus and Sergius may have undergone was evidence that the attitude of Christianity toward homosexual union has changed over time.[371] The relationship of these saints is said to have gone beyond a "brotherly" one, though there is no concrete evidence that any sort of sexual act occurred between them. Still, sex is by no means a necessary requirement for love, and Severus, the Patriarch of Antioch from 512-518 A.D., openly stated that we must not separate in speech they who were joined in life.[372]

Allan A. Tulchin of Shippensburg University drew upon more historical evidence – including documents and gravesites – to suggest that loving homosexual unions existed in Late-Mediaeval France. The "brother-making" contract there – termed *affrerement* – was a pledge made to live together sharing *"un pain, un vin, et une bourse"*; "one bread, one wine, and one purse." Tulchin explained that this meant all of their goods generally became the joint property of both of them, and that each usually became the other's legal heir, adding that...

"They also frequently testified that they entered into the contract because of their affection for one another. As with all contracts, affrerements had to be sworn before a notary and required witnesses, commonly the friends of the affreres."[373]

The union of affrerement was not just for brothers. In a number of cases the affreres were single unrelated men. Thus Tulchin argues that these contracts provide a significant amount of evidence that the affreres were using the union of affrerement to formalize their same-sex

---

371 *The Marriage of Likeness: Same-Sex Unions in Pre-Modern Europe* (New York: Villard, 1994).

372 "When Same-Sex Marriage Was a Christian Rite" Reproduced by Gwinna in the blog "anthropologist" on December 11th, 2009. http://anthropologist.livejournal.com/1314574.html Retrieved June 18th of 2013.

373 Allan Tulchin, "Same-Sex Couples Creating Households in Old Regime France: The Uses of the Affrerement." *Journal of Modern History:* September 2007.

loving relationships. He suspects that some – though by no means all – of these relationships were sexual, yet also admits that this is both impossible to prove either way and also somewhat irrelevant to understanding their way of thinking. Sexual desire most-assuredly existed in Mediaeval France as elsewhere, however the constant presence of sexual objectification did not need to exist there as people seem to think it does here. Tulchin stresses that the importance dwelt with the fact that they loved one another, and that the community accepted this. The existence of affrerements thus shows there to have been a radical shift in Christian attitudes, and that this shift occurred between the 16th Century and the rise of modern antihomosexual legislation in the 20th.[374]

These unions were not called "marriages" per se – after all, the Bible strongly suggests that marriage is a union of the male with the female – but they were otherwise virtually identical socially, legally, and spiritually. One may thus wonder how much such same-sex relationships have changed since they were acceptable in a Christian environment. Has the decadence of modern culture confused or altered them?

I know a gay couple whom I visited almost weekly for over a year. One of the partners – whom I shall call David because his appearance, mannerisms, swift wit, and the fact that he was pursuing a PhD in psychology caused him to remind me of David Tennant's portrayal of *Doctor Who* – would have long discussions with me during a difficult period of transition (which, though neither he nor I considered him my psychologist, would inevitably involve psychological analyses on both our parts). His life partner lived with him; a long-haired school teacher whom he once described as a "mermaid" when swimming in their pool. They were charming, loving, and took great care of all that was entrusted to them, which for a time even included my secret and myself.

One day I saw a neighbour briefly visit and ask David – out of entirely respectful curiosity – how his "wife" was. This caused David to become very (albeit courteously) cross in a way I did not entirely understand, but which I suspected had something to do with the shoe-horning of homosexual couples into one of the two traditional gender roles. After some follow-up discussion this proved to be the case; and I

374 Ibid.

learned from him more fully that loving same-sex relationships, while somewhat mysterious even to me, were as deep and intense as those between men and women...while simultaneously being quite different.

The Biblical understanding of marriage between two human beings is that it is a covenant of partnership between a man and a woman so long as they exist upon the earth. Though there is no shortage of polygamy in the Bible, the statements regarding the institution of marriage in Genesis 2:24, reiterated by Jesus Christ as He answered the questions put to Him by the Pharisees, strongly indicate its intent to be between a single man who shall "leave father and mother, and shall cleave to his wife...." (Matthew 19:5, KJV). In His responses to the questions asked of Him by the Sadducees, Jesus also added that "in the resurrection they neither marry, nor are given in marriage, but are as the angels of God in heaven." (Matthew 22:30, Mark 12:25, KJV) From the perspective of the inspired human writers of the Bible, a union between two loving, consensual, adult, and Christian homosexuals was not considered due to the prevailing assumption that all such relationships must be sexually-driven toward carnal ends or the result of idol worship. However, all love is beautiful, and we shouldn't complicate the matter.

Now, while my making that innocent statement sounded lovely when I was nineteen, I must note that Christian denominations differ greatly regarding how (and sadly, if) homosexuals should be accepted. Fortunately, the attitudes possessed by many of these denominations is actually in something of a state of flux. The purpose of this book is to provide theological and historical cause to choose love over hate, and perhaps the new discoveries shall eventually – as my gentle Dean suggested – help many people to change. However, Rome was neither built nor overcome by Christian thought in a day, and now it is we of the LGBT community who suffer persecution.

Due to the many different Protestant denominations and churches, one must approach them on something of a case-by-case basis; not every one is represented by the vocal minority who brandish such slogans as the pejorative (not to mention wholly-inaccurate) "God Hates Fags (sic)!" of the (in)famous Westboro Baptist Church.[375] For a greater

---

[375] A small church in Topeka, Kansas which is well-known for its vocal condemnation of "doomed America." One may read more about it at www.

understanding of the situation of the various churches in America, I recommend Jeff Chu's *Does Jesus Really Love Me? A Gay Christian's Pilgrimage in Search of God in America*, which is both a partial-memoir and a very well-researched survey of the contemporary Protestant world regarding its position(s) on homosexuality. Here in Canada the situation is similar, depending upon which denominations are represented, yet as an individual one should proceed cautiously at this point in the quest for acceptance.

For instance, the Metropolitan United Church Senior Minister whom I consulted informed me that 75% of the United churches in Canada would not only accept homosexuals but would also perform homosexual unions. He later suggested, in fact, that United had something of a reputation for "bleeding hearts." However, he also told me of his own church's predecessor; a Minister who, when asked if he would ever accept homosexuals, "slammed his fist down on the table and cried 'Never!'" There is much left to be done, but progress is being made.

The situation is rather intriguing regarding the major denominations of Christianity in the two countries from which Canada drew its official languages; England and France. In the former, Anglicans have experienced a sort of schism due to orthodox teaching with regard to human sexuality. Thus a wide variety of attitudes exist within the Church, ranging from the less-tolerant ones of England and Ireland to the more accepting ones of Scotland and Canada.[376] The Episcopal Church in the United States of America defined its understanding in a compelling document entitled "To Set Our Hope on Christ." It states the belief that God has been opening the Church's eyes to His acts which it had previously not known how to see. Taking a rather liberal stance, it even suggests that those living in same-gendered unions could be eligible to lead the flock of Christ, as...

godhatesfags.com, which features a constantly-updated counter of "people whom God has cast into hell since you loaded this page" (though I have my doubts that it is actually privy to such information).

376 Christopher Craig Brittain and Andrew McKinnon, "Homosexuality and the Construction of 'Anglican Orthodoxy': The Symbolic Politics of the Anglican Communion," *Sociology of Religion* (2011), pp. 1–3.

> "...members of the Episcopal Church have discerned holiness in same-sex relationships and have come to support the blessing of such unions and the ordination or consecration of persons in those unions ... Their holiness stands in stark contrast with many sinful patterns of sexuality in the world."[377]

As for France...well, we shall soon attend to the matter of France....

The Roman Catholic Church disapproves of homosexual acts yet does not condemn homosexuals themselves, and actually decrees that....

> "They must be accepted with respect, compassion, and sensitivity. Every sign of unjust discrimination in their regard should be avoided."
> (*Catechism of the Catholic Church*[378], *Paragraph 2358)*

However, the Catholic Church has very high standards of sexual purity; so high in fact that no sexual desire should be acted upon unless it be between a married couple for the purpose of reproduction. This is very demanding upon the will and has caused much scandal when it came to light how many within the Church have proven unable to meet such demands. Still, it is a restraint placed not only on homosexuals, but everyone with any kind of sexual urge that is not likely to result in a child, for chastity is a very important virtue. Unfortunately, the belief that homosexual acts are inherently sinful has allowed for a wide range of attitudes which have originated from the Pontiff and trickled down via the virtue of Obedience. As I noted earlier, in the 1990s under Pope John Paul II, there existed a cautious debate on the matter of the LGBT community – even in my own Catholic high school. However, this debate closed in 2005 when John Paul II passed away and the Papacy passed to the more right-wing Benedict XVI, who as a Cardinal had

---

377 Jill Lawless, Associated Press, 21 June 2005. "U.S. Episcopals Defend Openly Gay Bishop."

378 "PART THREE: LIFE IN CHRIST. SECTION TWO – THE TEN COMMANDMENTS. CHAPTER TWO – YOU SHALL LOVE YOUR NEIGHBOR AS YOURSELF. Article 6 – THE SIXTH COMMANDMENT. II. The Vocation to Chastity." http://www.vatican.va/archive/ENG0015/_P85.HTM

been nicknamed "the Enforcer" of traditional doctrine. Fortunately, the election of Pope Francis has brought about the re-opening of this debate, and its urgency has resulted in His Holiness doing something that has never before been done.

A synod is, historically, a council of Bishops who have convened to decide upon a doctrine, administration or application. However, in late 2013 Pope Francis called a synod which was open to the entire Roman Catholic Church. Titled the "Synod on the Family", it gave especial attention to marriage according to the natural law and unions of persons of the same sex. I noted that the attitude toward the LGBT community has created something of a schism within the Church, with some openly condemning homosexual unions and others (probably the majority) seeking a way to validate them. I offered the recommendation that, if the Church already performed same-sex affrerements in the Middle Ages – "as I imagine the Vatican would be best-equipped to confirm or deny"[379] – then a modern equivalent could be introduced. After all, if God acknowledged the love between Saints Sergius and Bacchus, then so must the Church.

It is important that these religious institutions not turn a blind eye to Sacred Scripture merely to satisfy growing trends toward inclusion, for that would cause them to appear as inconsistent as weather vanes which shift direction with any prevailing wind. However, it is equally important that they not be so blind to the meaning of the Scriptures as to assume that their condemnations can be expanded to include those who are doing nothing wrong.

One may then ask how it is that these two courses are so easily confused in the modern world. How can people confuse loving relationships with sexual debauchery?

Western civilization has been quite-noticeably moving from the sexually-repressed Victorian and Edwardian periods to a time of heavy sexualization since the First World War, as it has become more and more apparent how materially profitable it can be to do so (to quote the popular maxim, "sex sells"). In the highly-competitive environment which free capitalism fosters, to be successful it is constantly necessary to be

---

[379] Um...me, in my contribution to the Synod on the Family (responses were emailed to the Bishop of our Diocese and sent by him to the Vatican).

"cutting-edge", that is, to be more new and innovative and even at times controversial than anything that has come before. In an increasingly-sexualized environment, it is thus often found necessary to erode what remains of the moral modesty of past centuries a little further each time one wishes to have particular attention paid to one's work.

To provide a prime example by narrowing our focus to the diameter of a pin-point, let us leap in time at approximately-30-year intervals as we briefly examine the effects of this trend by using as our depth-marker blonde female celebrities (though this is not to suggest that such effects manifest only through women; after all, our first example experienced her fame simultaneously with controversially-hip-swaying Elvis Presley). Marilyn Monroe was rather controversial in the 1950s – a decade of forced and artificial perceptions of conservative gender roles – and became an inspirational symbol of sexual liberation. While the singer known simply as 'Madonna' endeavoured to occupy a similar niche and level of fame in the 1980s, she could no longer do so without deliberately adding additional elements to spice up her repertoire, including (as her very name suggests) religious imagery (even to the extent that the Pope reportedly took notice), and she too was rewarded by becoming a sex symbol (who inspired such well-intentioned artists as the Spice Girls). Now in the 2010s, we have Lady Gaga; who is overtly aware of what precisely she must do to occupy the position of her predecessors and in so doing pushes into the realms of both the bizarre and the shocking. Nevertheless, Gaga also champions the worthy cause of the homosexual and trans- communities in her own way...specifically with her opus, "Born This Way." This affirmative and inspirational piece reminds us that – as we have just seen – God indeed makes no mistakes, though its approach and presentation are of course those of the cutting-edge sexualized style of the singer and thus less than religious in nature. Unfortunately, this causes both conscious (as evidenced by her line about "the religion of the insecure") and unconscious association with her shocking and at times inappropriate use of religious imagery, whether it be wearing an inverted cross upon her crotch as in her "Alejandro" video or virtually everything in the video for her 2011 hit "Judas". This latter piece seems especially engineered so that religious people such as myself will write about it, for in it she declares herself to be in love with the titular character [who is sadly the betrayer Iscariot and not Maccabeus or the loyal Disciple of Jesus] even as she declares that Jesus is her virtue and refers to said Judas as a "devil". The result is some degree of confusion; even if it was not the artist's intention, Gaga's displays contribute to the portrayal of the media as a whole, which appears to pit those she champions against the religion she disparages.

As a result of this mounting movement of increased consumerism, there are now a great many grandmothers who have been encouraged to be "sexy" since they themselves were little girls.[380] However, even while the "sexual revolution" became a sexual *institution*, the free world continued on its course of gradual social progress; oppressed minorities such as homosexuals and transpeople began to have their voices heard and receive rights which were formerly denied them. Under normal circumstances, Christians would be at the forefront of such social change, as was the case with the abolition of slavery. However, thusfar this has apparently not been the case, and this is due both to those who accept only the face-value of limited Scriptural translation and the media which propagates images of such people.

The media is not inherently immoral; it is simply trying to sell to us what "it" thinks we want. However, to sell us what we want, it must first convince us that we are wanting.

The media does not exist simply for the purpose of selling things, either, and as it has evolved it has become a sounding board for attitudes broadcast throughout its sphere(s) of influence. As such, the media can both raise awareness of and perpetuate hostile attitudes.

The most effective way to deprive someone of something is to make them believe you have given it to them.[381] If one wished to try to destroy Christianity, then one would paint the Church as an archaic tyranny

380 This has recently given rise to a new recurring phenomenon: the 'growing up' of starlets. For example, just as Justin Timberlake, Britney Spears and Christina Aguilera found it necessary to become overtly sexual to shed the *New Mickey Mouse Club* image of their childhood last decade, Miley Cyrus has now found it necessary to do the same with her Disney image as Hannah Montana. Of course, this now means that she feels the need to be more extreme and 'adult' than her predecessors, as it is a new decade.

381 The Second Rule of Exploitation. Don't even ask how I learned that....

depriving the people of freedom, and then paint servitude to sin as true freedom. The would-be destroyer[382] would need to paint Christianity as having betrayed its own values, so they would focus as much attention as possible on those who joined the Church not out of noble self-sacrificing love, but out of a desire for power and influence. If Christianity is seen as part of a corrupt establishment, then revolutionaries will try to take it down.

A particularly overt case in point is found in the recent legal rulings that have prevented some Christians from wearing a cross at their places of work. One of several articles in the United Kingdom's online newspaper *The Telegraph* upon the subject is quick to note that:

> "The Government's refusal to say that Christians have a right to display the symbol of their faith at work emerged after its plans to legalise same-sex marriages were attacked by the leaders of the Roman Catholic Church in Britain."
> – "Christians have no right to wear cross at work, says Government", March 10th of 2013[383]

It is a horrible thing that we Christians are not permitted to display our faith. After all, in Luke 9:26 Jesus Christ clearly states that: "whosoever is ashamed of me and of my words, of him shall the Son of man be ashamed, when he shall come in his own glory, and in his Father's, and of the holy angels." (KJV) However, this statement does what so many other news articles have so recently done: **given the impression that condemning homosexuality is an inherent part of being Christian, and that the support of homosexuality is inseparable from the condemnation of Christianity.** Those great many Christians who are coming to support the LGBT community are ignored, and instead homophobia and Christianity are woven together in a most tangled web. In short, it appears that the government is simply Anti-Christian; and that it will eagerly punish those of the Faith who would dare resist their encroaching power. This is becoming increasingly-easy to believe,

---

382 *Asmodeus* in Aramaic. See Tobit 3:8.

383 *The Telegraph.* David Barrett, Home Affairs Correspondent, March 10th of 2013. http://www.telegraph.co.uk/news/religion/9136191/Christians-have-no-right-to-wear-cross-at-work-says-Government.html Retrieved Sunday, July 7th of 2013.

for this sort of thing is not an isolated incident: it is happening even in Quebec here in Canada.[384]

Thus we have the other side displayed. Christianity has become associated with all things conservative, and this is easily used to incite us to extreme stances against even those things which we might otherwise champion. So it is that "siege-mode Christianity" is born; holding fast to established doctrine until the bitter end.

In fact, one commentator on the above article jocularly mentioned that he had been on the telephone to his best friend about this small persecution. This friend needed to fly to Dubai of the United Arab Emirates in a week's time, and proposed to express his persecuted faith by traveling dressed as a Knight Templar.

One wonders how he got past the metal detector dressed in the armour of one of these 12th-14th Century Crusaders. Once known as The Poor Fellow-Soldiers of Christ and of the Temple of Solomon, these French-founded Knights were also affected by the twisting of Church and politics. After serving for centuries as protectors of Christian pilgrims, they had built fortifications across Europe and the Holy Land and also utilized an early form of banking to become arguably the world's first multinational corporation, managing a large economic infrastructure throughout Christendom (despite remaining individually poor). The French King Philip IV, deeply in dept to them, pressured Pope Clement V to disband the Knightly Order in 1312, though only after having many of the Knights arrested, tried and burned alive. Among the numerous articles (such as charges of apostasy, idolatry, heresy, and secrecy) – the false confessions for which were extracted via torture – was...

> "Fifthly, that the Order's receptors kissed new entrants on the mouth, the navel, the stomach, the buttocks and the spine, and that homosexuality was encouraged and indeed enjoined on them."

---

384 The Quebec 'Charter of Values', still in a state of debate and proposal at the time of this writing, would render it illegal for government workers to wear head coverings or all but the smallest signs of their faith. My personal comments on this particular example of religious "Don't Ask, Don't Tell" may be found at: http://www.youtube.com/watch?v=w1G1xlz56c0

– Malcolm Barber, *The Trial of the Templars*, Cambridge University Press, Ch. 7, "The Charges", p. 178

The Chinon Parchment, discovered in September of 2001, revealed the Pope's attempt to clear the Knights of the charges against them even as the King of France continued to burn them, and the position of the Roman Catholic Church is that the persecution against them was unjust. As for the man flying to Dubai dressed as a Knight Templar, he was seeking sponsors for world's largest cleft-palate charity Smile Train, but the act of potentially offending Muslims for the sake of charity still suggests a pinch of Christian schizophrenia. Christian counter-antagonism is a sad thing, for it encourages onlookers to view it and its opponent as two sides of the same coin. Such is particularly regretful when its opponent is Islam, as ideally Muslims should have far more enmity for those who would suppress Christianity than for the Christians themselves:

> "And you will find the nearest of them in affection to those who believe [Muslims] (to be) those who say: Lo! We are Christians. That is because there are among them priests and monks, and because they are not proud."
>
> – *The Quran*; shura 5, aya 82[385]

It is possible for a true desire for peace to end any conflict. On that note, let us proceed to....

The Matter of France

> "(President) Hollande wants blood, and he will get it!"
> – *Frigide Barjot* ("Frigid Looney"), leader of France's primary anti-gay marriage group *La Manif Pour Tous* ("The Protest for All")

> "The most telling part of this story is that it is the so-called loving Christians/Catholics who are violent. Much like here

---

385 *The Quran Translated*: Message for Humanity. Based on the English Translation of M. Marmaduke Pickthall. First Edition: 2005.

> in the USA. You don't see gangs of gay people attacking Christians."
> – Commentator on Martine Nouaille's *Agence France Presse* article titled, "France's Gay Marriage Legislation: Why It's Polarizing The Nation", April 21st of 2013[386]
>
> "To every...bigot...compelled to tell us how to live our lives, my disgust towards you is greater, and more justified. May your Christian synagogues of hate pay for the investments that have wrought discrimination and deliberate lies against an entire classes of people. May the French police bash your brains in."
> – Commentator on *The Washington Post* article titled, "Demonstrators March Against New Law Legalizing Gay Marriage in France", May 26th of 2013
>
> "Lots of violence on both sides, it would seem. I think every one needs to chill out and discuss this like human beings."
> – My correspondent Roman Catholic Priest, April 25th of 2013

All of the above converges in France. Tensions rise amid a desperate economy, fear of Islamic immigration and concern over cultural identity, and the ages-long issue of Christian values in a country that converted to secularism in a rather brutal fashion. The battleground: homosexual rights. Yes, you read correctly.

This matter of homosexual union and adoption is a little thing; it shall destroy neither France nor the Church, and it is very unlikely to harm anyone. Why then has the Roman Catholic Church opposed it so vehemently? Why has embattled France suddenly become the perfect arena in which everything used against Christianity is thrown into stark relief?

Christians are not suffering from a persecution complex, but rather a complex persecution. This complexity is such that at times Christians even play into its hands.

---

[386] Martine Nouaille. "France's Gay Marriage Legislation: Why It's Polarizing The Nation" *Agence France Presse.* Sunday, April 21st, 2013. http://www.huffingtonpost.com/2013/04/21/france-gay-marriage-debate_n_3125696.html Retrieved Sunday, April 21st, 2013.

Due to the seemingly-losing war that Christianity has fought against promiscuous lust for the last hundred years, the perception of apostatic battalions amassing against everything which the Christian Church holds dear, and the preconceptions and stereotypes associated with homosexuality, conservative religious groups have entered full siege mode.[387] They are concerned that acceptance of homosexuals is a part of the increasing moral decadence of our society. A perfect example of this – and thus of why I have written this book – is the conflict "which is dividing France"[388] and which His Holiness Pope Emeritus Benedict XVI has called "a threat to world peace."[389]

It all began in November of 2012, when the call of His Eminence Cardinal Andre Vingt-Trois, Archbishop of Paris, was answered, and on the 17th of the month many French conservatives had appeared to protest atheist French President Francois Hollande's efforts to legalize 'gay marriage' *en masse. "Mariage pour Tous"* ("Marriage for All") was one of Hollande's campaign promises, and his goal was to properly and finally legalize same-sex union by the first anniversary of his May 15th of 2012 election.

By November 17th of 2012, I had nearly entirely written this book, but I felt mightily compelled to add a section on this newly-emerging matter of France. Since then, I have found the need to update this section several times as the situation has deteriorated.

As I began to write it, hundreds of thousands of Roman Catholics and other French conservatives, inspired by the words of the Archbishop of Paris[390], were marching from the countryside and in cities across

---

387 Also referred to as "bulwark mode Christianity". 1 Timothy 3:15 (*"Hedraioma*" in the original Greek.)

388 *The Globe and Mail.* "In Christmas speech to Vatican bureaucracy, the Pope denounces 'manipulation' of sex, gender" Nicole Winfield, VATICAN CITY – The Associated Press. Published Friday, Dec. 21 2012, 7:44 AM EST. http://www.theglobeandmail.com/news/world/in-christmas-message-the-pope-denounces-manipulation-of-sex-gender/article6626645/ Retrieved January 7th, 2013.

389 Ibid.

390 *Diocese de Reims.* "Archbishop Andre Vingt-Trois: 'On the' marriage for all, 'I call on Christians to manifest". http://catholique-reims.cef.fr/spip.php?article3658&lang=fr and http://www.la-croix.com/Religion/S-informer/

France[391] (including Toulouse, Marseilles, and Lyon) and fighting – engaged in actual physical scuffles/skirmishes in some cases – in the streets of Paris over the very matters of which I have just been writing. In response, the protest was assailed by Femen; a worldwide group of young self-proclaimed feminists who use extreme sexual imagery to protest far-right activities. They are not without nobility in their deeds, for they do try to bring to the world's attention issues of misogyny that might otherwise have gone unnoticed.

However, the methods of Femen leave much to be desired. In this case they were marching topless – save for black imitations of nuns' veils – and spraying foam from canisters marked "Sperm" while chanting "in gay we trust." Lest one be somehow uncertain of their stance with regard to religion, these protest-protesters had such antagonistic slogans written upon their naked torsos as "F*** CHURCH".

I am not sure if this was quite what Lady Gaga and her predecessors intended. Nevertheless, it provides a living caricature of feminists and of the LGBT community in a world where even the term "sexual" is bane (support for "gay men and lesbians" has been shown to be at least 17% higher than support for "homosexuals") – a caricature that might have been drawn by those who would condemn the LGBT community.

So it is that such is the image which we of the LGBT community receive broadcast throughout the world; an offense to that which we as devout Christians value above all. Yet when some of the supposedly-Catholic protesters take the bait – as they have, knocking out the tooth of one Femen member and possibly breaking the nose of another – an

---

Actualite/Cardinal-Andre-Vingt-Trois-Sur-le-mariage-pour-tous-j-appelle-les-chretiens-a-se-manifester-_NG_-2012-11-08-873726 November 8th of 2012. Both sources retrieved Monday, December 31st of 2012.

391 Mpelembe Admin. "Thousands march in Paris against gay marriage." 17 November 2012. http://world-news.mpelembe.net/home/thousands-march-in-paris-against-gay-marriage Retrieved 18/11/2012 and "French march against gay marriage." *IrishTimes.com* http://www.irishtimes.com/newspaper/breaking/2012/1118/breaking2.html Sunday, November 18th of 2012. This latter article reveals the final destination to be the final resting place of Napoleon Bonaparte, as his civil code states that marriage is a union between a man and a woman.

image is painted of two sides in a war which is not in fact real...and which must never be treated as though it were.[392]

> "You wanted war, and you've got it." – One of many anonymous and violently-threatening letters sent to those French politicians who remain loyal to the President[393]

I dearly hope that those who have described this as a French "civil war"[394] are merely spouting hyperbole. However, it has been neither without its combatants nor its casualties. In the months that followed November 17th, the protests became increasingly violent. Demonstrators threw smoke bombs and lobbed glass bottles, cans, and metal bars at police, who responded with tear gas[395], water cannon[396], and the occasional light clubbing[397]. In one case a protester actually broke into the Assembly as the measure was about to be legalized on April 23rd. General anti-gay violence has also increased; gay bars have been

---

392 *Femen: Sextremism Women's Movement.* "An Eye for an Eye, a Tooth for a Tooth" (November 19, 2012) and "Femen Calls to Ban the Organization of the French Religious Fascists" (November 21, 2012). http://femen.org/en/news/page/3#post-content Retrieved Friday, December 14th of 2012.

393 *The Montreal Gazette.* "France: Anti-gay terrorists continue to threaten politicians" Jillian. May 3, 2013. http://blogs.montrealgazette.com/2013/05/03/france-anti-gay-terrorists-continue-to-threaten-politicians/ Retrieved Monday, June 24th of 2013.

394 *la Croix.* "Are we crazy?" Bruno Frappat. April 19th of 2013. http://www.la-croix.com/Actualite/France/Sommes-nous-devenus-fous-Par-Bruno-Frappat-2013-04-19-950114 Retrieved Tuesday, June 25th of 2013.

395 *CBCnews|World.* "Protest turns violent after France legalizes gay marriage" The Associated Press. April 23rd of 2013. http://www.cbc.ca/news/world/story/2013/04/23/france-passes-same-sex-marriage-law.html Retrieved Tuesday, June 25th of 2013.

396 *Yahoo! NEWS.* "French gay marriage: Water cannon, police legions" Associated Press/Michel Euler, Tuesday, April 23rd of 2013. http://news.yahoo.com/french-gay-marriage-water-cannon-police-legions-092606866.html Retrieved Tuesday, June 25th of 2013.

397 "*Incidents Manif pour Tous Champs Elysees / Paris 24 mars 2013 Line Press.* March 24th of 2013. http://www.youtube.com/watch?v=3KphxSwz-J4&feature=player_embedded Retrieved Wednesday, June 26th of 2013.

attacked[398], the Spring LGBT Trade Show in Paris was vandalized on film[399], and anti-homophobia helpline calls have tripled.[400] Just for walking arm in arm, Wilfrid de Bruijn and his boyfriend were brutally beaten in Paris by several men shouting homophobic epithets. He sustained the loss of blood and a tooth as well as broken bones around his eye; the photos of his injuries which he posted on Facebook were so provocative that the French Interior Minister called Bruijn to express his personal shock. Bruijn himself had this to say:

> "'It was not Frigide Barjot who was hitting my head, or the bishop of Avignon lurking in that street to attack us,' he said. 'But they are responsible.'"[401]

As for Frigide Barjot (real name Virginia Tellenne), whose "stage name" is a play on that of anti-Islamist actress and human/animal rights activist Brigitte Bardot, led the French anti-gay movement inspiringly for six months. Her charisma and inflammatory "one-liners" gained her great fame, including such statements as her April 12th response to the government's accelerating the parliamentary timetable to pass the same-sex measure:

---

398 "French PM urges calm as gay marriage heads to final vote" *Agence France-Presse.* 04/18/2013. http://www.rappler.com/world/26686-france-parliament-vote-gay-marriage Retrieved Tuesday, June 25th of 2013.

399 *AMERICAblog.* "Not-very-bright anti-gay bigots in France film selves vandalizing Paris' LGBT center" John Aravosis, April 8th of 2013. http://americablog.com/2013/04/gay-marriage-vandals-paris-lgbt-center-video.html Retrieved Wednesday, June 26th of 2013.

400 *AlaskaDispatch.* "Divisions exposed as France prepares to say 'I do' to gay marriage" Paul Ames, May 14th of 2013. http://www.alaskadispatch.com/article/20130514/divisions-exposed-france-prepares-say-i-do-gay-marriage Retrieved Tuesday, May 25th of 2013.

401 *AMERICAblog.* "French religious right promises to spill blood over gay marriage push" John Aravosis. 4/14/2013. http://americablog.com/2013/04/gay-marriage-france-frigide-barjot-hate-crime.html Retrieved Monday, June 24th of 2013.

> "The President of the Republic has decided to guillotine us.
> If tonight we fuse of 'Hollande resign', unlike at other times,
> I will not prevent the slogans,"[402]

and perhaps her most famous statement:

> "Hollande wants blood, he will have it! Everyone is furious.
> We live in a dictatorship."[403]

However, in the end the deeply-Catholic Barjot refused to attend the grand May 26th protest in Paris which she herself had organized[404], to avoid escalating the violence and disturbance, and urged...

> "...all those who follow me since November 17, 2012...[405]"

...to join her in protest elsewhere. Now, less than a year later, she is no longer even a part of the actions of *Manif pour Tous*, saying instead that "Human dignity cannot be defended in violence and in shouting."[406]

Perhaps she took to heart the open letter from her brother-in-law, Karl Zero, which he posted online three days after Barjot's April 12th statements above. Barjot wept publicly[407] at the nature of Zero's plea,

---

402 *Le nouvel Observateur.* "Frigide Barjot: 'Hollande wants blood, he will have it!'" April 12th of 2013. http://tempsreel.nouvelobs.com/mariage-gay-lesbienne/20130412.OBS7832/le-senat-vote-le-mariage-homo-frigide-barjot-hollande-veut-du-sang-il-en-aura.html Retrieved June 26th of 2013.

403 Ibid.

404 "Rainbow Warriors" *The Economist.* April 27th of 2013, Paris. From the print edition, found online at http://www.economist.com/news/europe/21576692-frances-parliament-votes-legalise-gay-marriage-and-adoption-rainbow-warriors Retrieved Monday, June 24th of 2013.

405 *English Manif.* "A sad, sad turn -- Frigide Barjot decides not to march with the grand Manif today!" Posted by RO Lopez on May 26th of 2013. http://englishmanif.blogspot.ca/2013/05/a-sad-sad-turn-frigide-barjot-decides.html Retrieved Monday, June 24th of 2013.

406 *Le Parisien.* "*Manif pour tous*: Manuel Valls will not tolerate 'any overflow'". Saturday, February 1st of 2014. http://www.leparisien.fr/societe/video-sans-frigide-barjot-la-manif-pour-tous-retourne-dans-la-rue-dimanche-01-02-2014-3549895.php Retrieved Saturday, February 1st of 2014.

407 *GENTSIDE.* "Frigide Barjot: Woman evokes Karl Zero and [Barjot] bursts

which suggested that her vision had been "dimmed at this point by the media" and advised her "to get off thy glorious destrier, like Joan of Arc[408]" and "stop the charge," for "Hollande does not want blood."[409] Perhaps there is a bit of Joan of Arc in her after all.

The Archbishop of Paris may not have had such an overt change of heart, yet he has become disgusted with what the protests became. In November, when he reminded us of why the Bishop is a potent Chess piece through his influence over Catholics, he appeared to be holding to the simple statement he made on August 15th of 2012, "the family... includes...a father and a mother in enduring love...there is no place to debate."[410] On April 16th of 2013, at his speech of the Plenary Assembly of Bishops of France, His Eminence complained that this violence came from the President's decision to "drive this process" through rather than open it up for more debate (although considering that the legalization of full homosexual union was one of Hollande's campaign promises, one might argue that the decision was made by the French voters, if only

---

into tears on D8" Posted by Solene Grandclaude on April 16th of 2013. http://www.gentside.com/frigide-barjot/frigide-barjot-elle-evoque-karl-zero-et-fond-en-larmes-sur-d8_art49888.html Retrieved June 26th of 2013.

408 The Maid is such a popular figure – especially in France – that she inspires much comparison. I recall even having a dream to that effect shortly before this Matter of France began: a crowded stage was addressed by a voice asking, "Who will play the role of Joan of Arc?" I guess one of the people at the front of the stage looked a *bit* like Barjot, whom *English Manif* described as "the children's rights movement's Joan of Arc" in the above article, but I only saw her from the back! As for me, I was mostly hidden behind the curtain, and I rather hoped we weren't putting on Shakespeare's *Henry VI, part i*!

409 *Le Huffington Post. "Lettre -- ma belle-soeur Frigide Barjot* Karl Zero, 15/04/2013. http://www.huffingtonpost.fr/karl-zero/lettre-ouverte-frigide-barjot_b_3081428.html Retrieved Saturday, September 28th of 2013. Translated from the original French in part by myself, as Zero apparently intentionally used the archaism "thy" instead of "your" to describe Frigide's metaphorical steed.

410 "Mariage des homosexuels : 'Ce que veut l'Eglise, c'est qu'il y ait débat'" http://www.lemonde.fr/societe/video/2012/08/15/mariage-des-homosexuels-ce-que-veut-l-eglise-c-est-qu-il-y-ait-debat_1746248_3224.html Retrieved November 8th of 2012. Translated from the original French by the author.

on a secular level). The Archbishop also gave his own explanation as to the cause of the violence in France, which according to him is in a condition in which it...

> "...is preparing for violence. What we already see is the fact that the failure to accept a number of differences in social life leads to the crystallization of categorical demands of small groups or identity subsets, who think they cannot be recognized through any means other than by violence."[411]

Despite the expressed desire of some to have the French police bash in the heads of protesters, the LGBT community falls into the category of "small group or identity subset" and as such has gotten the worst of this French "civil war." Nevertheless, one must not look upon the Archbishop as a bitter enemy, no matter how much anger, frustration, or despair one may feel at this apparent reminder that the manner of love one may feel is somehow not good enough for the God whom we love. His Eminence Cardinal Vingt-Trois honestly thought it necessary to be involved in actions that might change the situation positively in the long term.[412] As for those of us in the LGBT community, we know that God's will was always one of love for those who love, and that comes before all else.

Considering how closely tied this matter of France is with my own work, identity, and faith, one may wonder how I chose to act. While working on this book, I initiated my "Little Shower of Roses" letter-writing campaign and posted several message videos online, each with a slightly-less-incomprehensible French accent than the last (fortunately, I generally included English versions as well). Nevertheless, my effectiveness was limited by my remoteness and by the fact that letters of war gain more attention than letters of peace. It is considerably easier

---

411 "Opening speech of Cardinal Vingt-Trois of the Plenary Assembly of the Bishops of France" *la Croix*. Tuesday, April 16th of 2013. http://www.la-croix.com/Religion/Actualite/Discours-d-ouverture-du-cardinal-Vingt-Trois-de-l-Assemblee-pleniere-des-eveques-de-France-2013-04-16-945214 Retrieved Saturday, April 27th of 2013.

412 Ibid.

to stir people to the point of violence than it is to calm them down from that point.

As a case in point, I received an intriguing response to the first of my French-language videos, titled "GOD LOVES HOMOSEXUALS: Bible Proves It (English subtitles)".[413] As one might imagine, such a bold stance proved somewhat inflammatory, and it attracted the attention of *ODYS-7*, a small Catholic production studio allied with *Manif Pour Tous* from the city of Lyon in east-central France. Rather than attempt to assault my position directly, this company invited me to view a video titled "No homosexuality in Lyon, or in France, or in the world"[414] and by association their entire channel. I was particularly disturbed by the studio's Christmas message to Christian families, titled "[ODYS-7] Father Christmas has been sacrificed as a holocaust"[415], which shows an effigy of the popularized Saint Nicholas in a standing position being slowly consumed by fire.

I confess that I am not 100% certain as to why *Santa had to burn,* yet I can only assume that there was an important political and possibly religious reason for it. Like Frigide Barjot, *ODYS-7* endeavours to at times have humourous qualities, but if that was the case here I cannot personally be certain. Perhaps I am biased, as I personally have been threatened with death by fire if I but go to Russia.

One must think twice what one does in the name of Christianity when these actions bring out the worst in people. One must recall Jesus Christ's statements recorded in Matthew 24:45-51 (KJV, emphasis mine):

---

413 "DIEU AIME HOMOSEXUELS: Bible Il Prouve (English subtitles)" *YouTube.* Tiamat Michelle Hart, January 28th of 2013. http://www.youtube.com/watch?v=2C7qUX1-r88 Retrieved Thursday, June 27th of 2013.

414 "[ODYS-7] Pas d'homosexualité à Lyon, ni en France, ni dans le monde" *YouTube.* ODYS-7 Productions, February 2nd of 2013. http://www.youtube.com/watch?v=k5aF-lDIGpQ Retrieved Thursday, July 4th of 2013.

415 "[ODYS-7] Le Pére Noël a été sacrifié en holocauste." *YouTube.* ODYS-7 Productions, December 22nd of 2012. http://www.youtube.com/watch?v=8A6WIosRQW4 Retrieved Thursday, July 4th of 2013.

> "Who then is a faithful and wise servant, whom his lord hath made ruler over his household, to give them meat in due season?
> Blessed is that servant, whom his lord when he cometh shall find so doing.
> Verily I say unto you, That he shall make him ruler over all his goods.
> But and if that evil servant shall say in his heart, My lord delayeth his coming;
> And **shall begin to smite his fellowservants**, and to eat and drink with the drunken;
> The lord of that servant shall come in a day when he looketh not for him, and in an hour that he is not aware of,
> And shall cut him asunder, and appoint him his portion with the hypocrites: there shall be weeping and gnashing of teeth."

The catharsis of our world is displayed in its media, and while the majority of us would not wholly imitate what we see therein, we still find ourselves tempted to take – however more moderately – one of the sides which we are shown. The very reason for the existence of these protests was to make the anti-LGBT opposition appear larger than it truly was, so that it would seem that the LGBT community could never coexist with Christian France. The subtle message to reach our minds is that we can only choose one of the apparently diametrically-opposed positions, and that there exists no effective mediation between them. Thus the conflict in Paris is reflected throughout the world.

So long as there is a perception of opposing sides, no matter which one prevails, the other shall feel that their country has betrayed them... and betrayal is among the worst feelings imaginable.

However, if Christianity really can exist in harmony with the LGBT community, why would our Holy Mother Church choose to instead be represented by such a fanatical attitude?

I beg you to let me indulge in a brief anecdote. When I was nineteen – and still in the guise of a man – my high school drama teacher assigned me the part of 16th-Century Cardinal Bellarmine (now Saint Robert Bellarmine) in Barrie Stavis' 1947 play *Lamp At Midnight.* As an analogy for modern intolerance, I was to play the role of Inquisitor opposite Galileo and convince him to abandon heliocentricism. As

I read over the script, I became intrigued by the argument I was to employ. The play appeared at first to be biased against the Church, as is all-too-common in the realm of drama, yet it instead portrayed even the Inquisitor Saint I was to play in a somewhat sympathetic light. Rather than merely resort to close-minded coercion, I was obliged to point out that the new and radical idea that the earth actually rotated around the Sun threatened the authority of the clergy of the Church. Because such a concept contradicted their understanding of the Scriptures (though said Scriptures actually do allow for the heliocentric model when examined carefully and in-context[416]), I had to claim that if the concept were spread now, "the evil would be too great"; the peasants would not understand.

A similar approach is now being taken in France. Political forces have manipulated French Catholics into standing with the far-right against the LGBT community. Yet now the "peasants" *can* understand, the authority of the clergy of the Church *is* threatened, and God understands better than any of us, as He always has.

Wait a minute, one might at this point interject; if the Catholic Church actually performed same-sex unions – even ones sanctioned by the Pope – in the Middle Ages,[417] how does the matter of France threaten the authority of the clergy? The answer is that it doesn't; the Church will eventually grow far more accepting of the LGBT community. The actual threat to the Church's authority – and thus the cause of its apparent threatening of the LGBT community – is twofold.

The virtue of Obedience and the universal acceptance of doctrine is very important to the Roman Catholic Church. It is through these that – despite the existence of approximately 33,000 different denominations of Christianity – fully half of the 2.2 billion Christians in the world remain Roman Catholics. One would imagine that, being able to maintain such a high level of cohesion, the Catholic Church is not a

416 The controversial verses here include such examples as 1 Chronicles 16:30, which states that God "has made the world firm, not to be moved." (NAB) It is neither appeasement nor apology to suggest that the Scripture referred to the fact that humans could not move the planet themselves; it is simply truth.

417 "When Same-Sex Marriage Was a Christian Rite" Reproduced by Gwinna in the blog "anthropologist" on December 11th, 2009. http://anthropologist.livejournal.com/1314574.html Retrieved June 18th of 2013.

thing easily manipulated. One might also assume that the Church would be unaffected by political rulings which are secular in nature; that it would stand strong and alone.

This is precisely the problem. What we see now in France is a climactic clashing of forces which have been building up for well over a hundred years, and which have been especially active recently. The separation of Church and state had been an integral part of the French Revolution, in which advocates of a radically secularistic and atheistic philosophy had violently wrested away the privileges and property of the Church, enabling these revolutionaries to sell the latter to cover the deficit of the state. This had a very lasting effect upon French Catholics, as many viewed the imperial government as necessarily connected to the Catholic Church, and were thus very suspicious of the new, secular government and the new direction in which French society was moving. The result was, as described by Sister of the Sacred Heart Mary Frohlich, Associate Professor of Spirituality at the Catholic University of America:

> "Almost a hundred years later [1890 A.D.], many French Catholics...still configured their personal lives in terms of **a black-and-white division between a holy, Church-centered life and the utter moral corruption they perceived in the mainstream culture.**"[418]

To varying degrees, this division occurred not only in France but throughout the whole world where Christianity was circulated and practiced, and it meant that the political ironically became associated not with the Church but with the aforementioned mainstream culture. In the modern era, this meant that the governments of some countries where Christians were a minority – such as communist China – would suppress, control, and limit the spread of Christianity. However, in more democratic countries where Christianity had already been practiced by the majority – such as the United States, Canada and France – this meant

---

418 *ST. THÉRÈSE OF LISIEUX: Essential Writings.* "Introduction: The Religious Milieu of the Time" Mary Frohlich. 2003 Orbis Books, Maryknoll, NY. p. 17. Emphasis mine.

that the entire citizenry was legally free to worship (or not worship) as they pleased.

Yet one hundred years after 1890, a strange thing had happened in France. Despite the law separating Church and state having been enshrined in 1905, 80% of the French were still Catholic by the early 1990s. However, in the last two decades that number has plunged drastically to a mere 51% in 2007 (most of this drop – which has continued – occurred in the 2000s, especially after 2004).[419] This is an immense concern for the Roman Catholic Church, for France is rightly considered to be her "eldest daughter".[420] This has been the case since ~499 A.D., when France's first king, Clovis I, was baptized by Saint Remi – then Bishop of Reims – who anointed him with a statement which proved eerily-prophetic for France, "love what you have burned, burn what you have loved."[421]

Thus Pope Benedict XVI was very interested in French President Nicolas Sarkozy's desire to once again pursue the theory of the "two swords"[422]; the traditional approach in which the Church has power over all issues of a spiritual (and by association, moral) nature, while the political government is in charge of its own temporal affairs. However, Sarkozy is no longer President; he was unable to pull France out of the

---

419 *EXPATICA.COM – French News.* "Pope backs Sarkozy over church-state divide" 12th of September 2008. http://www.expatica.com/fr/news/local_news/Pope-backs-Sarkozy-over-revamp-of-church_state-divide.html Retrieved Saturday, June 29th of 2013.

420 *National Catholic Reporter.* "Extracts from Sarkozy on church/state relations in France" John L. Allen Jr. September 10, 2008. http://ncronline.org/news/extracts-sarkozy-churchstate-relations-france Retrieved Saturday, June 29th of 2013.

421 Gregory of Tours, *History of the Franks*, Book II, Chapter XXXI. This collective baptism of Clovis as well as 3,000 warriors occurred during Christmas between 496 and 511 A.D.. This statement probably referred to the Pagan burning of Christians and the Christian burning of idols, respectively and in the context of its time.

422 Fr. Evaldo Xavier Gomes. "CHURCH-STATE RELATIONS FROM A CATHOLIC PERSPECTIVE: GENERAL CONSIDERATIONS ON NICOLAS SARKOZY'S NEW CONCEPT OF LAÏCITÉ POSITIVE" http://www.stjohns.edu/media/3/37319585863d4c94a5f6bc531defe3af.pdf Retrieved Saturday, June 29th of 2013.

great recession and the country turned away from the conservatism that seemed so sensible a decade ago. The current President, Socialist Francois Hollande, is considerably less interested in ties with the Church than his more conservative predecessor, which widens the rift between the religious and the secular. Economically, France shall be restored when America is restored, and as was apparent in the 2012 U.S. Presidential election, whichever political party is in power when this happens will claim credit for the recovery. As such, the conservative right will seize any opportunity to undermine Hollande's authority, and it is more than happy to paint him as a Godless tyrant if doing so can gain it the support of the still-great number of French Catholics.

In addition to the matter of French political power, the other factor is that within the Roman Catholic Church itself, for it has also been affected by the immense wave of conservativism that engulfed the world at the turn of the Millennium. In retrospect it is ironic that when John F. Kennedy became the first Catholic U.S. President in 1961, people were worried that the Pope could influence American interests, for the opposite might well have happened forty years later. After seeing Pope John Paul II holding his head in despair in response to the 9/11 terrorist attacks on the World Trade Center and the Pentagon in 2001, one could not help wonder if the Catholic Church might take a right-wing turn in response to that of the U.S. of A..

The election of Pope Benedict XVI on April 19th of 2005 suggests that this proved to be the case. As His Eminence Cardinal Joseph Ratzinger, Dean of the College of Cardinals, he was nicknamed "the Enforcer" for his vehement defence of traditional doctrine. He was strong, steadfast, and stalwart in maintaining vital concepts of Christianity, such as salvation being found through Jesus alone. However, Cardinal Ratzinger also supported more controversial attitudes. This is found in such areas as his claim that Protestant churches were not actually churches but rather "ecclesial communities" lacking the elemental "fullness" of the Catholic Church[423] and in his stance on the LGBT community.

---

423 *Dominus Iesus.* The Vatican. 16 June 2000. http://www.vatican.va/roman_curia/congregations/cfaith/documents/rc_con_cfaith_doc_20000806_dominus-iesus_en.html Retrieved Sunday, June 30th of 2013.

Homosexuality was viewed as particularly problematic to His Eminence Cardinal Ratzinger, and he espoused his perspective on it both vocally and tacitly whenever the opportunity presented itself. This did not change when he became Pope Benedict XVI and gained the Church Militant's absolute doctrinal authority over the 1.2 billion Roman Catholics of the world.

According to its doctrine, the Church believes – as officially does the Eastern Orthodox Church, despite current attitudes in Russia (which have more to do with distancing itself from the "decadence" of the West than with religion) – that homosexuals should be treated with understanding and love. However, homosexuals would be swift to suggest that it possesses only a limited understanding of their love. Examining the *Catechism of the Catholic Church* reveals the nature and purpose of the traditional marriage, and it is interesting to compare them to those of homosexual union. Both are based upon a covenant by which two baptized people establish between themselves a partnership for the whole of their lives, and both are ordered toward the mutual good of the partners. The sacrament of marriage has by its nature an additional component, however, that it is also by its nature ordered toward the procreation and education of offspring.[424]

Intriguingly enough, the issue of the presence or absence of sexual acts has not been addressed as a major part of the anti-homosexual marriage argument encountered in this current matter of France. After all, one cannot be absolutely certain of what if any sexual acts will occur during a marriage, though any sin must of course be confessed. Rather, the focus has been placed upon two areas.

The first is the preconception that homosexuality is unnatural. This is a belief which is permitted to remain due to attitudes possessed by our society of sexual exaltation. Within approximately three decades homosexuality has been transformed from a fairly taboo subject

---

424 *Catechism of the Catholic Church,* "PART TWO: THE CELEBRATION OF THE CHRISTIAN MYSTERY. SECTION TWO – THE SEVEN SACRAMENTS OF THE CHURCH. CHAPTER THREE – THE SACRAMENTS AT THE SERVICE OF COMMUNION. Article 7 – THE SACRAMENT OF MATRIMONY." Paragraph 1601. http://www.vatican.va/archive/ENG0015/__P51.HTM

to one which has achieved worldwide acknowledgement and fame. Unfortunately the media has not always treated this new information responsibly, and at times people find themselves even encouraged to experiment with homosexuality as though it were a mere sexual fetish. Hence it seems to some that acceptance of the LGBT community is not so much the result of groundbreaking understanding as it is part of the reckless acceptance of all things sexual. However, those who are indeed naturally – and unchangeably – homosexual will swiftly point out the evident faultiness of this assumption.

The second is that no homosexual partnership – no matter how monogamous or loving – could possibly replicate the dynamic of masculine and feminine, male and female, present in a traditional Biblical marriage. His Holiness Pope Emeritus Benedict XVI made this statement a prime component of his final major addresses:

> "The natural structure of marriage must also be recognized and promoted...[defined as] the union of a man and a woman, against attempts to render it juridically equivalent to radically different forms of union which, in reality, contribute to the destabilization of the natural, eclipsing its particular character and its irreplacable social role."
>
> – *Diocese de Reims.* "Message of the Holy Father for the World Day for Peace 2013." (Translated by the author from Section 4. "*The Peacemakers are those who love, defend and promote life in its entirety*")

Reims, where I first encountered this message, is one of a number of cities in France to be especially bold in its contrast between the attitude of the Church and that of the state. While the former openly adheres to the above statement, the latter is represented here by the Socialist Mayor of Reims, Adeline Hazan. Loyal to the President and his policies, and a world-class mayor in her own right, she not only supported homosexuals but also was the first French politician I have seen to consider the effect that this conflict has had on France's transsexual community.[425]

---

425 *ADELINE HAZAN, Maire de Reims.* "International Day Against Homophobia and Transphobia" May 17th of 2013. http://www.adelinehazan.net/2013/05/

Additionally, despite the presence of skirmishers (who apparently were not part of Barjot's *Manif Pour Tous*)[426], Hazan personally presided over Reims' first homosexual wedding (between lesbians Danielle and Daphne).[427]

Thus we see before us the concern of the Roman Catholic Church, who worries that broadening the definition of marriage could confuse as much as expand the understanding of gender relationships and thus the mother and father parental roles. It is a concern with which my own homosexual friends and acquiantances might – as we have already seen – agree, were it not phrased and approached in such a hostile manner. As I wrote to the Vatican in the Synod on the Family: "France has not 'fallen'; we must never look upon it that way, for God would not allow its spiritual destruction. If ever it seems that France has fallen, that only means that God wishes us to take a different approach in its defense."

The ironic paradox is that if and when 'gay marriage' is universally accepted, the only way in which it might create chaos is by forcing an attempted pigeon-holing of homosexual relationships into heterosexual terms. This will result in such uninformed inquiries as that to which my own friends have been subjected, such as "which of you is the 'man' (or would you prefer 'butch') and which of you is the 'woman' (or would you rather be addressed as 'femme')? Which of you is 'the husband' and which is the 'wife'? We of the LGBT community really do not need any more labels.

Then why do people consider it so important that homosexual union be referred to as 'marriage'? There are two reasons for this. Firstly, if the semantics of the word 'marriage' are not employed – even though they

---

journee-internationale-de-lutte-contre-l%E2%80%99homophobie-et-la-transphobie/ Retrieved Monday, July 1st of 2013.

426 *Champagne-Ardenne.* "Reims: Some clashes against a group of protesters from the Protests for All" Lionel Gonzalez. June 22nd of 2013. http://champagne-ardenne.france3.fr/2013/06/22/reims-quelques-heurts-contre-un-groupe-de-manifestants-de-la-manif-pour-tous-275459.html Retrieved Monday, July 1st of 2013.

427 *Champagne-Ardenne.* "The first gay marriage in Reims celebrated by Adeline Hazan" Lionel Gonzalez. June 22nd of 2013. http://champagne-ardenne.france3.fr/2013/06/22/un-premier-mariage-homosexuel-reims-celebre-par-adeline-hazan-275125.html Retrieved Monday, July 1st of 2013.

do not apply in the Biblical sense and a different (however legally-equal) term might better apply – then gay and lesbian couples are at risk of being viewed as legally and socially inferior. Secondly, as marriages have a religious association and are performed in a religious ceremony, there exists the potential for some measure of eventual religious validation for the loving homosexual relationship, as homosexual couples appear to have enjoyed several hundred years ago.

Then, of course, there is the question of the homosexual couple's ability to raise a family. Arguments suggesting the disadvantages of homosexual union and adoption have often been stated, however there seem to be advantages also, for homosexual couples display – for all the world to see – a mysterious manner of love which is nevertheless real. I have seen this with my own eyes; I know too many homosexuals and have seen too much of their potential to doubt that theirs is a true and spiritual love quite worthy of being shared.

Would a same-sex couple provide a worse upbringing than a widowed single parent, or even the one-gender environment of a convent? There may not yet be enough evidence to be certain one way or the other, but the outlook is positive. Would a same-sex couple not provide a more stable familial environment if it was properly recognized as a couple? It is safe to state that this is the case. Are the orphanages of the world so well-furnished that children are better off in them? I cannot say; perhaps the orphans might decide for themselves.

It is true that male and female influences are both necessary for a child's moral development, whether these are provided by the parents or whether it is possible that this exposure could come from elsewhere. It is also true that, as homosexual couples cannot become pregnant accidentally, every child in the care of same-sex parents is a child who is wanted.

One wonders why the Roman Catholic Church seems never to have considered any of this. In actual fact, it...started to. The question of homosexuality was often considered by Pope John Paul II during his papacy. In fact, it was in the Roman Catholic 2003-2004 Edition of the Holy Bible which I have so often referenced that I first found evidence of the homosexual defence. There is a cross-reference regarding Romans 1:27 (in which Paul writes of men who "burned with lust for one another") that links it, not only with the other verses condemning the *tow'ebah* of homosexuality,[428] but also with the verse of Wisdom which is immediately followed by the absolute clarification that idol worship is the cause and extent of all *tow'ebah* evil. However, whatever advances were on the verge of being made regarding the understanding of homosexuals' relationship with God were halted.

We can only speculate about what aspects of his background influenced Prefect Joseph Ratzinger's attitude toward homosexuality, but he used his position to great effect, as is evident in the introduction to his *CONSIDERATIONS REGARDING PROPOSALS TO GIVE LEGAL RECOGNITION TO UNIONS BETWEEN HOMOSEXUAL PERSONS,* circa 2003. Therein, the Prefect referred to the fact that various questions relating to homosexuality had been frequently addressed by Pope John Paul II and the relevant Dicasteries of the Holy See. However, he himself viewed homosexuality as a troubling phenomenon both morally and socially, and described it as being of greater concern in those countries that intended to grant legal recognition of homosexual unions and perhaps the possibility of adopting children, which was precisely the case in France during the final days of his Pontificate. Thus, when Pope John Paul II desired the input of his trusted advisor Prefect Ratzinger regarding the matter, the latter sought to reiterate the previous arguments rather than provide new doctrinal elements. His stated aim in this was to aid Bishops in preparing more specific interventions, and also to direct Catholic politicians in dealing with proposed legislation in this area.[429]

There we have our explanation as to why, nine years later, the Pope Emeritus advocated not only Catholic refusal to acknowledge homosexual unions but also interventions in those secular nations which would legalize them. Both of these apply in the case of France, for it is still a half-Catholic nation yet is also one governed by a self-proclaimed

---

428 "Lv 18, 22; 20, 13; Wis 14, 26; 1 Cor 6, 9; 1 Tm 1, 10" p. 1211.

429 *CONGREGATION FOR THE DOCTRINE OF THE FAITH.* Joseph Card. Ratzinger, Prefect. Approved by the Sovereign Pontiff John Paul II in the Audience of March 28th of 2003. Published June 3rd of 2003. http://www.vatican.va/roman_curia/congregations/cfaith/documents/rc_con_cfaith_doc_20030731_homosexual-unions_en.html#fn1 Retrieved July 2nd of 2013.

"non-believer" who wrote, "I defend secularism not as a value of leftism, but as a legal and policy framework."[430] The fact is, since the legalization of same-sex union as a marriage equivalent was in France utterly devoid of religious consultation, Roman Catholics could not accept as sacramental what was made to be a purely secular institution. Thus it was difficult to question what, as Dean of the College of Cardinals, Prefect Ratzinger had stated earlier....

> "When legislation in favour of the recognition of homosexual unions is proposed for the first time...the Catholic law-maker has a moral duty to express his opposition clearly and publicly and to vote against it. To vote in favour of a law so harmful to the common good is **gravely** immoral.[431]"

When the Prefect became Pontiff, no Catholic who wished to serve the Church Militant first in all of France could disobey. To do so was, according to him, to commit a grave (or mortal) sin and thus risk being consigned to the Fire.

However, history has shown that those whom one Pope would have burned, another Pope might have saved. Pope John Paul II was known for having a much different approach from that of his successor, and one which would prove useful to see again. I cannot help but remember a 2012 encounter I had with an elderly Muslim who thought me a Missionary. After a brief discussion, she confessed that she would even have been happy to attend Mass had it been given by Pope John Paul II, for, in her words, "he was a Pope for everyone."

---

430 *la Croix*. "Francois Hollande wishes to appease relations with cults" March 3rd of 2012. Bernard Gorce. http://www.la-croix.com/Actualite/France/Francois-Hollande-souhaite-apaiser-les-relations-avec-les-cultes-_EP_-2012-03-06-775678 Retrieved July 2nd of 2013.

431 *CONGREGATION FOR THE DOCTRINE OF THE FAITH. CONSIDERATIONS REGARDING PROPOSALS TO GIVE LEGAL RECOGNITION TO UNIONS BETWEEN HOMOSEXUAL PERSONS.* V. POSITIONS OF CATHOLIC POLITICIANS WITH REGARD TO LEGISLATION IN FAVOUR OF HOMOSEXUAL UNIONS Joseph Card. Ratzinger, Prefect. Published June 3rd of 2003. http://www.vatican.va/roman_curia/congregations/cfaith/documents/rc_con_cfaith_doc_20030731_homosexual-unions_en.html#fn16 Retrieved July 2nd of 2013. Emphasis mine.

It is true that John Paul II accepted Cardinal Ratzinger's proposals; this was due to the immense trust which he placed in the Dean. If another had been in his place, a more tolerant view might have been adopted. However, the conservative time apparently called for a conservative Pope, and thus His Eminence Cardinal Ratzinger become His Holiness Pope Benedict XVI, and spent seven years and nine months as Pontiff.

Thus we have before us a very difficult and complicated situation. It is because of this tight-lipped conservativism that very few understand how God always intended for good Christian homosexuals to be accepted and embraced, and those conservative Christians who might understand have thusfar been fearful of taking a stand against the tide of condemnation.

French President Hollande called the full legal acknowledgement of homosexual union an "irreversible movement in history"[432], and some have even considered it the most significant legal move in France since the 1981 abolition of the death penalty.[433] Yet conservative French Catholics, and their conservative Christian counterparts in all the world, do not feel that they are on the wrong side of history. They feel that they are standing strong against a siege to the bitter end.

Despite Hollande's legalization of full same-sex unions, nearly half of France's municipal leaders – 14,900 mayors – are opposed to same-sex ceremonies, and many have flatly refused to hold such ceremonies in their towns. The government's response has been quite firm. Bertrand Mathieu, a specialist in French constitution, stated that should any member of the council be unable to or refuse to "marry a gay couple, the prefect could intervene" and force the mayor "to proceed

432 "Gay marriage in France – Rainbow warriors" *The Economist.* April 27th of 2013. http://www.economist.com/news/europe/21576692-frances-parliament-votes-legalise-gay-marriage-and-adoption-rainbow-warriors Retrieved Thursday, July 4th of 2013.

433 "France Gay Marriage Protesters Arrested As Bill Moves Forward" *HUFFPOST GAY VOICES CANADA.* Reuters. Reporting by Marine Pennetier and Chine Labbe; Writing by Brian Love; editing by Mike Collett-White. April 15th of 2013. http://www.huffingtonpost.com/2013/04/15/france-gay-marriage-protesters-arrest-_n_3083926.html Retrieved Thursday, July 4th of 2013.

with the wedding. The mayors who refuse will be outside the law."[434] Punishments for disobedience are up to three years imprisonment and a fine of 45,000 euros.

This is not the sort of thing which is terribly effective on those of a religion filled with martyrs. Far-right French Catholic film group *ODYS-7* (whom you will remember as the ones who burned Santa Claus at the stake in effigy; one imagines that perhaps he now wishes he had not given them so much coal in their stockings) states this clearly in their banner-video from June 3rd of 2013:

> "Your repression will not stop our convictions!"[435]

Similarly, some French mayors are prepared to defy the President's egalitarian law. Mayor Abjat-sur-Bandiat in Dordogne, Jean-Claude Massion, stated simply, "I am ready to become a criminal by refusing a wedding."[436]

Pope Emeritus Benedict XVI did all he could to keep the Church strong. It is a sad thing that his approach fomented such ill-directed zealotry, however, as most of the LGBT community appears to view his Papacy as what I have heard described as a "Dark Age." Mediaeval or no, however, Saint Theresa of Lisieux promised that something would happen that had not been seen since the time of Joan of Arc, and she was not speaking about Frigide Barjot.

As it was predicted, on February 11th of 2013 His Holiness Benedict XVI became the first Pope to resign since 1415 A.D. (also the year of the devastating Battle of Agincourt, when Joan of Arc was three years

---

434 "Local mayors veto gay marriage law" *The Riviera Times.* Isabelle Younane, May 22nd of 2013. http://www.rivieratimes.com/index.php/provence-cote-dazur-article/items/local-mayors-veto-gay-marriage-law.html Retrieved Thursday, July 4th of 2013.

435 "[ODYS-7] Votre répression n'arrêtera pas nos convictions ! / 03-06-13" *YouTube.* ODYS-7 Productions, Published on June 5th of 2013. http://www.youtube.com/watch?v=7gj2aCobTrY Retrieved Thursday, July 4th of 2013.

436 "Local mayors veto gay marriage law" *The Riviera Times.* Isabelle Younane, May 22nd of 2013. http://www.rivieratimes.com/index.php/provence-cote-dazur-article/items/local-mayors-veto-gay-marriage-law.html Retrieved Thursday, July 4th of 2013.

old). It was France's Patron Saint Theresa of Lisieux who helped install His Holiness Pope Francis, as surely as Joan of Arc helped crown King Charles VII.[437] If any Saint shall save France this time around, it shall be her, for it pleases God that the biggest church in the world shall be saved through the Little Way.[438]

Pope Francis has taken a very open and frank approach. He recently confirmed that there had in fact been a "gay lobby" in the Vatican, though unfortunately this lobby may have been associated with the purchase of courtesans and thus done little for the advancement of gay rights.[439] How much more open-minded Pope Francis will be toward the LGBT community as more is learned about it remains to be seen, but the outlook is very hopeful indeed.

As for France itself, the fact that it is currently suffering from a sort of identity crisis may seem strange to those of us who were born elsewhere in the world. France has spent its history between other empires such as those of Rome and Britain while remaining mighty in its own right, and its culture has inspired the world. Even those who only

---

437 What Pope Francis Carries in His Briefcase: It is not the secret to the atomic bomb, but extremely powerful nonetheless". Mary Anne McElroy. *beliefnet.* http://www.beliefnet.com/Faiths/What-Pope-Francis-Carries-in-His-Briefcase.aspx__See also http://en.wikipedia.org/wiki/List_of_devotees_of_St._Thérèse_of_Lisieux Both retrieved Friday, January 24th of 2014.

438 The Little Flower of Jesus, who remained a Novice by choice, believed that great deeds were forbidden her, and that she could best please Jesus her Spouse through little, day to day actions of piety and love. Saint Theresa of Lisieux, after whom Mother Teresa of Calcutta named herself, found God to be more tender than a mother, who is always ready to forgive trivial and involuntary misbehaviour on the part of her child. She was greatly disturbed by the preachers of her time who stressed sin and the sufferings of purgatory and hell, and wept when told that noone knew whether they were worthy of love or hate. At times such darkness caused her to wonder if Heaven even existed. Her heart expanded with the desire for mercy and that no soul be lost. She described her way as being all confidence and love.

439 "Pope Francis: 'Gay lobby' exists inside Vatican" *CNN Belief Blog.* Daniel Burke, June 11th of 2013. http://religion.blogs.cnn.com/2013/06/11/pope-francis-gay-lobby-exists-inside-vatican/comment-page-20/#comment-2416817 Retrieved Thursday, June 4th of 2013.

speak English cannot help but feel the French influence and admit that it has a certain *Je ne sais quoi,* if you will. It is heartbreakingly wonderful to see that France is still so Christian that it would go to such lengths to march forth for its beliefs...if only its actions – and its understanding – reflected the true desires of our loving God.

Therein lies our problem. In this time of (let us face it) depression, the emptiness of a purely material existence is most keenly felt. In dark times such as these, people always tended to turn to religion for a sense of community, hope, and love. Yet now our beloved Church has become vilified.

This is why those who support same-sex union speak as their anthem the phrase, "Love has won out over hate." It seems almost as though Christianity now represents the latter quality. Ah, but as we have discovered, there are other forces at work in France. When one can convince them that their situation shall be improved, it is easy to incite people with words of war. Hate is not stronger than love, but it can often be easier.

To bear the cross upon one's neck, standard, books or buildings, or indeed to display one's Christianity in any way, is in a sense literally to "bear the cross"; to take upon oneself the very representation of Christianity. The actions of those who have done so led Mahatma Gandhi to never become Christian, just as they helped a young homeless man I knew to easily convert to Christianity after realizing that the only ones who helped him in his time of need were Christians. Thus, as the violence increased, a great paradox became more and more apparent: the supposed servants of the God of Love seemed in the world's eye to become champions of hate.

The result of this chaos is that, in their desire to stand firm against the increasing moral decay of society, religious leaders have barred their doors against the perceived siege of traditional morality, shutting those of us who are and wish to be good Christians but have had the misfortune to be associated with such preconceptions out in the cold.

It is possible to open the gates again; to mend this massive rift between the LGBT community and Christianity, to reunite not only France, but all the world in love. This path does take the Little Way; even something as insignificant as the "GOD LOVES HOMOSEXUALS" video which I mentioned earlier has touched someone, and as he wrote in response:

> "...I did not understand much, because of your accent [I am well and truly humbled – Author], but...I believe the key is initially knowing why sin is sin...[otherwise] it will be unfair to our eyes and the Love of God will seem cold...[He didn't] create homosexuals then ban them for His own pleasure; God is not a sadist..."
>
> – A commentator calling himself simply "Little Boy Looking for True Love and True Freedom", Thursday, January 23rd of 2014; translated from the original French (and fortunately, he *did* understand my French writing)

In the midst of France's web of power and politics, in-fighting and intricate intrigue, it is we of the LGBT community who are used as scapegoats. What then are we to do against such reckless hate? We must prove – to France and the world – that we are not goats.[440]

So long as the LGBT community is associated with the immoral, the doomed, and those who are not people of God, it will be quite difficult for the Christian community to accept us. It is deeply ironic that it is for seeking moral and monogamous relationships that French homosexuals have drawn so much ire from French Catholics. However, the truth shall bring ultimate succor in this matter of France, just as it shall set us all free.

The defense of homosexuality may not seem easy, but it is perfect, and for ease of understanding I have summarized it below:

1. Homosexuality is only sinful through association with idol worship; the Book of Wisdom makes this explicit.
2. Homosexuality was afforded special treatment among the ancient crimes of the old Mosaic law; the Hebrew wording used for it associates it not with other sexual crimes such as incest and bestiality, but rather with crimes such as cross-dressing.

[440] Matthew 25:31-46.

Again, these *tow'ebah* crimes are sinful in and of themselves through association with Paganism/idol worship.

3. As such, homosexual acts should not be condemned any more than certain other sexual acts not approved of by one's particular Christian church. If a denomination condemns masturbation or other non-reproductive sex as well as homosexual acts, then that is one matter. If a denomination does not condemn such things, then that is quite another.
4. This is not a coincidence. Only God can see all ends, and it was always His plan that these secrets be discovered, so that homosexuals might be saved, and with them all of Christianity.

To those of us who have at one time or another been tempted to blindly obey the scriptural passages dealing specifically with homosexual acts without considering their context or origins, I beg of you to recall Wisdom (14:27) and understand that monogamous Christian homosexuals are not truly abominations, for any evil that homosexuality may have contained in and of itself ended with the embrace of Christianity. Let us concern ourselves not merely with the letter of the law, but with the spirit; for our salvation is with the Spirit. (Romans 7:6, 2 Corinthians 3:6)

To those of us who have suffered ostracisation or condemnation for our apparent homosexuality at the hands of those who presume themselves to serve the God we love (and *want* to love), please remember that the secret truths of the Book of Wisdom are not yet such common knowledge that they can change the world. Thus most of our oppressors do not fully understand just what they are doing.

It is imperative that one understand that those of our Holy Mother Church – such as the Archbishop of Paris – are only doing what they think is right, and once they understand that to accept the LGBT community is to champion love rather than corruption, they shall accept us. It is important also that we all realize that the Christian Church is built upon a rock that will remain for all time, and that when Christian churches do accept the LGBT, they are not abandoning the Scriptures to obey some gathering trend, but rather they are obeying the Greatest Commandments:

> "Jesus said unto him, Thou shalt love[441] the Lord thy God with all thy heart, and with all thy soul, and with all thy mind.
>
> This is the first and great commandment.
>
> And the second is like unto it, Thou shalt love thy neighbour as thyself.
>
> On these two commandments hang all the law and the prophets."
>
> (Matthew 22:37-40, KJV)

When hateful deeds are done – in France or anywhere else – in the name of the Church, they are but politics. It is the work of humanity, not of God.

Finally, I shall note that I mentioned "casualties" in this matter of France; you may be wondering if there were any fatalities. There were at least two, yet neither of these were specifically from the homosexual community.

One was a transwoman named Mylene. Little about her is known save her nationality and her name, and the fact that she was bludgeoned to death with a hammer on July 24th of 2013 in the city of Limoges in central France. The transgender are the rarer and oft-forgotten "T" of the LGBT community, more recognizeable than homosexuals and thus usually in far more danger, and in this matter seemingly forgotten by all of France save for the shining city of Reims.

The other ended his life by his own hand: a man named Dominique Venner; a man who shot himself before the altar at Notre Dame Cathedral before a shocked congregation. He was a man who took his life to be a symbol of a cause. That alone means that we must at least explore the meaning of that cause.

Marine le Pen, President of France's far-right National Front party, suggested that "he wanted to wake up the people of France"[442], and in

---

441 Original Greek: αγαπαω ("*agapao*").

442 "Man kills himself at Notre Dame Cathedral" *CNN.* Stephanie Halasz and

a sense she was correct. He was a 78-year-old historian – a mere child when Hitler attacked the Alsace-Lorraine Rhineland and eventually occupied France – who had watched his nation's movements, phases, and tumults with a very conservative but also very educated eye. He was concerned about the legalization of proper homosexual union and wrote of such, yet he was more concerned that all those centuries of crusades would receive their final answer in an imminent Muslim conquest of France. However, he was not a Christian.

Examining his blog – generally a Spartan affair decorated only with the picture of a lone stag – reveals that he believed the life he led was the only life he would ever have. Indeed, he and I have virtually nothing in common save for a concern for France's future and a mutual fondness for Joan of Arc. Still, he had an intriguing grasp of the nature of the matter of France, and so in tribute to his memory I give Dominique Venner the final statement:

> "[The Protesters, who are often quite young, are partially] non-violent Catholic bourgeois...seduced by the new tolerant discourse of the Church in matters of conjugal love. Their references are Gandhi and Martin Luther King ... [The others, however, are young people whose] identities are mobilized by the insolent dynamism of protests. The future will show which components will prevail over the other by their vitality and determination."
>
> – *The mysteries of the 'French Spring'*[443]

Which will it be?

Jessica King, Tuesday, May 21st of 2013. http://www.cnn.com/2013/05/21/world/europe/france-cathedral-death/?iref=obnetwork Retrieved Thursday, July 4th of 2013.

443 "Les mystères du 'printemps Français'" *Dominique Venner.* May 14th of 2013. http://www.dominiquevenner.fr/2013/05/les-mysteres-du-printemps-francais/ Retrieved Thursday, July 4th of 2013. The article includes of a photograph of the French Spring in Lyon.

Chapter the 7th

The Two Shall Become One Flesh[444]

Issues of Biblical Gender Identity and the Conclusion of the Work

The Epistles of Peter and John speak of those who have known the light and then fallen into the darkness.[445] It is a different experience for those of us who have known the darkness first.

The midsummer light had begun to dwindle as I approached the door, upon which was emblazoned the image of a naked woman reclining on her hands, one leg extended seductively skyward. Taking a deep breath, I plunged through the portal into a wide room suffused with light vaguely reminiscent of red wine, or fresh blood. The gentlemen's club had just opened, and the women employed there were milling about as they awaited their male clientele of the evening. Garbed the way I was, I must have appeared part of that clientele as I approached one of them and asked, in a tone of voice which mixed the nonchalant masculinity I had long practised with the seductive femininity I was beginning to adopt:

"I'm looking for B---. I've been told he frequents this place."

"Oh yes," replied the young woman helpfully. "He usually comes just after we open. Wait about fifteen minutes and he should be here."

I thanked her and proceeded to the second tier of the building, where I found the washroom and changed therein. I had journeyed here discreetly from the Royal Ontario Museum where I had been doing volunteer work for the Head Archivist. I had spearheaded the

---

444 Genesis 2:24, Matthew 19:5-6, Mark 10:8, 1 Corinthians 6:16, Ephesians 5:31.

445 2 Peter 2:20-21 and 1 John 1:5-7, respectively.

construction of an electronic record of the Dr. T.G.H. Drake Collection, which consisted of artifacts relating to femininity and motherhood throughout the ages, including (I had just learned) idol statuettes of the Egyptian fertility goddess Isis dating back to ancient times. However I was earning no money from this, and what I was about to do here promised definite coin.

Thus I removed my dress pants and turtleneck to don an entirely different set of work clothes. I put on a leather bondage corset, a crushed velvet miniskirt, and PVC thigh-high stiletto-heeled platform boots; all black (relics from my time involved with the Gothic subculture a few years earlier). I did not truly wish to partake of that which I was poised to do – I had adamantly refused to even appear nude before now – but all of the mainstream modeling offers I had received had been rescinded immediately upon my informing my agent(s) that I was a 'pre-operative transwoman.'

Therefore I was about to step down the path trod by a great many of my trans-sisters. The first transwoman I had ever met, after complaining of the difficulty of finding a job when one is trans, had enthusiastically expressed the desire to experience the supposed vindication of femininity which comes from being desired by a man to the extent that he will offer money for her. It was as though this were considered a rite of passage of sorts for those such as I. We had been brought up to view women through the "male gaze" with our constant exposure to everything from sensuous centerfolds to scantily-clad superheroines to sexy succubi (and thus learned to sexualize our own womanhood in a like manner). We had also been thoroughly assured that in terms of intimate relationships with men, this was the only thing for which we could ever hope.[446]

---

446 It is for this reason especially that I would later become so fond of Joan of Arc's method of dealing with prostitutes. According to Squire Simon Baucroix, Joan would never permit women of ill-fame to follow the army. None of them dared to come into her presence; due presumably to her reputation for striking them on the backside with the flat of her blade. However, what made this especially righteous was the ultimatum Joan had given to her troops. She made the prostitutes depart **unless the soldiers were willing to marry them.** *St. Joan of Arc's Trial of Nullification: Arrival at Chinon and the Trial of Poitiers*, http://www.stjoan-center.com/Trials/null05.html Retrieved Monday, October 1st, 2012. Emphasis mine.

When I had been but sixteen a muscular soldier/classmate named Dave (who had just returned from the Canadian Armed Forces) had, due apparently to the shape of my lower lip, offered me $400 in cash if I would perform fellatio upon him. I had declined and delivered a speech about integrity which felt as much trepidatious as self-righteous in response, but I knew not how much of that sprang from the "Paladin" persona of which I had skirted the adoption since the age of thirteen and how much was part of whatever constituted my true nature. I knew not where "Sir Ted" (a nickname I received in my teenage years) ended and Tia Michelle began, but I was quite certain I could fetch a fine price.

I descended once more into the main room, now dressed in a manner likely to attract the attention of my prospective employer, and sat at a table that was frontal and central to ensure that I would. I did not need to wait long.

B--- was a clean-shaven young man with short-cropped dirty-blonde hair. He saw me as soon as he entered, and grateful that he was not more intimidating I called him over and propositioned him, trying to seem like the kind of woman who might be running an establishment such as this rather than the terrified virgin I truly was:

"I have been told you film porn, and I am interested in doing some tgirl[447]-on-girl work." For fear of being labeled "homosexual" before I was finished puberty, I had attempted to psychologically banish all desire for men eleven years earlier...mere months after the last time I had ever shed tears; the blood of the soul.

"Do you know anyone?" He asked in response.

What kind of question was that? Did the man want me to drag someone *else* into this?

After informing him that I did not, I received his explanation/lamentation that (unlike transwomen such as myself) "(genetic) girls are so expensive." Thus in his eyes I saw my apparent value as a human being, and found it wanting.

I politely-yet-briskly thanked him and, with a slight air of haughtiness to provide me with yet another mask, climbed the stairs on my high

[447] Tgirl: "Trans-girl"; one of the less-offensive nicknames that we transwomen are given. Still, I would not recommend using it outside of the darker industries in which we are all-too-often involved.

heels. Whatever I was, it wasn't this. At least when one strikes rock bottom, one has a rock upon which to stand.

I was desperate and distraught as I changed back into my male clothes. I could not share the attitude of those with whom I worked: there is nothing feminist, liberating, or empowering about pornography or prostitution. Perhaps I had been too disgusted by the crass emptiness of it all, perhaps my pride had been wounded, or perhaps I simply did not have the stomach for this profession, but for whatever reason my hypothesis had been proven: I simply could not go through with it. Desperately I tried to tell myself that the seemingly-arbitrary rules of Christian morality which I was half-convinced I had transgressed already simply by existing must be upheld; that it could not be worth selling the body I had to buy the body I needed. I would be able to return to work as a man for an indefinite time. I would be able to perpetuate the lie that was my male guise. I would be...damn.

"Oh my God, what am I going to do?"

A change of costume cleared me of this deed, and unsexed me in every sense of the term. Dressed as a man, I was no longer seen by the dancers and "escorts" as one of their own, and I was again safe from B--- and his ilk. I was perceived as predator rather than prey, and that is how the lovely ladies of the club saw me once more.

When I was mere feet from the exit I was approached by a pretty woman of Hispanic descent wearing a sequined pink minidress. As this was a 'tgirl night', she was almost definitely a transwoman, but she was so soft, pleasantly-plump and voluptuous that it was difficult to be certain of this. Smiling warmly, she bid me farewell, and my heart went out to her as she enfolded me in her gentle arms. Who in all the world could put a price upon her?

This transition from the ages-old roles of highly-literate male transcriber to somewhat-desperate female "prostitute" reflects the reality of life for a vast number of transwomen like myself who have been forced to face a society that shuns us and struggle with a God who supposedly condemns us.

However, there is nothing in the Bible that condemns transsexuals, and thus this is going to be a rather unusual chapter. Indeed I shall draw upon my own experiences multiple times herein, for as we have seen I have done so many times over the course of this book already, which is among the reasons why it sometimes mixes what may be considered Sunday School fare with Scriptural insight never before seen. Though I was raised a Roman Catholic and had a loving family, the secrets I needed to keep from everyone caused me to feel, in a sense, very much alone. When I had been afraid of being rejected by the world and losing even the love of my own family should they learn the truth, I desperately clung to He who is Love in faith that He still loved me, for who else would?

Male *and* Female He *also* Created Them

Why, one asks, are we ostracized, deemed immoral and insane? Not for any mortal sin, but incongruity of body and brain.

Paragraph 2333 of the Catechism of the Catholic Church states that "Everyone, man and woman, should acknowledge and accept his sexual identity."[448] That is well and I would gladly have complied... had said sexual identity always been readily apparent to me. However, this passage does not precisely cover what one is to do when one is physically both *man and woman!*

Herein lay my lasting anguish. You see, unlike homosexuals (the origin of whom has not yet been scientifically determined), transsexuals exist at varying points on a sort of intersex spectrum; meaning those who have some combination of attributes unique to each of the normal sexes. On one end of the spectrum are the very rare "true hermaphrodites", who have the primary and secondary sexual characteristics of both genders, and on the other are those unfortunate souls who have only the physical characteristics of one sex but are nevertheless certain that they belong to the other. These more-common examples feel the way they do

[448] THE HOLY SEE. *Catechism of the Catholic Church.* Part Three: Life in Christ, Section Two – The Ten Commandments, Chapter Two – You Shall Love Your Neighbor As Yourself, Article 6 – The Sixth Commandment, I. "Male and Female He Created Them..." Copyright Libreria Editrice Vaticana. http://www.vatican.va/archive/ENG0015/__P84.HTM Retrieved Sunday, October 14th of 2012.

because the only feature of their true sex is the neuron component of the bed nucleus of the stria terminalis...at the very core of their brains.[449]

When one is born closer to the invisible end of the spectrum, one may be experiencing chimerism, mild androgen insensitivity syndrome, mosaicism, de la Chapelle (apparent male with double-X chromosomes) syndrome, Klinefelter's syndrome, or some undiscovered condition from whose grasp many have suffered but of which nothing is yet known. There are very many complications and variations which can occur in human development, for the human being is a magnificently complex creation. It is usually necessary to undergo a "transition" in the form of hormone replacement therapy to properly align the gender of the less-cooperative parts of one's body with that of one's brain. This is an endocrinological metamorphosis and, as my friend and fellow transwoman Isis has attested quite publically, the process of transitioning requires all of one's mental energy; it becomes everything in one's life, for it affects the mind as well as the body.

I shall now offer two other examples of transwomen from my personal experience at various points within the spectrum. The first is a close friend of mine named Jenna, whom I first met a few years ago at a transperson support group and who has been searching for a Christian church which will properly accept her as a woman. She also has Silver-Russell syndrome with uniparental disomy on chromosome 7, causing her to have received two copies of said chromosome from her mother.

Though lacking a vagina and breasts, Jenna is otherwise a true hermaphrodite, having fully-functional male genitalia yet an internal fully-functional womb. Had she so chosen (via technology normally used in artificial insemination and a donor egg), this beautiful miracle of

---

449 "Male-to-Female Transsexuals Have Female Neuron Numbers in a Limbic Nucleus" http://jcem.endojournals.org/content/85/5/2034.full Retrieved Thursday, August 23rd of 2012. Though part of the limbic system and thus endocrinological (hormonal) in nature, the effects of the bed nucleus of the stria terminalis would likely be partially countered by such a testosterone-emitting powerhouse as even a sterile set of testicles. Among female-to-male transsexuals – despite the human body being more receptive to change via testosterone than estrogen – the limbic region associated with the bed nucleus would not be capable of providing testosterone to counter the level of estrogen produced elsewhere.

God could have impregnated herself with her own seed, borne it within her own womb, and (via Caesarian section) given birth to her own child; all without ever having known the touch of a man.[450]

Yet the world in its prejudice was convinced that she herself was a man, though she possessed no desire to be one.

Despite all the internal proof that she was indeed a woman, Jenna had no means of convincing external viewers of her femaleness. All she possessed to reassure herself for the first three decades of her life – until the assistance of a fortuitous ultrasound test – was her own mental certainty of her sex.

Now as for me, I am a classical hermaphrodite who suffers from androgen insensitivity syndrome, which is the largest single entity that leads to intersexuality. I have not quite such primary reproductive characteristics as Jenna, but my femaleness was made more immediately apparent. My personal area of the intersex spectrum is that of the "mermaid problem" if you will (for after all, if the fabled Little Mermaid had been a bull shark or male seahorse beneath the waist, would she not still be called a mermaid and thought of as female?). Beneath the waist I possess nonfunctional male genitalia, yet above the waist my glands and organs are entirely female.

However, it took me quite a long time to become aware of this, for it was not immediately noticeable until I was past my masculinized puberty. Though I was never able to impregnate a woman, my lower genitalia was – after an inordinately long time (ie. the age of 18 or 19) – able to produce enough testosterone to disturb me to the point at which I needed to shave my face once every week or so lest I grow detectable hair there. I sympathized with "visible" women of course, and embraced feminism, despite the limitations of mid- to late-20th Century Women's Lib. However, I otherwise did all I could to be the man the world apparently wanted me to be.

---

450 Please note that I am in no way suggesting what the reader may now be pondering; the Immaculate Conception and miraculous Virgin Birth of Jesus Christ required neither artificial insemination nor Caesarian techniques, nor did the Seed originate from Mary herself!!!

Thus it was that at 15 I found myself sitting in the library of Cardinal Newman[451] High School, trying desperately to identify with the male perspective while reading a book with very distinct attitudes regarding the respective sexes...and berating myself for not being entirely able to do so. How dare I think of myself as "female at heart" simply because I was gentle, docile, submissive, sensitive, caring, peaceful, nurturing, and longed to bear a child in the womb I was for whatever reason denied? For some hypocritical reason, though our society was so advanced that it was considered wrong to hate people based upon their race or sex, it was apparently still OK to hate people for being what I was...whatever I was.

Two years earlier I recalled that my mother had once told me a story about an apparently-male child who had such a high level of female hormones that she actually had begun to grow breasts, and that gave me a small sense of hope. So it was that on a midsummer afternoon when I was thirteen, seven months before my Confirmation, I worked up the courage to ask God to grant me this deep desire. I distinctly remember saying,

> "LORD, I pray that I have more female hormones than male hormones so that I can show the world that I really am a woman."[452]

Yet by the time I had left my sixteenth year it seemed certain that God would not answer my prayer; such a request was simply too impossible...and though with God all things are possible, surely a wretched abominable monstrosity such as myself was unworthy of

---

451 Perhaps this was ironically appropriate considering the angelic (his beatification was proclaimed by Pope Benedict XVI on 19/09/2010) quality of the Cardinal for whom this school was named: Blessed John Henry Newman, whose sermons were described as "so simple and transparent, yet so subtle withal; so strong yet so tender; the grasp of a strong man's hand, combined with the trembling of a woman's heart...laying the most penetrating finger on the very core of things". ([Wikipedia] Roden, p. 16).

452 I beseech you to consider Psalm 38, which I stumbled upon accidentally while seeking another (Psalm 34), but which I believe speaks true to the plight of the trans community (esp. vv. 7, 11, and 15).

such miraculous mercy. I resolved to thoroughly banish all femininity from body, mind, and soul. I even lost the ability to shed tears of sorrow.

I was not the first transwoman to pray to God to let me awaken in the body of a woman, nor even in this time of apostasy shall I likely be the last. However, such is the nature of this world's malleability[453] that one must be certain that that for which one asks will be granted.

> "Now faith is the substance of things hoped for, the evidence of things not seen." (Hebrews 11:1, KJV)

I did not receive a womb, nor did my breasts fully mature until I had been on a hormone-balancing regimen for months. However, even before I had begun this regimen my "oddly-shaped" (as I had previously noted them to be) nipples had grown into functional female ones. Despite my unnaturally-high masculine hormone levels (low for a man, yet high for a woman), my breasts had already begun to grow and could apparently (under certain circumstances according to my physician) lactate. Thus I am quite pleased that the word *feminine* stems from the Latin word for woman/female: *femina,* which means literally "she who suckles." Thus I am – according to the actual definition of the source word – quite female.[454]

> "Even by the God of thy father, who shall help thee; and by the Almighty [ידש לא *El Shaddai*], who shall bless thee with blessings of heaven above, blessings of the deep that lieth under, blessings of the breasts [דש *shadayim*], and of the womb [מחר *racham*]:" (Genesis 49:25, KJV)

Life was very confusing for both Jenna and myself; people rely upon that which they can see and touch, and when one's thoughts and feelings speak of something that cannot be immediately proven in material terms it is often impossible to inspire belief...even within oneself. Every piece of physical evidence of our femaleness was further proof that we were not insane. For me it was quite a relief when I learned that I would not

453 Matthew 21:21.

454 Harper, Doublas. *Online Etymology Dictionary.* http://www.etymonline.com/index.php?term=feminine Retrieved September 17th of 2012.

actually be able to impregnate a woman as a man would; I found the alternative frightening. In terms of primary sexual characteristics (ie. bottom genitalia) I may have been not unlike a eunuch. However, in terms of secondary sexual characteristics (top genitalia) and primary components of the brain I was slowly becoming a fully-functional female, even before taking medication to balance out my physical and mental hormone levels and place them safely within the female range.

The process which produces transwomen such as we can of course work in reverse, causing the brain to masculinize in the womb while the body remains female (as all mammalian embryos originally are female). However, the transman's trial is quite a bit different from that which is endured by transwomen. Since the human body is especially receptive to testosterone, hormones are far more effective at masculinizing feminized bodies than vice-versa. For example, I knew a transman who went to the same endocrinologist as I and began hormone replacement therapy the very day that I did. Upon that day, he looked and sounded simply like a short-haired, haggard young woman dressed in men's clothes. However, when I met him again little over a year later he was deep-voiced, bearded, and muscled to the point of being unrecognizeable.

The technology available to reproduce sexual characteristics that cannot be naturally "grown" is far more primitive where male genitalia are concerned, however. It is a sad thing that so many countries still require sex-reassignment surgery for legal change of gender marker, for modern medicine can construct a working womb no more than it can a pair of fully-functional testes. Still, medical technology has placed far more emphasis upon assembling a vagina than it has a penis, and has met with considerably more success in that endeavour. This has led to the popular phrase, "Transmen pass [ie appear to be normal members of their desired gender] on the streets; transwomen pass in the sheets" (however little comfort this may provide).

With the consideration of the relative rarity, variety and often invisibility of the conditions which produce "transsexuals" comes the understanding of why there is no specified method of dealing with us in the Bible; its inspired authors were concerned no more with them than with aerospace engineering (as both were generally discovered approximately 1,500 years after the Bible was written). Thus, unlike with homosexuality, there was no attempt therein to condemn, embrace, or explain "transsexualism" (as it is called in some medical circles) in any of its manifestations.

Being Trans versus Being Sexual

Transsexual/transgendered is the anomalous T associated with the LGB (Lesbian, Gay, Bisexual) community, for it was (and in some areas still is) inaccurately assumed to be related to sexual attraction. This unfortunately has led to some truly vile misconceptions of transpeople as sexually disturbed to the point of madness; that to satisfy our desires we must envision ourselves as a gender contrary to what all external (in the case of those less fortunate and more frequent specimens) evidence would indicate. As is so often the case, a lack of understanding is responsible for this mistake. The accurate term for sexual or erotic interest in cross-dressing is "transvestic fetishism", the occurrence of which is uncorrelated to that of gender identity disorder and – intriguingly enough – has been described only in heterosexual men.[455]

A possible explanation for this was suggested earlier: due in part to the fact that sex does indeed sell, young men (and those encouraged to think like them) tend to find themselves inundated with exposure to the sexualization of the gender to which they are presumed to be attracted. This age-old attraction led to the potential mental association of anything visually and tactilely feminine with such sexualization. The result is that men tend to view women's dress in terms of either modesty or "sexiness" (and in some cases I have encountered they actually find a clothed woman more erotically appealing than a naked one).

Acclaimed author James Joyce states in his 1918 novel *Ulysses*[456] that "Fashion [is a] part of their [women's] charm."[457] Later in the

[455] American Psychiatric Association. (2000). *Diagnostic and Statistical Manual of Mental Disorders* (4th ed., text rev.). Washington, DC: Author.

[456] Considered the #1 best English-language novel of the 20th Century according to the Modern Library Editorial Board of authors and critics. http://www.modernlibrary.com/top-100/100-best-novels/ Retrieved Wednesday, October 31st of 2012.

[457] Ulysses. Episode 13, Nausicaa (named for the girl who assists Ulysses in

book, he delves quite graphically into transvestic fetishism and its sister indulgence: feminization. In the sexual sense, feminization is defined as...

> "enforcing behaviors on a male submissive or slave that are normally associated with a woman. For example: cross-dressing him in female clothes....[It] Can be used for humiliation play or for empowerment depending on the context."
>
> – Morpheous, *How to Be Kinky: A Beginner's Guide to BDSM* (an acronym for Bondage/Discipline, Dominance/ Submission, and/or Sadism/Masochism)[458]

Joyce has his *Ulysses* protagonist, Leopold Bloom, kneel before brothel-keeper Bella Cohen – even calling her "Empress" – while various items of her attire such as her fan and boot (or "THE HOOF" in the text itself) are so fetishized that they are actually given speaking parts(!).[459] Once Bloom has begun being referred to with feminine pronouns and is "unmanned...a thing under the yoke", (s)he is told in detail how (s)he is to be dressed, including being "laced with cruel force into vicelike corsets of soft dove coutille, with whalebone busk"[460] to add elements of masochism to Bloom's submissive role. This scene continues for quite some time, yet the essence of Joyce's take on

---

Homer's tale). p. 480.

458 Morpheous. *How to Be Kinky: A Beginner's Guide to BDSM.* 2008, Green Candy Press. p. 69.

459 *Ulysses.* Episode 15, *Circe* (named for the deceptive sorceress of transmutation). pp. 642-644.

460 Ibid. p. 647. In the modern resurgence in popularity the corset now enjoys as an openly-fetishistic device, the busk (corset front) and stays (boning) are best made of spiral steel rather than whalebone, and it is used primarily as an outergarment as women tend to wear considerably less clothing than once we did. In the Turn-of-the-20th-Century time in which Joyce sets *Ulysses*, however, the corset was still an undergarment of severe shapewear common to women of the upper classes as it had been for centuries, and thus it if anything had even more potency as fetish fuel than it does now (albeit somewhat more secretly so).

transvestic fetishism and feminization is most effectively displayed in the passage immediately following Bloom's being purchased by "*Caliph Haroun Al Raschid*"[461]. By this point, Bloom's dominant whoremistress Bella has been masculinized as Bello by Joyce. From this position, she gives him an exceedingly-detailed account of how to use every piece of feminine clothing to his alluring advantage, from the peep of white pantalette visible beneath a daringly short skirt to the emerald-gartered transparent stockings to the smooth mincing walk upon four-inch Louis XV heels. While utilizing feminine imagery in effort to make Bloom more attractive to men, Bello's monologue is laced with references to Pagan cultures in which unrestrained homosexuality was common; the bend of Bloom's movement is described as "Grecian", and he is instructed to pander to the men's "Gomorrahan vices."[462]

Of course, the sexualized aspects of femininity are based upon conventional social images of women as filtered through the male gaze (or that of anyone else sharing such fetishes). In the realm of the truly misogynistic, the Marquis de Sade's *120 Days of Sodom* also contains some instances of transvestic fetishism and forced feminization (and de Sade does what he can to associate them with far darker debaucheries), but as always while Joyce is thought-provoking de Sade merely manages to be disturbing and crude. Still, as we now have both the Sodomite and the Gomorrahan represented in these two authors, one can understand the demonizing effect of affiliation with the sexual; here lies such "guilt by association" as that about which Abraham was so worried in Genesis 18:23-32 ("**Abraham Intercedes for Sodom**").

Upon that subject, I have also encountered the assumption that those who transvest are detrimental to the cause of feminism. The argument is that if the traditional garb of females is associated with the sexual, then females will be more at risk of being viewed as objects and inspirers

---

461 "Aaron the Upright/Just/Rightly Guided," an 8th-Early 9th-Century monarch of a region that encompassed modern Iraq. Haroun is known for establishing the legendary library *Bayt al-Hikma* (Arabic for "House of Wisdom"; note the sound similar to the Hebrew *Chockma(th)*) and having many stories of *The Book of One Thousand and One Nights* related to his magnificent court or to he himself.

462 *Ulysses*. Episode 15, *Circe*, p. 652.

of the immoral (specifically of the sin of lust). This particular anti-transvestite concern, I have found, is due to the caricatured sexualization of women found in drag shows and among "female impersonators" and the like. The condition of "transsexualism", as it is better understood as a physical condition than a mental one, is most certainly not of the like. However, we ourselves do often stumble into such territory for a time, as we seek any means by which to express our true selves in a society set against it.

Transitioning: A Journey of Self-Discovery

It is highly important to be aware that gender expression is by no means limited to the physical realm. The mental journey of understanding takes far longer and is far more difficult, and early on we are desperate for any scraps we might be given.

The increasingly-popular pastime of role-playing, for instance, is one often indulged in by the trans community. Games that incorporate this provide an especially-desirable form of escapism, whether in the classic pen-and-paper format or in the form of video games such as celebrity transman Chaz Bono often played prior to his transition. Such games are very appealing, for they allow one to take on a fantasy identity as a member of one's secret gender without immediately drawing condemnation from one's peers...if one is careful.

My own first experience with such things came in the late autumn of my 13th year. I became inordinately excited over the prospect of playing *Dungeons & Dragons*[463] because a) one was actually permitted to play as a female character and b) the older boys were doing it and thus it was socially-acceptable (a number of my friends had already joined in and were trying to coerce me into using dice as is normal, though I found the concept abhorrent). So far as I remember, however, none of the boys were playing female characters, for to do so was to invite *incessant*

---

[463] Specifically, this was the 2nd Edition of the *Advanced* version of the game, which I found particularly attractive due to its historical references to Paladins and whatnot. As for those who might now fear for my soul, I shall mention that I did later actually confess this to a priest. While he was proud not to have played the game himself, he did not consider doing so a serious sin.

fantasy sexual harrassment. Thus, so careful was I to avoid a *faux pas* that my first character was a maiden knight whose hair was just short enough and whose armour was just concealing enough to render her apparent sex ambiguous.

Despite all of this having taken place in Saint Agatha Catholic Elementary School, I hadn't the foggiest idea who Joan of Arc was, or who Eowyn from *The Lord of the Rings* was either, for that matter. So far as I knew, I had taken the concept of the "androgynous woman in plate armour" from the armoured interstellar bounty hunter Samus Aran of the *Metroid* series (and possibly Princess Leia from *Star Wars Episode VI: The Return of the Jedi* to a lesser extent). I thought that transposing this androgyne into a Mediaeval setting was simply the result of my sheer clever *brilliance* (in addition to not hating you, I am also fairly certain that God has quite a sense of humour). However, so vain and proud to even be *playing* a female character was I that I did not have her wear a face-concealing helmet...and thus it was perhaps for the best that I couldn't draw terribly well....

This is very common for transwomen, and one area where they do bear similarity with gays. Dwelling among men, it is important that one removes oneself from the sexual, so that one shall not be desired or abused by one's peers. In a sense it is the more militant side of the mermaid fascination also common among transpeople[464], which exists

[464] This is so common in fact that a U.K.-based transgender support charity has actually called itself *Mermaids.* Its focus is upon transgender children and its website is http://www.mermaidsuk.org.uk (Retrieved Sunday, January 26th of 2014). The mermaids (both professional and recreational) on mernetwork.com are also very trans-friendly. It has even been suggested that *The Little Mermaid* is (perhaps unintentionally) "an allegory for transgenderism." Though it is at best semi-serious, this interpretation was offered by Donna Dickens at *Buzzfeed rewind,* in an April 9th of 2013 article titled "14 Epiphanies You'll Have Re-Watching 'The Little Mermaid'". It is found at http://www.buzzfeed.com/donnad/14-epiphanies-youll-have-re-watching-the-little-mermaid and was retrieved Sunday, January 26th of 2014. In a very-similar vein, Disney's first feature-film foray into mermaids, 1984's *Splash!,* gave inspirational support for the trans community in a semi-serious remark. At one point Tom Hank's character indicates to Daryl Hannah's mermaid "Madison" that he would still love her even if her secret were that she "were once a man."

not only due to the beauty of the mermaid but also to its annihilation of the damning lower genitalia. The armour was thus both figurative and literal.

Of course, this concealment was all rendered moot anyway once I learned that one was obliged to place one's gender marker on one's identification (called a "Character Sheet" in gaming) even in the realm of fantasy; which is a problem that plagues transpeople quite often in the real world. This is especially troublesome when we face the results of more dangerous real-world self-expression, as it can result in our imprisonment.

Due in part to often being refused employment on the basis of gender identity (26% report being fired because of it), transpeople sometimes find themselves in less-than-legal situations. 16-33 percent of transpeople as a whole are in prison (as opposed to less than 4 percent of the general U.S. population). There they have found it necessary to stage protests for such basic rights as "the return of appropriately gendered clothes that had been taken from them, [and] an end to [sexual] harassment by staff..."[465]) In some regions transwomen are not legally allowed to even be placed in the women's area, and are instead imprisoned with men.

Every expression of transition is a part of our desperate quests to truly know ourselves, the goals of which must be achieved upon even the most basic level of identity. After all, the first categorization, classification, and judgement pronounced upon an infant is summed up in that question asked when first the baby emerges from the womb: "Is it a boy or a girl?"

There are social conventions which are especially challenged by transmen. As we are by now quite well-aware, for a female to don traditionally-masculine garb and perform traditionally-masculine roles – imitation being, after all, the sincerist form of flattery – is considered empowering and even desirable in a traditionally-partriarchal society. However, for an apparently-female individual to actually seek to *be* a man is heavily frowned upon. Such a desire can be seen as threatening by "normal" males, as it destroys all barriers between men and the

---

465 *In These Times With Liberty and Justice for All...* "Trans Prisoners Fight Abuse" by Toshio Meronek. November 10th, 2012. http://inthesetimes.com/article/13990/trans_prisoners_fight_abuse

'women' whom the transmen originally appeared to be. It also may even be viewed as a sort of 'betrayal' by some women; that somehow being female is not "good enough"; that actually becoming male might even be the ultimate step by which to completely break the glass ceiling through the assumption of traditionally masculine roles (despite the fact that transpeople generally have the most difficulty acquiring any sort of work).

Such are, however, merely social attitudes that do not run nearly so deep as a transperson's desire to be properly recognized as his or her true gender. However, the fact that a traditionally-partriarchal society places such emphasis on the supposed superiority of manly roles, and that – especially within the past hundred years – women have been increasingly encouraged to fill such roles, has caused considerable confusion in terms of what exactly constitutes a "gender identity."

I recall one particularly alarming example from the same transgender support group in which I first met Jenna. A short-haired woman with a moderately-deep voice and a penchant for pants had been with us for several months, and had all the while identified as a transman. However, one night she announced to us that, rather than beginning to take testosterone and perhaps even undergo a mastectomy as she had been poised to do, she had instead determined that she was happy simply being "a butch lesbian." Her attitude was actually apologetic, which prompted me to remind her that we weren't going to "cast her out" due to her nonconformity to our specific social circle. To know oneself is one of the greatest challenges which one may face, and the loving counsel she had received had enabled her to do just that...in a way that could never have been accomplished with ostracization from her community and the limited comfort of black-market hormones.

Briefly examining that latter subject, one might wonder exactly how much of an effect additional male or female hormones might have upon a brain that has already been 'hard-wired' as that of one sex or the other at its very core. The hormones cannot alter the brain itself, but they do offer the serenity which comes from chemical balance. In addition to electrical signals, the endocrine/hormone system is the most important influential factor upon the human body, and the body does follow the mind.

Hormone replacement therapy, when properly administered, usually has considerable noticeable effect. In the interests of science, I posted my physical transition in the form of a time-lapse video on *YouTube*;[466] as I am rather skinny the primarily-visible occurrences consisted of a major loss of muscle tissue and a more minor redistribution of fatty tissue (to the buttocks, hips, and breasts).

As to how much the hormones may alter one's mental attitude I cannot say with absolute certainty, even when delving into my own personal experience. However, I can offer what may be gleaned from the one specific example which I found most striking. When I first saw the titular character of Shakespeare's *Henry V* go to war over an insult from the French *Dauphin*, I did so but shortly prior to receiving testosterone-reducing hormone therapy. King Henry's motives seemed somewhat sensible then. However, they do not seem so to me any longer, and it rather shocks me that I ever thought otherwise. One may take from this whatever one wishes.

The transwoman who has concealed her identity most of her life faces confusion when she transitions as an adult and, reaching within herself to whom she really is, finds a terrified little girl. We are thus left to explore what society's perceptions of femaleness are and use them to help us as we try, in a sense, to grow up in mere moments. I know many who have either pounced upon the most flamboyantly feminine things available or who settle for a 'butch' exterior, unwilling or unable to leave behind their male personae. I once saw one who, perhaps desiring distance from the label of 'transsexual', called him/herself instead a "gender illusionist". S/he believed that the 1950s offered the height of the feminine image. I myself found solace with Saint Theresa of Lisieux. She both embraces the child aspect of the human experience and represents the sort of brilliant and gentle woman who helped save the world.

---

466 "Male to Female REAL Transsexual Time-Lapse Transformation Full" Tiamat Michelle Hart, December 24th of 2009. http://www.youtube.com/watch?v=iONM3BZDiPI Retrieved Friday, July 5th of 2013. It is one of a number of videos documenting my transition/development which together have received approximately 2 million views.

Thus being trans is both quite complicated and quite different from being among those who cross-dress merely for entertainment or sexual gratification. We are happy for any evidence discovered which helps explain why our bodies and minds are as they are. Transwomen (and transmen) are however just as prone to being duped by the media as any other women (or men), and as I have already discussed to some degree, we are if anything more so. Transboys, forced into the roles of girls, find the 'liberation' of taking on roles reserved for males all the more appealing. Transgirls, of course, have the opposite experience. When the 'other boys' we were encouraged to play with were looking at the female characters catering to them (usually visually and supposedly unintentionally) as potential sexual partners, we were instead looking at them as potential role models.

In my case, this eventually resulted in an instance wherein my adopted masculine guise seemed to fuse with my natural sympathy with the female sex. I had become a life guard for the Red Cross and thus found myself surrounded by noble souls who had chosen a noble profession. After all, life guards are not only vigilant rescuers and healers, but they also often go on to become paramedics, law-enforcement officers, or firefighters. Still, they were nevertheless not immune to the oversexualization of society, and in this instance they were all male save for my close friend whom I shall call Alana. While looking at an erogenous but mainstream magazine, the male life guards asked me if I would "do her" (ie. have sex with one of the women pictured therein). Trying to avoid appearing "gay" I replied, "Maybe... after getting to know her first." Alana, a beautiful co-worker of nineteen who had quietly endured such macho displays even to the point of nigh-sexual harassment, then placed her arm upon me and told me something I would find very awkward indeed:

"I'm glad there are still men like you left in the world."

This positive response seemed almost strange because I favoured the supposedly more-archaic chivalrous attitude over the more modern and oblivious "if you want to be like us, you must act like us" attitude.

I must admit that I found her statement perplexing. I was a shy twentysomething virgin nerd merely maintaining the "Paladin" persona I had fully adopted when I was seventeen. I was then courting a shy poetess whom I shall call Catherine[467], and gained quite the reputation for chivalry, as I enjoyed nothing else which was remotely masculine. As for my male personality, it was (and, I worried, obviously) a fabrication of sorts. I was endeavouring to be the kind of man I myself wanted to marry: strong and intelligent without abusing those gifts, protectively passionate of his woman without stifling her, and able to restrain his passion not because of any sort of weakness, but because its intense and possessive force was held in check by the might of his will[468].

A bisexual female Roman Catholic friend of mine once replied to this, "If you ever find a man like that, could you send him my way?" However, these I believe are qualities that Jesus Christ exemplifies infinitefold, though I could not honestly claim to have fully possessed them myself. The psychological voyage of the "transsexual" requires much consideration and reconciliation of how much of one is nature and how much of one is nurture, and the dissonance this generates for a time in the psyche is one of the reasons the condition was originally thought to be psychological in nature.

This is also the reason why some religions still consider it a choice. Sadly, the most prominent example of such seems to be the Roman Catholic Church, however this is mostly due to the trans community's association with the homosexual community. Hence, when delivering his 2012 Christmas address to the Vatican, then-Pope Benedict XVI described the 'gay marriage' matter of France (and Britain and the U.S.) as people manipulating their God-given identities to suit their sexual choices. It is in this context that His Holiness suggested that people are

---

467 This high-school relationship was I believe a powerful example of the ability to love without any physical component, for neither Catherine nor I were lesbians. She shared my taste for escapist/romantic fantasy, however, and as a result much of our courtship consisted of us writing poetry, role-playing scenarios and fanfiction to one another. When I was 19 she made me a Christmas gift of a poem she had written entitled, "The Hero," but I could not be certain what to make of it as she had originally credited it to her gothic and brooding elven bard named Devin Ravenlocks....

468 A tall order to fill perhaps, yet no more so than all the extremes to which women have gone in the quest for desirability to the opposite sex over the centuries. Perhaps like Christine de Pisan, Alana enjoyed the ideals of chivalry.

disputing the idea that bodily identity serves as a defining element of the human being. He said that God made man and woman as a duality, an essential aspect of what being human is all about, and that man is treating the deplorable manipulation of nature as a fundamental choice. This is most ironic, for every true "transsexual" knows that we have no choice at all.

If I now stood before the Archbishop of Paris or Pope Emeritus Benedict himself, I would do what I imagine most of my trans- readers would do. I would tell them how unchangeable gender truly is. I would tell them how I spent nearly 30 years trying to change my gender to that of a male. I would tell them of how bittersweet it was to hear Mass and receive Communion each Sunday as a child when my appearance and my name felt like such a falsehood in the eyes of the Most High. In short, I would tell them that they're right.

I have done so. Not before the Archbishop of Paris (yet) or Pope Emeritus Benedict (who is now cloistered), but before a high-ranking Priest of my own Diocese. He has accepted me for who I am, in the spirit of the new Pope whose Patron Saint I share, and is even helping me to join the Carmelite Order.[469] There is hope. It *will* get better; for in the long run, the Church is not truly opposed to science.

Understanding of the LGBT Community versus Nazi Barbarism

"Transsexualism" is a clinical term coined by German physician Magnus Hirschfeld, who also earlier invented the word "transvestite" (in 1910). It would later be developed by his colleague Harry Benjamin, a Berlin-born Ashkenazi[470] Jewish endocrinologist who moved to the United States with the outbreak of World War I. Benjamin became

469 This offer was actually requested and received on the same day that Saint Theresa of Lisieux requested it of the Pope (ie. November the 20th), yet this was perhaps coincidence.

470 After Ashkenaz of Genesis 10:3, a kingdom of whom were called together with Ararat and Minni against Babylon in Jeremiah 51:27. Other Ashkenazi Jews include Sigmund Freud, Albert Einstein, mathematician Emmy Noether, nuclear physicist Lise Meitner, Franz Kafka, and Anne Frank.

involved with transsexualism and intrigued by its difference from sexual classifications.

Benjamin later related that his first encounter with a transperson was due to sexologist Alfred Kinsey, who worked primarily with homosexuals. Kinsey had come to California and consulted with Benjamin regarding a very effeminate 'boy', who had stated that he (sic) wished to become a girl, and who was supported by his (sic) mother in this. Kinsey had never encountered such a case, and it was even new to Benjamin, for it went far beyond transvestism (which was by then recognized). This first case helped the concept of transsexualism to gradually take shape in Benjamin's mind, and he introduced the term in 1954. In the meantime, the 'boy' received "female" hormones that "had a calming effect."[471]

Harry Benjamin was inspired to create the "Benjamin Scale" for the purpose of distinguishing transvestic fetishists from transsexuals and trying to understand both[472]. He would also be instrumental in many transitions, including that of Christine Jorgensen, who became quite famous in the 1950s after receiving the procedure[473]. However, in his modest honesty he credited his colleague and old friend Magnus Hirschfeld with making transvestites visible as a special group, while he himself helped to distinguish the transsexuals from them. As a result, the social acceptance of transpeople has been greatly helped, though as according to Benjamin:

> "I have also seen how this whole hopeful science fell victim to Nazi barbarism. Still, it came back to life here in America, but also in Europe. It is simply indispensable."[474]

---

471 Erwin J. Haeberle's interview with Harry Benjamin on the occasion of his (Benjamin's) 100th birthday. Published in "*Sexualmedizin*", vol. 14, 1/1985. Retrieved from the *Archive for Sexology* http://www2.hu-berlin.de/sexology/GESUND/ARCHIV/TRANS_B5.HTM on September 21st of 2012.

472 Benjamin, H. (1966). *The Transsexual Phenomenon.* New York: The Julian Press, p. 22.

473 ChristineJorgensen.org (2006). http://www.christinejorgensen.org/MainPages/Home.html Retrieved September 22nd of 2012.

474 Erwin J. Haeberle's interview with Harry Benjamin. "*Sexualmedizin*", vol. 14, 1/1985.

Magnus Hirschfeld, also a Jew, remained in Germany and thus was not nearly so fortunate. Despite support from such prominent people as Albert Einstein, he was unsuccessful in his efforts to overturn Section/Paragraph 175 of the German penal code, which punished homosexual acts with imprisonment[475]. He apparently even considered exposing some of the prominent secretly-homosexual lawmakers who had remained silent...until the Nazi Party seized power and intensified the very law he was trying to repeal. Now the law no longer even required homosexuals to touch one another to be declared guilty and given – rather than the gold Star of David given to the Jews – the Pink Triangle. Now Gestapo officers had the excuse to round up homosexuals and send them to concentration camps; now a simple confession of love was sufficient incrimination for them[476].

Additionally, the world's first Institute of Sexology, which Hirschfeld founded and was designated director for life, was plundered by a mob of Nazi "students" on May 6, 1933 (just over three months after Hitler had come to power in Germany). On the famous book-burning day of May 10, 1933, its library was consigned to the flames along with the works of many other "Un-German" authors (such as Sigmund Freud). After its closure, the institute was reopened as a Nazi office building, housing various antisemitic organizations until its destruction by allied bombing raids.[477]

---

475 § 175. "www.Schwulencity.de – beginning (or an attempt) to a historic gay Labyrinth" <translated from German by Google> http://www.schwulencity.de/strafrecht175.html Retrieved 24/09/2012.

476 Heger, Heinz. *The Men with the Pink Triangle: The True, Life-And-Death Story of Homosexuals in the Nazi Death Camps.* Translated by David Fernbach. 1980, Gay Men's Press, London, England. pp. 4; 104; 8. Whereas Jews were forced to wear a golden Star of David to identify them, homosexuals were instead required to wear an inverted pink triangle. In those cases in which a Jew was also homosexual (such as would have applied to the woman who helped me legally change my name to Tiamat or the 'David' I mentioned in the previous chapter as an example of a homosexual partnership) the two would be combined so that the pink triangle actually formed the frontal portion of the Star of David.

477 *Archive for Sexology.* "Magnus Hirschfeld (1868-1935). The Institute for Sexology (1919-1933)". http://www2.hu-berlin.de/sexology/GESUND/

It is lamentably true that the common mainstream association between homo- and trans-sexuals has been both boon and bane. The camaraderie transpeople enjoy as a part of the LGBT community has been useful to a group whose members often feel very much alone, and it has also meant that as people gained more awareness of homosexuality, they also eventually became curious as to the truth about transpeople. It is, however, important that people understand that sexual preference and gender identity are two vastly different things. Gays, lesbians, and bisexuals desire social acceptance and legal equality without any thought of need for a 'cure.' Due to the gender incongruity within our own bodies, we of the trans community do indeed desire a cure; yet due to the fact that the root of our identity is at the core of our brains, the only cure is either to allow our bodies to be changed to the point at which balance is achieved...or to exterminate us.

I suspect that I need not mention which of the two solutions I favour; and which one God commands against[478].

However, due to the large number of transpeople who are for whatever reason attracted to their identified sex, the LGB association is often appropriate. Being mistakenly associated with what were once (and still at times are) considered "psychosexual disorders" for a physical abnormality, however, has been a tremendously archaic disservice to us.

Bible Verses Used Against Us (and Against Saint Joan of Arc)

It is not accurate to assume that these factors are exclusive cause for our ostracisation, however; there are two passages in the Bible which, when wielded hamfistedly enough, have been misinterpreted as follows: I) 1 Corinthians 6:9...

> "Know ye not that the unrighteous shall not inherit the kingdom of God? Be not deceived: neither fornicators, nor idolaters, nor adulterers, nor **effeminate**, nor abusers of themselves with mankind," (KJV)

ARCHIV/MHINS.HTM Retrieved September 24th of 2012.

478 Exodus 20:13; the Fifth Commandment.

Such a terrifying passage this appears to be! It seems that, if interpreted broadly enough, some of its condemnations could apply to virtually *anyone!* I spent literally decades frightened of transgressing this vague decree. *I mustn't behave differently from the boys, even if they are being unkind to the girls and/or to one another; it might be deemed "effeminate." I mustn't cross my legs a certain way; it might be deemed "effeminate." I mustn't dress in women's clothing...except when the 'other' boys are dressing in women's clothing*[479]*...and then I must act as they do and thus pretend to don such garb as mockery rather than flattery of femininity; to do otherwise might be deemed "effeminate." I mustn't allow my spectrum of expressed emotions to extend beyond mirth and anger – though as I didn't like anger I seldom expressed that either, thus earning the nickname "Spock" – or shed tears; that might be deemed "effeminate." I mustn't reveal my desire to watch that new television show* ***Touched By An Angel****; it looks like it would be deemed "effeminate."* The list went on (and on), yet we dared not question the Sacred Scripture; it was necessary that we simply submit *(though not in the social/relationship sense; that might be deemed "effeminate"....)*

However, it appears that we were indeed deceived; not by the Sacred Scripture, but due to a mistranslation of it. Apparently, its 17th Century translators had a grasp of Ancient Greek that was no more perfect than that which they held on Ancient Hebrew.

The King James Version of the Bible translates the original Greek word *malakos* as "effeminate" (perhaps due to a limited understanding of Corinthian culture at the time of translation), which probably seems strange to even a casual reader. It does not make sense to use an adjective in place of a noun; after all, the Fifth Commandment does not read "Thou shalt not homicidal". When actually used as a noun, "*malakos*" refers specifically to male (usually boy) prostitutes. As a result of this new

[479] Perhaps I should clarify: the cross-dressing in question was for a Christmas play (as opposed to a Christmas *pageant*) at Saint Agatha Catholic Elementary School when I and my classmates were twelve years of age, for it was a very confusing season (specifically, the production was a modern re-telling of Dickens' *A Christmas Carol*...liberally reinterpreted). It may be noted, however, that only one of the interested boys was actually *required* to wear those stiletto-heeled pumps/court shoes....

understanding, the word is translated as such in the New American Holy Bible. Thus Saint Paul the Apostle was not condemning effeminacy but rather prostitutive pedophilia; quite a different (and more reasonable) concern indeed!

However, there is another verse wielded against transpeople, and indeed it was wielded against me by a stranger upon the internet when he attempted to vex me with the following statements:

> "You talked about chastity, which is certainly a great thing. Hypothetically if one can have a brain "stuck" at opposite sex (I still need to read some Church docs about the whole thing), how come you're dressing as a woman etc. I'm pretty sure that was never allowed."

II) Deuteronomy 22:5...

> "The woman shall not wear that which pertaineth unto a man, neither shall a man put on a woman's garment: for all that do so *are* abomination unto the LORD thy God." (KJV)

Oh my...this verse indeed takes being a "slave of fashion" to the ultimate level; I am glad it wasn't wielded against us those one or two times it was transgressed back when we were children at Saint Agatha Elementary! Blessed Cardinal Newman High School was similarly open-minded when I was a student there back in the 1990s. When a teacher first described the school uniform to us, she casually mentioned to the student body that it was well for boys who wanted to wear pleated skirts like the girls. When I mentioned her statement elsewhere, however, my listener amended the teacher's statement with "Not if they want to live!"

Indeed, Deuteronomy 22:5 is another passage open to an immense range of interpretation, which could even be so broad as to condemn such things as men wearing rugged Scottish kilts and/or women wearing delicate harem pants, depending upon the attitude toward fashion of any given society at any given time.

However, the word "abomination" (הבעות *tow'ebah*) is used again, which indicates that its sinfulness is due to an affiliation with idolatric practices. This is most likely due to association with pagan ritual cross-dressing, which was often intimately connected with ritual castration. *The Syrian Goddess* by Lucian, translated by Herbert A. Strong and John Garstang in 1913, offers specific examples of a variety of such procedures and their motivations. One such motivation came from Attes, a priest of the Titan Rhea, wife of Chronos and mother of Zeus. When Rhea deprived Attes of his powers to teach her mysteries, he ceased to dress as a man and assumed the garb and appearance of a woman. He then roamed across the land and performed his mysterious rites, all the while narrating his sufferings and chanting praises to Rhea. The men called "Galli" of Grecian temples were said to castrate themselves in imitation of Attes, and in honour of Rhea.[480]

Lucian offers another explanation for this procedure. An Assyrian named Combabus, fearing that while they were together building a temple he and the king's wife Stratonice would become enamoured of one another, 'unmanned' himself. This plan was successful and the king even granted him a brazen statue of himself to stand in the temple which he helped to construct. Its form is that of a woman, but its garments are those of a man (however it is generally believed that this statue is not of Combabus himself, but rather of an Amazon who may or may not be representative of him). Castration, performed out of sympathy for Combabus, was said to be inspired by the goddess of his temple, with the intention that her lover should not be the only one to lament the loss of his virility. The wearing of women's garb is explained as being due to a foreign woman who had joined a sacred assembly and, seeing Combabus' extreme beauty when he was dressed in men's attire, became violently enamoured of him and took her own life when she discovered that he was castrated. To avoid such deception in the future, Combabus donned women's attire, as did those who imitated him. Thus those in the cult castrated themselves and ceased to wear the garb of men, instead donning women's raiment and perform women's tasks.[481]

For those who may be curious as to precisely the process through which this radical change in lifestyle came about, Lucian generously provided a graphic account just after a description of the same culture's live animal sacrificial burnings. Recalling the actions of the 'prophets

---

480 Lucian, *The Syrian Goddess*, pp. 55-56.

481 Ibid., pp. 61-66.

of Baal' with whom Elijah dealt in 1 Kings 18:28, the Galli would on certain days perform the ceremonies of the men, gashing their arms and turning their backs to be lashed before a multitude which had gathered. As the Galli sang and celebrated their orgies, frenzy fell on many of the spectators and each would, as narrated by Lucian, strip off his clothes with a shout and pick up one of a number of swords supposedly kept ready for many years for this purpose. Then he would perform a rather impressive feat, given the resulting blood loss....

> "He takes it and castrates himself and then runs wild through the city, bearing in his hands what he has cut off. He casts it into any house at will, and from this house he receives women's raiment and ornaments. Thus they act during their ceremonies of castration." (Ibid., pp. 84-85)

One can begin to understand why the Jews and early Christians were so wary of such practices as these. They offer explanation for Deuteronomy 23:1, "He that is wounded in the stones or hath his privy member cut off, shall not enter into the congregation of the LORD." (KJV; in a part which is a section focusing on the exclusion of foreign influences.) However, the wondrous Book of Wisdom again comes to the rescue of the oppressed 'abomination' in Ch. 3, v. 14, which states that the pure eunuch is blessed. This paved the path for the events of the Acts of the Apostles 8:26-39, in which one of the first converts to Christianity was an Ethiopian eunuch, and thereby provided further proof that Christians are not abominations.

It is possible that Deuteronomy 22:5 also arose from a desire to preserve traditional gender roles, and thus I must also address a possible explanation for it that was suggested to me: that the verse was intended to thwart males attempting to avoid – or females attempting to enter – military service. The words for articles (ילכ *keliy*) and man (רבג *geber*) regarding "that which pertaineth unto a man" have meanings rather focused upon the "weapons/armour" of a strong man or warrior (with an emphasis on fighting ability). In contrast, the words for "woman's" (השא *'ishshah*) "garment" (הלמש *simlah*) are focused upon a wife's raiment, including her wrapper and/or mantle. Logically, this gender-based division of clothing may have been intended to provide clearly-defined areas of defense and perpetuation for the people of Israel and their descendants via the reinforcement of traditional gender roles. However, as He so often has done, God chose a woman to (among other things) provide an exception to the rule and thus further display the versatility of humanity in general.

> "Alas! Oh! Must I pervert all order? Must I, forgetting my sex, dress myself as a man?
> '[Should I then] find myself pursued by everyone with justifiable accusations...? But, on the other hand, should the fear of men mean we do not keep faith with the God who made us?"
>
> – Joan of Arc, as portrayed in Father Fronton-du-Duc's verse tragedy *L'Histoire Tragique de la Pucelle d'Orléans*, performed September 7th of 1580)

Joan of Arc's mission was neither that of an intercessor as with Esther, nor that of an infiltrator/assassin as with Judith, nor even that of a military commander who would wield God-given elemental phenomena as with Deborah, for her military role was that of a front-line warrior leader and thus it necessitated the donning of the battle armour of the era. The costume of war was of course traditionally male garb[482] and the law of Deuteronomy 22:5 was difficult to work around. Thus the Maiden was hesitant to state by what authority she transvested, for to state that she received such permission from her visions would be to state that the Messengers therein had thus transgressed the Law (though she would eventually become so bold as to state just that).

Those who supported her in her cause were swift to excuse her from any such violation. However, those conducting her Trial of Condemnation were swift to pounce upon it. On a frigid Thursday, the 22nd of February in 1431, Joan of Arc's Second Public Examination was conducted, and even this early on the issue of her cross-dressing was brought to the fore.

---

482 *Jeanne d'Arc, son costume, son armure: essai de reconstitution.* Adrien Harmand. Paris, Editions Leroux, 1929. http://lerozier.free.fr/chausses.htm Retrieved Wednesday, January 29th of 2014.

Fortunately for history, Joan volunteered a great deal of information, especially for one in a situation wherein every word she spoke could and would be used against her. She spoke of her childhood, the Voices and visions she had received from God, and her mission, even ignoring her prosecutors' questions so that she might continue her story. She spoke of how the Voice she heard convinced her to go into France, how its information enabled her to convince the Squire Robert de Baudricourt to assist her[483], and how she was called to be taken before the Duke of Lorraine before returning to Vaucouleurs. She then casually mentioned how she departed from Vaucouleurs dressed as a man and armed only with a sword given her by Robert de Baudricourt, how she and her six companions (a Knight, a Squire, and four servants)[484] passed through the towns of Auxerre and Saint Urbain, sleeping in an Abbey and hearing Mass in the large Church counter-respectively, and that thenceforward she often heard her Voices. She was still cautious as to what she chose to reveal and when she chose to reveal it, though that would make no difference in the end. As was her policy, Joan guarded herself even as she plunged onward into the danger, yet she would eventually be caught regardless.

---

483 This is generally believed to have been due to her clairvoyant mention of a great loss suffered by Joan's gentle Dauphin, which she made on February 12th of 1429 and which referred to the Battle of Rouvray, as she reportedly stated that it was near the town of Orléans. Hundreds of kilometres away from Vaucouleurs, the Battle of *Rouvray-Saint-Denis* was also called the Battle of the Herrings as it was over food supplies en route to Orléans. When a French spy reported the emergence of 300 carts guarded by 1500 Englishmen from the city of Chartres, four thousand English and Scottish soldiers left Orléans to intercept them. The English, led by Sir John Fastolf, were able to circle their carts and wait out their enemies from that defensive position. An argument broke out between the French and Scottish commanders, Jean de Dunois and John Stuart Derneley, respectively, and the latter charged in with his cavalry independent of the French. Their enemies took advantage of this, and 600 defenders of France were lost that day.

484 These are stated in the document to be Jean de Novelomport, called de Metz, Bertrand de Poulengey, Colet de Vienne, the King's Messenger, and three servants. Robert de Baudricourt was Captain of Vaucouleurs in 1428, and afterwards knighted and made Councilor and Chamberlain to the King and Bailly of Chaumont, in 1454.

As though this were the most important thing of which Joan had just spoke, as opposed to her February 12th prediction or her *Voices from God*, her prosecuting Professor of Theology Maître Jean Beaupère asked her who counseled her to take a man's dress. The fact that the Inquisition chose to latch onto this of all things put Joan of Arc on edge, and this caused her to many times vary or avoid answers to this question. In the end she said that she charged noone for it, as she wished to protect her loyal friends, and that it was simply necessary to change her woman's garments for those of a man.[485]

This statement provided all the information which one really needs to understand why Joan of Arc dressed the way she did. However, it paints her as a logical young woman who simply behaved as was necessary to accomplish her mission from God – a mission of freedom, justice and peace for the people of France – and would not have been acceptable to the hostile English who purchased her, or to her chief prosecutor (Bishop Pierre Cauchon) who worked for them. Thus the nation's politics twisted the religious argument onto a most abominable path.

At the Third Public Examination, two days later, "Maître Jean Beaupère, a well-known Doctor" employed a different tactic. Going above and beyond the limits of Deuteronomy 22:5, he probed Joan to determine if she had any abnormalities which could suggest full gender nonconformity. This method of inquisition continues to some degree even to this day, and not only for those who express gender-nonconformist behaviour, but also for Joan herself. The question of whether or not Joan acted as she did out of deliberate defiance of the traditional female gender role has caused many to attempt to affix various labels to her – including that of "transgender."

In fact, this label would even be attached to her dear spiritual sister, Saint Theresa of Lisieux, due in no small part to her association with Joan of Arc. In acknowledgement of her place as Doctor of the Church, a position to which she had been newly-appointed by Pope John Paul II, Paul Halsall wrote a fascinating article titled, "The Transgendered

485 1903 English translation updated into modern English by Mathias Gabel of Trebur, Germany and Carlyn Iuzzolino. http://www.stjoan-center.com/Trials/sec02.html Retrieved 29/04/2013.

Sexual Imagery of St. Theresa of Lisieux" in August of 1997.[486] The primary source of this is Saint Theresa's autobiography, *The Story of a Soul*, in which she stated that in addition to her vocations of Carmelite Nun, Spouse of Jesus, and Mother of Souls, she also felt called to the vocations of Doctor of the Church, Apostle, Martyr, Warrior, and Priest. Halsall states that here the Little Flower proclaimed her *active desire* for essentially male roles (as they are usually understood culturally), and continues to use such terminology as he goes on to write....

> "She not only wants to be the receiver of Jesus, a conventionally female role, but to be a male hero for Jesus – to defend him, to present him to others, to actively *take him within [her] hands.* Theresa wants to be Jesus' husband as well as his wife."[487]

One might imagine that this gender "transgressing" could potentially get her into trouble. In fact, Halsall's essay was written partially in response to a detractor of Saint Theresa who warned that her being accepted as Doctor of the Church would promote the ordination of women, pointing out that Cardinal Ratzinger (yes, the one who was formerly Pope) had recently described it as a 'grave doctrinal error.'[488]

However, like Joan of Arc before her, Saint Theresa was able to outmanoeuvre ecclesiastical condemnation with honesty, writing that she would imitate the humble St. Francis of Assisi in refusing the sublime dignity of the Priesthood.[489] Nevertheless, Saint Theresa has occasionally been accused of association with 'gender nonconformity' of the most extreme nature. One internet commentator warned a preacher that "this saint is used as code for the transexual stronghold in the church who are eating up the Lord's children. It's code for them to enter...I don't know why the Lord allows the use of this simple saint by the enemy but HE does be forewarned..."

---

486 *The Jesuit University of New York.* http://www.fordham.edu/halsall/pwh/st-therese.asp Retrieved Sunday, July 7th of 2013.

487 Ibid.

488 Ibid.

489 Ibid.

Still, this commentator apparently believes herself to be one of God's Two Final Witnesses written of in Revelation 11:3-12, so one should probably take her statements with a grain of salt. There are those who would pluck down the very Saints from Heaven to try them for heresy over LGBT issues, yet we may rest assured that the Church Triumphant overrules all else.

The final transgender association given to one of the most feminine saints imaginable stemmed from her desire for martyrdom. In her autobiography *Story of A Soul*, Saint Theresa wrote to her Adorable Spouse Jesus that she was willing to be scourged and crucified like Him, and that she was willing to undergo all the tortures inflicted upon all the martyrs, and listed several of them as examples. However, she ended with one who had not yet even been declared Blessed: Joan of Arc. Calling Joan her dear sister, the Little Flower wrote that she too would whisper the name of Jesus at the stake.[490]

Halsall pays great attention to the order in which these martyrs are mentioned. The fact that Joan of Arc, whom he describes as being universally known for her masculine clothing and the fact that she retained it even rather than being allowed to receive communion, is the last one named is of particular importance to him. As he states, the apex of St. Theresa's desire – and the figure represented as her sister – is what he calls the most **flamboyantly transgendered** of all Christian heroines, Joan of Arc.[491]

"Flamboyant" may be an odd term to use when describing Joan of Arc (and I shall mention as an aside that in her time *all* Knights and Paladins wore bright and colourful costumes, especially in court), but like her dear sister she is a saint associated with the LGBT community. Unofficially, Joan is thought of as the patron saint of queers, Saint Theresa is thought of as the patron saint of women's liberation, and both are thought of as patron saints of the trans community. Clearly we are in excellent company!

Saint Theresa embraced her singular role without abandoning the idea that she was capable of all others, by choosing to embody the greatest of all: Love. This actually displays a unity of gender archetypes

490 Ibid.

491 Ibid., emphasis mine.

rather than exclusive restriction to one or the other; which is, in a sense, that which is undergone by those of transgender experience.

"Was Joan of Arc transgender" is actually the eighth most frequently-asked question about the 15th-Century battle saint, according to Google.[492] Transgender author Leslie Feinberg described her as "an inspirational role model – a brilliant transgender teenager leading an army of laborers into battle"[493] and suggested that "charges of transgender"[494] and its association with Pagan and heathen practices led to her execution. Transgender professor Joan Roughgarden describes Joan of Arc as "'a male-identified trans person' who chose to be burned alive rather than wear women's clothing – and who was so convincingly masculine that her executioners raked away the coals to display her naked body and remove people's doubts that she was a woman."[495]

Needless to say, there is inevitably some bias in these authors' analyses, as there has been in the more than ten thousand books which have been written on the saint. Joan of Arc is a different icon from the transperson's perspective than she is from that of the feminist or that of the consecrated maiden, but as I am all of these things myself I should be able to offer an intriguing analysis of my own. My feminist aspect wants to see Joan as a woman who is an excellent role-model for other females, my transgender aspect wants to see her (or *him?*) as a sainted champion of the LGBT cause, while my consecrated maiden aspect wonders why

---

492 The other often-asked questions are "was Joan of Arc" i) real, ii) a knight, iii) hot, iv) crazy, v) pretty, vi) beautiful, vii) insane, ix) French, and x) a Saint?" The answers are simply: i) Yes, ii) Essentially yes, complete with her own family Coat of Arms (now the Arms of her hometown *Domremy la Pucelle*), iii) Probably, despite it being the time of "the Little Ice Age", for Joan performed all of her most-significant manoeuvres in armour during the months of May-September (and yes, I know what the askers really meant by "hot"), iv) No, v) Probably, vi) Certainly on the inside; quite possibly on the outside also, vii) No, ix) Yes, and x) Yes.

493 Leslie Feinberg. *Transgender Warriors: Making History from Joan of Arc to Dennis Rodman.* Part One/Ch 4, "They Called Her 'Hommasse'" p. 36.

494 Ibid. p. 33.

495 Joan Roughgarden. "Transgender Professor Proposes a New Theory of Evolution Normalizing Homosexuality and Transsexuality." http://narth.com/docs/newtheory.html Retrieved 02/11/2012.

humanity makes such a big deal about sex in the first place. Thus my own biases counter each other and also provide a fulcrum upon which I may weigh the evidence and provide a unique understanding.

Joan of Arc, like Saint Theresa of Lisieux, is by no means the saint to have most expressed characteristics which could be considered transgender. There are a number of female saints who cross-dressed for such reasons as to gain entrance to monasteries, and perhaps the most distinctly transgender experience of the mind belongs to Saint Perpetua. Shortly before her martyrdom at the hands of the Romans in 203 A.D., she had a dream in which she was transformed into a man to better her chances of vanquishing an Egyptian warrior in gladiatorial combat. However none of these practices may be taken as effective proof that these saints were necessarily transgender.

Still, Joan of Arc is among the most well-documented saints in history, and her status as an almost-legendary icon has inspired much curiosity about her behaviour and how it might be interpreted. The prime sources of this documentation are the records of Joan's trials – both to obtain her condemnation and to nullify this condemnation 18 years later – and it is here that her apparent gender nonconformity is brought to the attention of the world. Examining it shall shed some light upon the two questions which we now have before us: how could Joan's Heavenly Council have advised her to apparently defy the Sacred Scriptures, and why was she asked such questions as this one delivered by Inquisition member and Doctor of the Church Jean Beaupère:

"When you had come into France, did you **wish to be a man**?"[496]

The question of whether or not Joan was transgender might have been answered most succinctly had she simply answered "yes" or "no" to this one. However, Joan manoeuvered her words as deftly as she did her swords, and thus she instead cryptically replied that she had answered this elsewhere. The statement to which she referred was that which I have already described – on the necessity of male garb to her mission – and by not providing a direct answer, Joan deftly evaded

[496] *Saint Joan of Arc's Trial of Condemnation*, "Third Public Examination." 1903 English translation updated into modern English by Mathias Gabel of Trebur, Germany and Carlyn Iuzzolino. http://www.stjoan-center.com/Trials/sec03.html Retrieved 29/04/2013.

a trick question. Had she answered yes, she would have nullified her status as the Maid of Lorraine/Orléans, for though her role as a military commander was generally like that of a man, no man could have been the Maid whom the prophecies foretold. Had she answered no, she would have prompted a torrent of interrogation aimed at calling into question Joan's womanhood based upon her actions. Anything she said could and would have been used against her, and thus to say as little as possible was the wisest course. This manner of interrogation is one with which most transpeople become intimately familiar, as we undergo psychological evaluation conducted by "gatekeepers"[497] to prove that we are not, in fact, mentally ill. However, had the circumstances been different, could Joan of Arc have honestly replied to the question with a "yes"?

She clearly assumed several roles which were normally reserved only for men. Joan wielded the horseman's lance, formulated military strategy and tactics, deployed troops and artillery, and even recruited mercenaries during her times of difficulty. Most iconically, she was Standard Bearer, an extremely dangerous position at the head of the army taken by those who expected to die rather than give quarter. Additionally, the immense sense of divine urgency which governed the last few years of Joan's short life must have made her seem fiery and aggressive even when compared to her fellow French military commanders. However, even as she did all this, Joan brought the touches of "the devout sex" to her work. Like the suffragettes she would one day inspire, she refused to allow gambling, prostitution, or even swearing among her troops. She herself also drank as little as possible (wine was virtually vital for hydration, for clean water was often unavailable).

Despite efforts to confuse the various waves of feminism, these particular forms of abstinence still retain some association with femininity. To draw from personal experience, up into my fourteenth year I was unique among the 'boys' at St. Agatha Elementary in that

[497] A term often used in the trans community, a "gatekeeper" is anyone – often a psychologist or physician – whose approval must be gained by a transperson if they are to progress in their gender-balancing "transition". If the transperson can prove themselves to them, the 'keeper will "open the gate" leading to opportunities such as hormone-replacement therapy or even surgery.

I seemed never to swear. When even the (other) girls drew this to my attention, I found it necessary to adopt such distasteful profanity merely to fit in. If Joan of Arc truly had wished to be a man, it is possible that she too might have adopted some of their 'manly' practices rather than make clear her distaste for them (but then, she had a stronger soul than I).

At the Trial of Condemnation, Inquisitor Beaupère was not satisfied with Joan's evasive response to the seemingly-simple question of whether or not she wanted to be a man. Thus he immediately resumed his cross-examination of the Maid's childhood for any evidence of gender nonconformity. He asked her if she had taken animals to the field, and Joan reminded him that she had already answered this as well (at the previous Examination; Joan had stated simply that she always attended to the cares of the house and did not go into the fields with the animals). She amended and elaborated upon her previous statement now, though. Joan stated that when she was bigger and had come to the years of discretion[498], she did not generally look after the animals, but she did help to take them to the meadows and to a Castle called the Island, to protect them from marauding soldiers. Joan then stated that she did not remember whether she had led them in her childhood or not.

Joan of Arc was described as a "shepherdess" by Grand Steward Raoul de Gaucourt and many others in her own time, and several works of art depict the Maid in the process of exchanging her shepherd's staff for a sword offered to her by Saint Michael. However, such an occupation was by no means unreasonable for a woman; Saint Margaret of Antioch, one of the saints who spoke to Joan, was a shepherdess herself. Still, working in the fields would suggest a lack of inclination toward working in the home, and one must be on guard when under such hostile scrutiny.

Joan had earlier pointed out that she did indeed work quite often in the home, and that she was as adept at spinning and sewing as anyone in Rouen[499] (the city of her trial and martyrdom). In fact, when confiding

---

498 *Saint Joan of Arc's Trial of Condemnation*, "Third Public Examination." Classically and by Mediaeval standards, this could have been as young as seven years of age.

499 *THE TRIAL OF JOAN OF ARC, Being the verbatim report of the proceedings*

in her first military advocate – the Knight Jean de Metz – Joan had even suggested that she preferred spinning with her mother to the arts of war to which she had been called, for the latter was "not [her] proper estate."[500] Yet as modern feminism has proven with at least limited success, her mother having taught her feminine activities did not in itself make Joan of Arc female any more than my father's being a military history buff and war games enthusiast makes me a General. It was such ambiguity that led Joan's prosecutors to wield their most tangible weapon against her.

After an unsuccessful attempt to use Joan's former practice of playing with the other village girls around a "Fairies' Tree" to accuse her of Pagan practices, the Assessors of the Inquisition asked her the final question of the Third Public Examination, which was whether she would like to have a woman's dress. Joan replied that if given one she would take it and begone; otherwise she was content with what she was wearing, for it pleased God that she wear it.[501]

That was a bold statement! In saying what she did, Joan suggested that she had received personal revelation from God that utterly defied the Mosaic Law of Deuteronomy 22:5. She was taking a stand against those she had identified as her enemies even as she attempted to discern their tactics. First assault (a blunt suggestion of gender nonconformity followed by a thinly-veiled suggestion of witchcraft), then charity (a potential offer of a woman's garment). What could have been their sinister scheme? It was obvious enough to Joan; they wished to further disarm the Maid of Lorraine. The question may have seemed more reasonable to the Inquisition, however; she should have been happy to resume women's dress now that she was no longer at war.

Yet were her days of fighting truly at an end? Yes, Joan of Arc was no longer leading people in combat, but she still needed to defend herself both mentally and physically. She did not simply call herself

---

from the Orleans Manuscript, translated by W.S. Scott, 1956, Associated Book Sellers. http://smu.edu/ijas/1431trial.html Retrieved May 5th of 2013.

500 Jean de Novelemport, Knight, called Jean de Metz. *St. Joan of Arc's Trial of Nullification: Vaucouleurs and Journey to Chinon*. http://www.stjoan-center.com/Trials/null04.html Retrieved Tuesday, October 2nd of 2012.

501 *Saint Joan of Arc's Trial of Condemnation*, "Third Public Examination".

"the Maid" to remind the people of the prophecy surrounding her; she considered the maintenance of her virginity – both bodily and spiritually – a condition of her salvation.[502]

As such, Joan's taking of men's clothes could be considered to be merely a matter of protection, whether or not these clothes literally consisted of armour. This began very early in her journey. When Joan traveled from her home village of Domrémy to the nearby Vaucouleurs, she was wearing a poor, worn red dress. It was in this woman's garb that she encountered Jean de Metz, who was quite impressed by her conviction to her divine calling. He then asked her if she could make this journey, dressed as she was, and Joan replied that she would willingly take a man's dress. He then gave her the dress and equipment of one of his men. The most logical explanation for Joan's swiftness to assume such garb is its functionality, but it is also possible that she took this as a sign or even that she had already been eager to assume male clothes.[503]

Throughout her period of imprisonment, Joan of Arc retained her male garb as much as she was able, even as she was torn between obedience to the earthly Church Militant and the Heavenly Church Triumphant. Perhaps if one who attempted to analyze Joan's life and motives had known how it felt to have vowed perpetual virginity to the Highest Authority and yet found oneself viewed as a vulnerable sex object, there would be no doubt as to the reason behind her behaviour.

---

502 *Saint Joan of Arc's Trial of Condemnation*, "Fourth Private Examination", Wednesday, March 14th, 1431, in the afternoon. http://www.stjoan-center.com/Trials/sec10.html Retrieved Wednesday, July 10th, 2013. Translated from the original French at http://www.stejeannedarc.net/condamnation/interro_prive4.php

503 ***Procès de rehabilitation.*** *V-2 "Deposition de Jean de Nouillompont dit 'de Metz'"* http://www.stejeannedarc.net/rehabilitation/dep_jean_de_metz.php. Added Sunday, August 21st of 2011. Accompanying this passage is a footnote which states that it is interesting to note that the clothing of a man appears appropriate to Jean de Metz, as Joan's feminine garments immediately seem incongruous with the mission which she wished to undertake. The inhabitants of Vaucouleurs even offered contributions of such clothing to him. It was with shamefully bad faith that the judges of Rouen and their accomplices made this grounds for the verdict of relapse and the sentence of death! Retrieved Wednesday, December 6th of 2012.

Under those circumstances, even a religious trans*woman* who spent the first thirty years of their life wanting to be accepted in women's clothing would likely have done just as she did; otherwise she simply would not have felt safe.

When Joan appeared to recant, she was made to sign an Abjuration schedule which included among her errors the breaking of the Divine Law as revealed in Holy Scripture, and of the lawful Canons; in wearing what they considered a dissolute habit, immodest for the feminine sex and against the propriety of nature, and having hair clipped round in the style of a man.[504] Lack of modesty was not her problem; she would have continued to wear a woman's dress had it not been for the reasons mentioned above. The value of male garb in this situation was twofold; with hosen closed at the crotch that would have taken some time to unlace (Joan's even had more laces than was customary), it would have slowed a sexual assailant, yet it also would have made Joan appear less attractive to them. This second purpose relates to all I have previously stated about the fetishization of the feminine; as hideous as it is to even imagine, the guards of the lowest sort who kept her would have found a begowned young woman immobilized in shackles far more enticing.

Assuming that Joan's refusal to resume a woman's dress came from a distaste for such garb thus is difficult to argue. As this truth of her statements became more and more evident along with the fact that she had not committed any crime worthy of execution, her prosecution became proportionately more desperate to transform her tendency to remain transvested into some sort of sinful violation of the sacred. By the Saint's Seventh Private Examination (ie. that conducted while she was shackled in her prison cell), in the morning of Thursday the 15th of March, 1431, the Inquisitors set up her transvesting against her very devotion to the Church.

Referring to Joan of Arc's voiced desire to hear Mass, they asked her if it did not seem more appropriate to her to be in female dress. Then the Inquisitors presented her with a conditional offer: would she rather have a woman's dress in which to hear Mass, or remain in male garb and not hear it?

---

504 ABJURATION. Wednesday, May 23rd of 1431. http://www.stjoan-center.com/Trials/sec20.html Retrieved Sunday, September 30th, 2012.

Joan didn't trust Bishop Cauchon or his ilk any further than she could have thrown them, though deep down she wanted to. She requested assurance that she would hear Mass if she were in female attire, and even after receiving it asked what they would say if she had sworn to her King not to take off her garb. Not receiving a recorded response, Joan acquiesced to the extent that she requested to have made for her a long (floor-length) dress, sans train. If given one, she would wear it to go to Mass, and then would resume the masculine garb she had upon her return.

Again it was apparent that, ironically enough, her *modesty* – and freedom from sexual predation – were of primary concern to Joan. Twice more she was questioned as to whether she would consent simply and absolutely to take female garb, and after agreeing yet again she specifically requested to be sent a dress like a daughter of their "*burgeis*/bourgeois" citizens, that is to say, a long 'houppelande'. I recall encountering the houppelande (whilst secretly reading every book on fashion history that Cardinal Newman High School's library had to offer), and being quite pleased that, while feminine by modern standards, it was rather unisex in the Middle Ages. It is a rather opulent gown, and a proper reproduction of one would cost hundreds of dollars even today. Understanding that Joan of Arc exemplifies how females can be quite versatile without in so doing sacrificing femininity, it is just possible that even in this vile situation she was somewhat intrigued by the chance to don the garb of a middle-class town-dwelling woman (as opposed to the rural peasant garb to which she was accustomed), for she had a fondness for fine fashion and gave further specific details as to what she wished to wear.[505] Though she was becoming increasingly exasperated by the line of questioning, instead of simply snapping back

---

505 Joan also requested to have a *chapperon de femme.* As much as the now more physically-vulnerable Joan of Arc might have enjoyed the accompaniment of a female chaperone, the *chapperon de femme* was actually a hood, the female version of which was distinguished by the neck (which was split from top to bottom and left open.) ***Procès de condamnation*** – *procès d'office Cinquime interrogatoire priv – 15 mars 1431.* http://www.stejeannedarc.net/condamnation/interro_prive5.php#notes and http://www.stjoan-center.com/Trials/sec11.html Retrieved December 11th of 2012.

a brief reply Joan took a surprisingly loquacious approach in her attempt to negotiate with her captors. Joan was fearless without being foolish; taking this particular manner of gown was her idea, and this revealed her to still have some control over the situation.

The Inquisition eventually turned the focus of the trial to merely the nature of Joan's visions and to her cross-dressing. Joan appeared to have noticed this as early as the Fourth Public Examination of her Trial of Condemnation, and she clearly stated just how insignificant she thought the matter of her clothing to be. When questioned yet again as to whether it was God or man who prescribed for Joan the dress of the latter, Joan replied that what concerns this matter of dress is a small thing – "less than nothing." It was a miniscule part of everything else she did, which was all by the command of God.[506]

Nevertheless, the Church authorities insisted upon making a big deal of this matter of cross-dressing or gender expression (just as so many are *again* making a big deal of it now). Even the English King Henry VI made this paramount in his letter regarding Joan *la Pucelle*....

> "...leaving off the dress and clothing of the feminine sex, a thing contrary to divine law and abominable before God, ...has seduced...simple people by giving them to understand that she was sent from God, and had knowledge of His holy secrets; ...scandalous and prejudicial to the Catholic Faith..."[507]

As we discussed previously with regard to Jezebel, political intrigues can thoroughly tarnish any sort of "trial" for heresy, and it is quite apparent that such was the case here. The motives for Joan's execution were clearly political, for she was both a beacon of hope to her people and a brilliant strategist (the campaign she initiated of swift, successive strikes followed by the establishment of a solid center of power being an excellent method by which to loosen the grip of an occupying force

---

506 http://www.stjoan-center.com/Trials/sec04.html Emphasis mine.

507 Ibid. "THE TENOR OF THE KING'S LETTERS CONCERNING THE SURRENDER OF THE PUCELLE TO THE BISHOP OF BEAUVAIS" January 3rd of 1430 (the date is Old Style; the year began at Easter). http://smu.edu/ijas/1431trial.html Retrieved Wednesday, July 9th of 2013.

as well as to bolster the spirits of those thus occupied, particularly with the liberating force drawn from among those to be liberated). However, mention of Joan's military activities – especially with regards to the damage she dealt to the English – were kept to a relative minimum during the trial. If the prosecution instead turned this into a religious debate, it would be more difficult for the people of any nation to argue against it. This religious element was thus employed as a screen for political shemes. The Earl of Warwick had openly stated that the King would not for anything in the world allow Joan to die a natural death; he had bought her too dearly for that, and he did not wish her to die in any way except by the 'justice' of the fire.[508]

However flimsy the argument of garb was, when coupled with Joan's prosecutors' refusal to accept the validity of her visions and Joan's own refusal to abandon her belief in them, the former believed they possessed sufficient excuse to pronounce final judgement upon the latter. However, heresy was a capital offense only in the case of a relapse (a fact of which Joan herself was left unaware). Thus, since the only apparently-solid Biblical law they could wield against her was that which condemned cross-dressing, the more unscrupulous Inquisitors needed to find a way to cause Joan to again wear male clothes after having supposedly promised not to. Knowing what they did, they chose to threaten her virginity.

After Joan's Abjuration, in which she signed a document which she had neither read nor of which she was properly made aware, she donned women's clothes and begged to be taken to an ecclesiastical prison. She was instead again betrayed, and returned to the prison in which she had spent so many months. There she was sexually assaulted by a 'great lord', and for that reason resumed her male clothing which had so perfidiously been left near her, as she later disclosed to Brother Ysambard de la Pierre. This same Monk heard the Bishop and some of the English exulting over Joan's re-donning of male garb and saying openly to the Earl of Warwick and others, "She is caught this time!"[509]

---

508 Parenthetical note regarding the April 18th of 1431 Private Exhortation by the Bishop. http://www.stjoan-center.com/Trials/sec19.html Quotation marks mine.

509 Brother Ysambard de la Pierre, Second Examination, May 3rd, 1452. Trial of

The argument used by the Bishop was in fact so flimsy that not all of the religious authorities present would accept it, yet Joan's enemies were so desperate to use it against her that their chicanery became quite clear. One of these religious authorities, Maître Andre Marguerie, hearing that Joan had resumed her male attire, went to the Castle of Rouen to find out why she had done so, stating that it was not enough for him merely to see her in such clothes. One of the English soldiers stopped him, calling him a traitor and an Armagnac (of the sect of French opposed to the Burgundians and loyal to the recently-crowned King Charles VII) and raising his lance against him, so that Marguerie fled, fearing for his life. The following day, after Joan had been seen again in her male attire, her woman's dress was restored to her.[510]

The Inquisitors did all they could to ensure that it was impossible for Joan of Arc to escape, physically or legally. As soon as her oppressors had the opportunity to do so, they provided Joan with a man's clothes after taking away her woman's garment, and refused to give up the latter no matter what supplications or prayers she might make.[511]

Whether Joan of Arc expected the Inquisition to make such a move, she was resigned to her fate when it did. Joan's voices had reprimanded her for her recantation, and she anticipated that she would share their

---

Nullification, Rouen Testimony. http://www.stjoan-center.com/Trials/null10.html Retrieved Wednesday, October 31st of 2012.

510 *Saint Joan of Arc's Trial of Nullification.* Rouen Testimony Part 3; Examination of Witnesses. Massieu: Second Examination, May 8th, 1452. http://www.stjoan-center.com/Trials/null11.html Retrieved Tuesday, November 13th of 2012.

511 MAÎTRE JEAN MASSIEU, Priest, Curé of one of the Divisions of the Parish Church of Saint-Caudres at Rouen, formerly Dean of the Christendom of Rouen. He described the Maid's imprisonment in detail, stating that she always remained guarded in the hands of five of the English, **three of whom stayed all night in her room.** He also knew for certain that at night Joan slept chained by the legs with two pairs of iron chains, and that these were fastened closely to a chain going across the foot of her bed which was held to a piece of wood five or six feet long; this was closed with a key, so that Joan could not move from this spot. (Emphasis mine.) *Continuation of the First Inquiry: 1449 – Examination of Witnesses* [Part of the Trial of (Rehabilitation) Nullification]. http://www.stjoan-center.com/Trials/null02.html Retrieved Sunday, September 30th of 2012.

fate of martyrdom as a result of her 'relapse'. For months now, Joan had in a sense been playing out her own version of the stories of Saint Catherine and Saint Margaret – both of whom had also been imprisoned virgins – more than one thousand years later. As the winter wind seeped into her cell, even as she went over in her mind everything she had said to her prosecutors from the Church she loved in the country she had given everything to save, sometimes wracked by illness, her own passion was excruciatingly visceral. Her visions – her belief – trumped even gender expression. Joan of Arc had reached that ultimate point in every martyr's life when she had nothing left but her faith...and her love.

She was quite aware of the falsehood of her enemies, however. Joan had stated earlier that her clothing and actions – being inspired by God – did not weigh upon her soul and were not against the Church.[512] Though this may have been a tremendous leap of faith on her part (or a reference to the Church Triumphant exclusively), she proved without doubt that her refusal to wear female clothes could not have been the true reason for her condemnation. On Monday, May 28th, 1431, Joan of Arc freely offered to "resume the dress of a woman."[513] However, she still would not abandon faith in her visions. As only her death remained, that was the final piece of compliance she could offer; to surrender anything else would be to betray her God-given calling.[514]

Bafflingly for the Inquisition, this surrender was also a request; Joan of Arc was not forced into a dress at the end, but rather asked for one. During her Sixth Private Examination (on March 17th of 1431), Joan stated that she would not yet take a woman's dress because it did

---

512 ***Procès de condamnation*** *– procès d'office Huitième interrogatoire privé - 25 mars 1431.* www.stejeannedarc.net/condamnation/interro_prive8.php Retrieved July 11th of 2013.

513 The original French version of this statement was that if the judges want, Joan would resume the dress of a woman; for the rest, she would do something else. In the end, it was her visions and her missions to which she held fast. ***Procès de condamnation*** *– la cause de relaps. Constat de relaps – 28 mai 1431.* http://www.stejeannedarc.net/condamnation/constat_relaps28mai.php Retrieved Tuesday, December 11th of 2012.

514 MASSIEU, Further examined December 17th 1455 and May 12th 1456. [Additional evidence:] http://www.stjoan-center.com/Trials/null11.html Retrieved Saturday, November 17th of 2012.

not please the Lord, however she then asked that if the Trial led to her condemnation the lords of the Church "give her the grace of wearing a woman's *chemise*"[515] and head covering. When asked why, since she wore men's clothes by the commandment of God, she would request to wear a woman's smocklike undergarment at death, Joan replied modestly and evasively:

"It suffices that it be long."[516]

Saint Theresa of Lisieux offered the most beautiful explanation for her spiritual sister's request. In her play *Joan of Arc Accomplishes Her Mission*, the Little Flower has Rouen Priest Maître Jean Massieu offer Joan the white dress she requested in which to die. Joan of Arc accepts it, saying that it seems to her that she shall thus have "a greater resemblance to [her] Beloved Saviour"[517], who was also clothed in a white robe in Herod's palace. She then adds:

> "I do not want to go to martyrdom as a warrior because peace is assured me forever; I want to prepare myself in the dress of a Virgin who goes in front of her Husband."[518]

However, as a side-effect of her Divine mission, Saint Joan of Arc revealed just how obsolete Deuteronomy 22:5 had become. In so doing she displayed the sort of courageous piety for which she is venerated even to simply state that it was God's pleasure and declaration that such an archaic law be openly defied, especially as she did so in the faces of those who sought her life.

There remains the question of Joan's gender identity, however. As effective as the evidence provided is, it does not utterly prove that she was indeed comfortable with her assigned gender marker, for she had little opportunity to be comfortable at any time after her seventeenth birthday.

---

515 **Procès de condamnation** - *procès d'office*
Sixième interrogatoire privé - 17 mars 1431. http://www.stejeannedarc.net/condamnation/interro_prive6.php Retrieved Sunday, February 2nd of 2014.

516 Ibid.

517 *Joan of Arc Accomplishes Her Mission*, Part II: The Captivity. The Martyrdom. Scène 10.

518 Ibid.

So what is the verdict?

In its 16th Article of Accusation, the Inquisition stated that Joan of Arc disdained to perform feminine work, conducting herself in all things rather as a man than as a woman.[519] This appears to fall flat in light of her past occupations. Yet such statements as her answer to this accusation, that regarding the women's work of which they spoke, there were plenty of other women to do it[520], and the statement that she preferred a man's dress to a women's dress[521] (despite that being due to her being vulnerable in the company of men) still could be considered evidence of transgender behaviour. Due to the limited understanding of the time, the question of "Was Joan of Arc transgender" must remain a mystery....

...For another seven seconds. Her Voices, whether one considers them to have come from God through the Saints (as I myself do), from some manner of paranoid schizophrenia, or even from her own 'conscience', addressed Joan of Arc as Jeanne the *Maid*, *Daughter* of God.[522] As any transperson knows, if she had not been truly female, they never would have called her that. That is the only way of being certain...just as it is with us of the trans community. We must trust the Saints at their word; for she did. Transpeople too, must be taken on faith.

Yet even though she was not a transman, the Maid of Lorraine is still a champion of the LGBT community because she *is* woman. As she herself said, the matter of her garb meant nothing, and her lack of sex

---

[519] *St. Joan of Arc's Trial of Condemnation.* "Continuation of the March 27th Reading of the Seventy Articles of Accusation" www.stjoan-center.com/Trials/sec15.html Retrieved Thursday, July 11th of 2013.

[520] Ibid.

[521] *St. Joan of Arc's Trial of Condemnation.* "Second Process: The Relapse, The Final Adjudication and the Sentence of Death" Monday, May 28th of 1431. www.stjoan-center.com/Trials/sec21.html Retrieved Thursday, July 11th of 2013.

[522] *St. Joan of Arc's Trial of Condemnation.* "Second Private Examination" Monday, March 12th, in the morning; in Jeanne's prison. Present: The Bishop, assisted by Jean Delafontaine, Commissary; Nicholas Midi and Gerard Feuillet; and as their witnesses: Thomas Fiefvet, Pasquier de Vaux, and Nicolas de Houbent. http://www.stjoan-center.com/Trials/sec08.html Retrieved July 11th of 2013.

meant her genitalia was likewise irrelevant. This is well, because there exists the small possibility that Joan of Arc was a partial hermaphrodite; outwardly entirely female yet lacking a womb.

This rather controversial revelation is due to the testimony of Joan's Squire Jean D'Aulon's at her Trial of Nullification. D'Aulon had heard from women with whom Joan stayed at night and who thus were privy to her 'womanly secrets' that, while Joan of Arc had developed breasts and was visibly entirely female, she had never been seen to menstruate.[523] If these observations were universally true, Joan of Arc suffered from amenorrhoea most likely caused by a genetic condition, for while she ate little when compared to her companions Joan's lifestyle was nevertheless far too robust for malnutrition to explain her lack of menses. It has thus been suggested that the most likely explanation is that Joan had *testicular feminization syndrome*, or rather a type of androgen (male hormone) insensitivity syndrome which is more complete than most.[524] While such a medical diagnosis is little more than a massive assumption based upon third-hand information, it would mean that Joan of Arc was an XY chromosomal genetic male, and it would change nothing.

Her bed nucleus of the stria terminalis would have remained female, and as records have shown her androgen insensitivity syndrome must have been sufficiently complete to give her a vagina and unbroken hymen, and even had she lacked a womb she would not have been physically or mentally masculine at all. Had this latter quality not been the case, Joan would have been born with external masculine genitalia and, however she may have developed in puberty, would probably have been permanently labeled "male." As a result, prophecy-supporting

---

523 The original French version of Jean d'Aulon's testimony may be found at http://www.stejeannedarc.net/rehabilitation/V-dep_jean_d_aulon.php Both retrieved Sunday, February 2nd of 2014.

524 Tomlins, Marilyn Z. "Joan of Arc...Jeanne d'Arc...Was she a he...?" January 6th, 2012. http://www.marilynztomlins.com/articles/joan-of-arc-jeanne-darc-was-she-a-he/#sthash.fSn3ABWR.NzbCqIwC.dpbs Retrieved December 7th, 2013. See also Patricia Nell Warren's article for *The Gay & Lesbian Review Worldwide*, titled "Was Joan of Arc genetically male?" Written on January 1st of 2009, it may be found at http://www.thefreelibrary.com/Was+Joan+of+Arc+genetically+male%3F-a0192646453 Retrieved Sunday, February 2nd of 2014.

courtiers such as Yolande of Aragon would have had to find another Maid of Lorraine; *bonne chance* to them. As for Joan, it is possible she would still have had military inclinations and – like Saint Francis before her – assumed her calling was to be a knight. She was interested both in religious crusades and in driving out foreign invaders, and it is generally believed that her land-owning father did know Sir Robert de Baudricourt, so it is just possible that she might have been sponsored and become a squire. She might have remained unkillable on the battlefield and lived to middle age, albeit not to become co-commander of anything until it was far too late for France. It is considerably more probable still that she would have spent her life tending her father's fields and flocks, and that while Joan of Lorraine would never have gotten into trouble for wearing men's clothing, neither would she or her brothers have been ennobled. Ironic as it may seem, *Jeanne la Pucelle* could achieve far more militarily as a woman than she ever could have as a man. Truly, God makes no mistakes, but He did intend the world to be far more complicated than one might like.

Beyond the evidence of her clothing and even the evidence of her physicality, what truly made Joan of Arc a woman – what made her the Maid to history and to God – was her mind, her heart, and her soul. Gender is indeed God-given and immutable; Joan of Arc was a woman, and no outward trappings could ever change that.

It is the same with true transpeople; those who do not suffer from a psychosexual disorder but rather exist at some point along the intersex spectrum. However, while Joan of Arc's womanliness and even virginity could be proven by external examination (as they were multiple times), a transgender's true gender is generally more difficult for others to detect. In my case, a careful visual examination would have revealed the slow budding of my breasts, while my friend Jenna's more-impressive physical femaleness could only have been detected very recently via an ultrasound. The majority of the trans community, however, lack the primary or secondary sexual characteristics of their actual gender. They require at least a state-of-the-art brain scan to reveal their true nature, and sometimes more than that; the bed nucleus of the stria terminalis is buried so deeply at the core of the brain (at the summit of the brainstem) that it may only be closely examined during an autopsy, and by then their vindication would come too late.

It seems presposterous that humanity could use apparent gender expression or simple cross-dressing as a religious excuse to put someone to death, but Matthew 5:17-20 is often misinterpreted....

> "Think not that I am come to destroy the law, or the prophets: I am come not to destroy, but to fulfil.
>
> For verily I say unto you, Till heaven and earth pass, one jot or one tittle shall in no wise pass from the law, till all be fulfilled.
>
> Whosoever therefore shall break one of these least commandments, and shall teach men so, he shall be called the least in the kingdom of heaven: but whosoever shall do and teach them, the same shall be called great in the kingdom of heaven.
>
> For I say unto you, That except your righteousness shall exceed the righteousness of the scribes and Pharisees, ye shall in no case enter into the kingdom of heaven." (KJV)

Fortunately, the Church Militant now possesses a distinct answer to this difficult passage. The 2003-2004 Edition of the New American Bible possesses a footnote for this section which reveals that the "passing away" of heaven and earth is not necessarily the end of the world, ie. the apocalyptic dissolution of the existing universe. Rather, the "turning of the ages" came with the apocalyptic event of Jesus' death and resurrection, meaning that those to whom the Gospel is addressed are living in the new, final age prophesied by Isaiah of "new heavens and a new earth".[525]

One is thus advised to see also Matthew 22:40 and Galatians 5:14; the latter of which reads, "For all the law is fulfilled in one word, even in this; Thou shalt love thy neighbour as thyself." (KJV)

---

525 Isaiah 65:17 & 66:22. (The footnote is found on p. 1015 of the 2003-2004 NAB)

The refusal to believe Jesus Christ – as would later be the refusal to believe Joan of Arc – was an example of valuing obsolete laws over the spirit of the Lord's teaching. Indeed, it is for such reasons as this that Jesus declared blasphemy of the Holy Spirit to be the greatest of sins.[526]

On the other hand, one cannot thereby assume that all of the Old Testament law should be considered no longer applicable and therefore ignored. It was given to humanity for a reason, and thus determining the reason why each individual law was given has occupied all Christian churches for millennia. 13th-Century Doctor of the Church Thomas Aquinas offered the following understanding of Deuteronomy 22:5....

> "...outward apparel should be consistent with the estate of the person[527].... Hence it is in itself sinful [for a woman or a man to transvest]; especially since this may be a cause of sensuous pleasure; [it is expressly forbidden in Deuteronomy 22] because the Gentiles used to practice this change of attire for the purpose of idolatrous superstition. Nevertheless this may be done sometimes [without the deed being sinful, due to necessity; the examples he gives include needing to hide from one's enemies, lacking other clothes, or a similar motive]."
>
> – Saint Thomas Aquinas, *Summa Theologica*[528]

This might seem like the writing of a bleeding-heart liberal to those more conservative Christians. Does this Saint – known as the "Angelic Doctor" – not know that the Bible (at least the ones translated into English) offers NO exceptions to Deuteronomy 22:5? According to

---

526 Matthew 12:31-32, Mark 3:28-30, Luke 12:10

527 Note that Joan of Arc even drew attention to the fact that her mission was not her 'proper estate', yet that she needed to fulfill it nonetheless, for it was the will of God. ***Proces de rehabilitation.*** *V-2 "Deposition de Jean de Nouillompont dit 'de Metz'"* http://www.stejeannedarc.net/rehabilitation/dep_jean_de_metz.php. Added Sunday, August 21st of 2011. Retrieved Wednesday, December 6th of 2012.

528 *"Second Part of the Second Part. Question 169. Modesty in the outward apparel. Article 2. Whether the adornment of women is devoid of mortal sin?"* http://www.newadvent.org/summa/3169.htm Retrieved Wednesday, October 31st of 2012.

the Good Book, any woman who wears men's clothes or vice versa is condemned to pay the ultimate price of...of....

Well, the Bible doesn't actually *have* a punishment for transvesting, but rest assured it is an *abomination!* That is to say, it is a *tow'ebah* – a sin due to association with idolatrous practices, as St. Thomas Aquinas stated – like homosexuality or (ironically) *burning people alive.*[529]

In this text written in the final years of his life, the 13th-Century Angelic Doctor thus offered defense for Joan of Arc's tranvesting more than 150 years before it needed to be heeded in her case, succinctly stated why cross-dressing was considered to be an "abomination" in the first place, and also separated religiously-acceptable transvesting from transvestic fetishism. Joan of Arc may not have been aware of the details behind the religious truths which vindicated her, but her insistence that her cross-dressing was endorsed by God is now most understandable.

As to the case(s) of the trans community, it is not altogether uncommon for those on the intersexed spectrum to be physically incapable of deriving sensuous pleasure merely from the wearing of female dress (or male dress either, though that is far less fetishized). Additionally, if being a transperson were truly about sensuality or even sexuality, I daresay one would never go through all the trouble of transitioning only to take a solemn Vow of Perpetual Virginity as I have! We ourselves have two choices: to either condemn without question, or do as Saint Thomas Aquinas did; consider the context and language of the text before passing judgement.

Even without noting all of this, however, it is reasonable to argue that the law does not effect transpeople due to our actually having the minds – and in many cases certain sexual characteristics – of the sex with which we identify.

With regards to gender-definition, the writers of the Bible made the same assumption made virtually everywhere else; those who were circumcised or eunuchs were considered boys or men, and those who had breasts and/or periods and/or gave birth were considered girls or women. One might thus assume that at least one of the aforementioned traits would necessarily be present for a person to receive any of those

---

529 Cf. Jeremiah 32:35.

classifications. However, as we have already discussed, it is rather questionable whether these constitute absolute definitions of gender, for actual definitions per se are not found anywhere in the Bible.

So different, so nonconformist, so difficult to fathom is the transgender that the default response among people was inevitably distrust. So too has it been among the religious as with virtually all other institutions, and so it was that I and countless other transpeople were made to feel as if our very existences were wrong. Nevertheless, if it were a matter of either serving the will of God or being true to ourselves, many of us would choose God. So it was for me for thirty years...until I fully realized that God would never force me to make such a choice.

Yes, I myself am a confirmed Catholic, and to be perfectly honest, I agree with the Church's stance that sex-reassignment surgery cannot change one's gender; gender and sex are not so superficial as that. Existing in a sense between genders is however very confusing and difficult in a civilization in which the gender binary has been so intrinsic. Yet transpeople are only physically between genders; deep down, even at our most distorted moments in life, in our hearts we know that which is our proper estate, even if the world will not accept it. Are we to remain guilty until proven innocent? It is for such reasons that God is constantly allowing further understanding of His will....

> "Therefore judge nothing before the time, until the Lord come, who both will bring to light the hidden things of darkness, and will make manifest the counsels of the hearts: and then shall every man have praise of God." (1 Corinthians 4:5, KJV)

Thus we have at last fully addressed Deuteronomy 22:5 and its effect upon the trans community. As for Joan of Arc, while she was not a transman and indeed did not feel the need to "transition" at all, it has been suggested that her transcendent gender expression was quite significant in another way. Though Marina Warner's book *Joan of Arc: The Image of Female Heroism* is rather oldschool in its approach to feminism, it presents an intriguing understanding of the result of her transvestism. It states that by wearing male clothes while never pretending to be anything but a woman and a maid, Joan of Arc came to occupy....

> "...a different, third order, neither male nor female, but unearthly, like the angels whose company she loved."[530]

The fact that angels were classically depicted as androgynes holds quite an intriguing meaning, especially in light of current understandings of gender and gender expression. Let us now address the angelic, for by now the stench of sexism mingled with transphobia has risen so high that it would attempt to mar the very image of Heaven itself.

The Disfigurement of Angels

Androgyny was something I sought whenever possible. It was perhaps the prime reason I originally wanted "Michael" to be my Roman Catholic Confirmation Name when I was 13; while clearly masculine in English, in French the name ("*Michel/le*") had a very androgynous sound. Also, like so many of the trans community I sought escapism through fantasy, and among all the beautiful things to which I was exposed in stories and games the ones I most wanted to be – more than fairies or even mermaids – were the angels. Angels, however, are not fantasy....

Yes, Christianity does contain beings which are depicted as existing between genders; the very angels themselves. In *Ulysses*, James Joyce even makes a brief allusion to the fact "that in the economy of heaven... there are no more marriages, [there is instead] glorified man, an androgynous angel, being a wife unto himself."[531] This androgyny, universally acknowledged in past centuries, has recently become noticeably lacking and at times even come under fire. Starting with the personal and extending outwards, let us examine the cause for this....

---

530 Marina Warner, *Joan of Arc: The Image of Female Heroism* (London: Weidenfeld and Nicolson), 1981, p. 146.

531 Episode 9, *Scylla and Charybdis* (after the monster and the whirlpool which Ulysses must carefully steer between), p. 274.

As a child I found the beautiful androgyny of angels a wonderful and highly desirable spiritual goal for which to strive. Indeed, considering myself a "(wo)man of science" when I was seventeen, I even devised a hypothetical hermaphrodital future evolution of humanity – members of which could control their own mutations and reproduce either asexually or with one another – whom I dubbed the "*Soalam* angels."[532] To one so accustomed to internal disharmony on the most basic level, the thought of deep and ultimate harmony in such a matter was truly heavenly.

The androgyny of angels is an intriguing concept, for it too initially proved difficult for humans to accept. Usually, when a Heavenly creature appeared in a humanoid form its viewer described it as having "the appearance of a man", as did the Archangel Saint לאירבג Gabriel[533] in Daniel 8:15-16, wherein the word *geber,* associated with "mighty warrior" was again used. However, in Zechariah 5:9 the Prophet identifies the two he sees as women (again using the generic word for "women", *'ishshah*) who "had wings like the wings of a stork." (KJV) This default description of masculinity may well stem from the inherent assumptions of a patriarchal society; just as even in modern times approximately 75% of true hermaphrodites are nevertheless raised as males, male may have been considered the 'default' gender due to it being considered the 'desirable' one. Yet if even angels are described using either masculine or feminine terms, from whence did this concept of angelic androgyny arise?

Gender roles were rigidly defined by human societies, as is quite evident in their descriptions in the Bible itself. Rather, the suggestion

---

532 *Soalam* was a word from a small logographic language I invented when I was sixteen; it means "soul armour" in the sense that the body is the armour of the soul. I became intrigued years later to read of the "eloi" ((Mark 15:34); apparently in this case from "מיהלא Elohim" "Sons of God" (as there is bit of confusion between the plural and singular in the Book of Genesis and elsewhere, I shall note that this word is plural when addressing angels, yet singular when addressing God Himself)) in H.G. Wells' *The Time Machine*, for they bore some similarity as beautiful human evolutions toward androgyny.

533 His name (*Gam bet resh yad El lam*) could be interpreted logographically as "ג Gather [the] ב Family [at/of the] ר First/Top/Beginning [to] י work [for]/ worship [the] א Strong/Power/Leader [Who is our] ל Shepherd/Teacher."

of an equality and even a unification of gender came from a Source that was not merely human: Jesus Christ:

> "For in the resurrection they neither marry, nor are given in marriage; but are as the angels of God in heaven."
> (Matthew 22:30, KJV; see also Mark 12:25 and Luke 20:35-36)

Maleness and femaleness, different but complimentary, were deemed inseparable; the man would leave his father and mother and cleave to his wife, and the two would become one flesh. If they were then to be seemingly cleft *apart* in the resurrection, how would the male receive the femaleness he needed and vice versa? It was thus presumed that these qualities are naturally provided to those of angelic form. Operating under this revelation that the union of male and female can reach a more perfect ideal in the Hereafter, the assumption was that the two in a sense literally became one being who embodied both masculinity and femininity. As both maleness and femaleness are necessary components of the whole being, it was also assumed that angels always embodied both traits.

Thus it was that admiration for the hermaphrodite – represented from Antiquity as a beautiful young creature with female breasts and male genitalia – was easily adopted in Christendom. Even in the Late-Mediaeval environment of the 15th Century, the hermaphrodite – also known as the androgyne – had only positive connotations. As Ross King wrote in his award-winning book *Leonardo and the Last Supper*, "its androgyny was understood to be a sign of the unity and the perfection of the self."[534]

Ross went on to note that the scholar Marsilio Ficino, a member of ruler of Florence Cosimo de Medici's circle, gave this conclusion in his commentary on Plato's 'Symposium'. Ficino wrote that the androgyne reconciled and united the masculine virtue of courage with the feminine

---

534 King, Ross. *Leonardo and The Last Supper.* 2012. Bond Street Books, a division of Random House of Canada, Ltd. p. 193.

virture of temperance.[535] In this view, the hermaphrodite was the perfect being: whole and complete. Ross also pointed out that....

> "[Leonardo's final patron] King François I of France, therefore did not object when [the painter Niccolò da Modena] represented him as an androgyne: he was shown to combine the warrior qualities of the male [and the] creative powers of a woman."[536]

It is sadly ironic that, now that real hermaphrodites of various types are being discovered in considerable numbers, we are received not with admiration but with revulsion. This is again due to the modern overly-sexualized environment in which we now find ourselves; we are less encouraged to think of the virtues of each sex than to think of their sexuality or of the very act of sex itself. Thus the state of being a hermaphrodite/androgyne/intersex/transperson is now often viewed simply as an extension of this environment; an extreme foray into the forbidden sexual pleasures beyond the limits of a single sex. However, if it was not associated with prostitution or other forms of sexual indulgence, the androgyne was an untainted ideal; it could be entirely spiritual, like the angels.

Now as for me (as a representative of an imperfect gender union in an imperfect mortal world), I suspect I would have heavily favoured femininity in any case. However, I must confess having some measure of affection for the chivalrous role I adopted as an attempt to apply my actual personality to a masculine image, and thus that exploring even the stern and stalwart hardness of manliness might have been a fond and fascinating experience...had I been raised in a society that treated both (and the expression of both from either sex) equally. Alas, however; things are not yet done on earth as they are in Heaven, and being forced into the masculine role from the very *beginning* of my life went quite a

---

535 Temperance is one of the Seven Heavenly Virtues, along with Prudence, Fortitude, Justice, Charity, Faith, and Hope.

536 Ibid. Emphasis mine. François I (1494-1547 A.D., crowned in Reims Cathedral in 1515), known as the "Knight King", is considered the monarch – and initiator – of the Renaissance in France.

long way toward poisoning any enjoyment I might have gleaned from the experience.

It would normally be quite inappropriate to even compare the glorious majesty of the angels to part of the LGBT community, but fear and hatred of the LGBT "agenda" and the possible infiltration of its idea(l)s into mainstream/heterosexual thought has led to a disturbing recent phenomenon: the de-androgynizing of depictions of angels. This ranges from the subtle to the extreme.

One example from the former end of the range is the Archangel Saint לאכימ Michael[537]. As his warrior role lends itself to a masculinized gender image, his classical image as a (moderately) long-haired beauty generally can only be considered feminine from a modern perspective. This is especially true in those illustrations which depict him in armour like that of a Roman soldier, yet even when he is depicted in a Mediaeval field plate cuirass any feminization of his appearance tends to be rather minor. Perhaps the most intriguing example of this latter approach which I have seen appeared on a holy card depicting Saint Michael offering a sword to Joan of Arc while she tended sheep; with long dark hair and wearing a full skirt beneath his armour, the Archangel looks for all the world like a futuristic reflection of the manner in which Joan herself would come to be depicted.

---

537 Possible logographical readings of Michael's name, *Mem yad kaph El lam*, include "מ [The] mighty/chaos [is] י thrown, כ bent/tamed [by the] א Strong/Power/Leader [Who is our] ל Shepherd/Teacher" or even "And they כי overcame him by the מ blood of the אל Lamb," (Revelation 12:11, KJV).

LEFT and CENTER: various androgynous fine art depictions of that most masculine of angels: the Archangel Saint Michael. Clockwise from top left: the aforementioned holy card, Stilke Hermann Anton's "Appearance of Saints Catherine and Michael to Joan of Arc" (The Left-Hand Part of *The Life of Joan of Arc Triptych*) circa 1843, Pietro Perugino's "Archangel Michael" circa 1499, and Josse Lieferinxe's "The Archangel Michael Killing the Dragon" circa late 15th Century, now located at the *Musée du Petit Palais*, Avignon. RIGHT: At a lower level of artistic ability, we have two depictions of attempts to feminize and masculinize androgynous-looking characters. The top is a drawing of Joan of Arc by Clément de Fauquembergue in the register for the Parlement of Paris following Joan's victory at Orléans (the man had never seen the Maid). Less significantly, at the bottom is my first attempt at a role-playing game character; a warrior-woman whom I was hoping would not draw too much flak for being such (I was twelve years old at the time).

For her part, Joan seemed to find the appearance of the Archangel to be entirely reasonable for an honest gentleman. When one of her prosecutors asked her about Saint Michael's hair, she simply asked in return if he had some reason to have cut it.[538]

One possible answer to the Maid's centuries-old question is found in depictions of the Archangel Saint Gabriel. The classical portrayal of the Annunciation reveals an Archangel who would be difficult to distinguish from the Blessed Virgin Mary whom he is addressing (were it not for the presence of wings on the former). However, in the same scene as shown in *The Action Bible,* a 2006 graphic art version illustrated by Sergio Cariello, the now-bearded and barrel-chested Saint Gabriel could perhaps be well-portrayed in film by Chris Hemsworth of *Thor* and *Avengers* fame.[539] This is by no means an isolated occurrence; the Mark Burnett/Roma Downey miniseries *The Bible* gives its angels similar hypermasculinization, and within the past few decades it has been seen as more and more important that the sex of an angel be distinctly and immediately apparent, especially if the angel in question is generally thought of as being male.

Clearly there are those who have their limits regarding what they deem acceptable in angelic expression, yet the reason that many centuries of androgyny has suddenly become unacceptable is seldom

---

538 *Sentencing trial – trial of Office.* "Fifth public examination – 1 March 1431"

539 Perhaps there is also a connection between the growing inclination toward a conservative approach to aggression/warfare and the increasing inclination toward depicting angels as being either distinctly masculine or distinctly feminine; I cannot say. However, on the subject of Thor (and the mounting popularity of other violent pagan gods – such as Zeus – also) I do recall an atheist demotivational poster depicting a picture of the Norse storm lord from a *Dragon* magazine advertisement with the caption: 'Our god has a hammer. Your God was nailed to a cross. Any questions?' The inherent social prevalence of this militant attitude had its effect upon me even when I was a child; I was amazed when my mother told me of how Jesus and His mother rode upon an ass or an ass' colt (Zechariah 9:9, Matthew 21:5-7, John 12:14-16), thinking that as an aspect of God "He could have ridden a tiger or a dragon if He wanted to!" (The dragon, coincidentally enough, is classically the mount of Marduk and of Asmodeus, Hellish Prince of Lust and villain of the Deuterocanonical Book of Tobit.)

overtly expressed. One prominent exception was provided in 2010 by a Catholic priest of the resort town of Jarabacoa in the Dominican Republic. This priest wanted to destroy a piece of artwork in his parish (a mural painting titled "Allegory of the Virgin of Carmen" by Roberto Flores) because the angels therein were depicted with "a homosexual expression" which "confuses the faithful".[540] As a result, the priest felt that the mural did not inspire religious sentiments, due to the angels having what he believed was a "diabolical, homosexual look" upon their faces. Finally, he contended that it was not clear whether the angels were male or female.[541]

At times it can be difficult not to picture a person taking aim at a celestial creature with a shot gun whilst remarking that stereotypical phrase, "We don't like yer kind around here!" They never showed that on *Touched by an Angel*!

(Though admittedly I am not 100% certain of this. I was a teenager when the show aired and saw only a couple of episodes during that time, for I tried to do so in secret due to the show being considered "too feminine" for a 'young man' to watch by oneself.)

One must question the moral authority of a world in which angels are persecuted. The twisting of the image of angels to better suit emerging attitudes of fear can only mark a drifting away from love.

Once More Into the Darkness

Love is a difficult thing to believe, give, and accept; especially for those of us who feel like anything but angels. I myself, like other "transsexuals" I have known, had learned also not to expect it. I was supposedly a creature of psychosexual disorder; a fetish and a freak

---

540 Solar, Igor I. "Priest wants church painting removed because 'angels look gay'." *Digital Journal.* Jun 3, 2010. http://www.digitaljournal.com/article/292901 Retrieved January 26th of 2013.

541 JD. "God's Androgynous Angels Looking Too Gay for Dominican Catholic Church". *Queerty: Free of an Agenda. Except that Gay One.* Jun 4, 2010. http://www.queerty.com/gods-androgynous-angels-looking-too-gay-for-dominican-catholic-church-20100604/ Retrieved Saturday, January 26th of 2013.

whose joy was thought limited to the flesh alone. As I have noted previously, I had been led to the false understanding that I must learn to settle for sexual encounters rather than hope for a lifelong union.

I would like to be able to say that the events described at the beginning of this chapter were the full manifestation of all the years of my life in which I was exposed to the distorted image of women and sexuality that is presented by the media and mutually shared amongst young men. I would like to be able to say that no more did I desire the sexual lifestyle upon which I had been 'missing out.' I would like to be able to say that no more did I have any interest in the supposed validation of femaleness that would somehow come from a carnal act with a man. However, one's life is not a Hollywood movie that all would be resolved in one climactic moment; there was one more similar temptation in my life.

Hormone replacement therapy – the balancing of chemicals to coincide with the primordial elements of one's brain – tends to lower the libido. Mine was no exception; for more than a year after starting hormones I had virtually no interest in sex (not that I was fully capable of such in any case). Then, in the autumn of the second year my previous desires returned with a vengeance, such that I was worried my dreaded masculine hormones might once again be on the rise. However, as it turned out, my *feminine* hormones were entirely responsible; my testosterone was too low to even register. So it was that in my most needful of times I consented to an encounter which seemed very modern and very "sexually liberated;" something that promised to vicariously fulfill at least some of my needs, if only in fantasy.

In both this case and the one which began this chapter, the danger came not only from my own weakness but also from my lack of understanding. For a long time I was at risk of becoming part of the stereotypical image of one who was brought up Roman Catholic yet become disenchanted by the apparent repression and reported corruption of the Church; that one who seemed unworthy to live within it was left with no choice but to try to live without it. I had been thoroughly deceived. Even now it is difficult to fathom how I ever was convinced by the media and my peers that being a porn star was somehow better than simply being a prostitute; how engaging in any of a plethora of possible "modern" sexually-explicit activities was somehow more acceptable than simply being penetrated vaginally.

> "But **it was in vain one was honest or a decent woman, one had to submit everything...."**
> (The Marquis de Sade, *The 120 Days of Sodom,* circa 1785. Translated 2002 by Richard Seaver and Austryn Wainhouse. p. 6)

It was with trepidatious excitement that I had changed my portfolio on *One Model Place.com* to describe myself as "willing to model in bondage; even extreme bondage such as *shibari*[542]" on (fittingly enough) April Fool's Day, 2006. Within twenty-four hours it had attracted the attention of a bondage photographer who had (as I would soon learn via instant messaging) "a soft spot for trannies (sic)." We had our first photosession later that same month (shortly before the time in which the previous story took place), and he had placed about my neck a stiff leather posture collar with an O-ring[543] attached, though I did not know at the time that this might have symbolized something more than a gothic fashion statement (despite his assistant having at one point stated that "this is where the Domme becomes a sub"). It was a chaste bondage shoot, yet it was a tactily erotic one that fueled my feminine self-image *(he used some of my pictures as part of his presentation at the Toronto, Ontario Kink convention that year; was it possible that someone could truly find a creature such as myself...BEAUTIFUL?*) and left my libido wanting more.

Let us flash forward a few years; years which were just as sexually uneventful as those preceding 2006. Now I had physically (though without surgery or artificial assistance) balanced my hormone levels, and now this "bondage lord's" stated goal was "to reshape [my] mind, body, and sexuality to suit men's desires." This was a man

---

[542] A Japanese term for rope bondage, which has evolved from swift methods by which Samurai might harmlessly subdue their quarry to incredibly intricate methods of restraint. When it is used for primarily aesthetic purposes, it is referred to as *kinbaku-bi*.

[543] As opposed to the similar "D-ring"; these are metal rings sewn into bondage gear so that chains, leashes, or other restraints might be easily affixed.

whose writings, as I would later learn, acknowledged such subjects as "polyamory" (erotic relations with others besides the one to whom one is married) and the belief that the Top/bottom --> Dominance/submission model found its ultimate and purest form in the 24/7 'Master/slave' relationship. However, it should be noted that, even while dealing with these commonly-held views within the community, he always espoused the BDSM[544] code of "safe, sane, and consensual" (even if that didn't necessarily mean that a submissive or slave was entirely aware of or prepared for what was to be done to them).

Nevertheless, I was only aware of this latter quality, and the 'bondage lord' had been very kind to me. He had offered to let me stay with him on the off chance that I was rejected upon "coming out" to my parents (though fortunately my family accepted me easily and forgave my earlier deceptions). He had protectively stated that I would not "pump" silicone[545] "on [his] watch" (though I never intended to do so). He had even offered to take me to the Dominican Republic and pay for breast implants if ever he could afford to (though he couldn't at the time and it was not necessary anyway due to my position on the intersexed spectrum, which allowed me to grow my own modest bosom). As I no longer lived in my birth-city of Toronto, his proposed intense training became limited to another photosession with the potential to become something somewhat more erotic. In our email and instant messenger-based three-month preparation for this experience, he stated something which profoundly proclaimed the limits of the purely-carnal existence: "You may adore me, you may worship me, but you may not love me."[546]

How easy it is to fall into sin when one considers *oneself* an abomination!

---

544 As a reminder, BDSM is a multiple acronym including the combinations "Bondage & Discipline," "Dominance & Submission," and "Sadism & Masochism."

545 "Pumping" is the disturbingly-common practice of injecting industrial-grade silicone beneath one's skin to give one's body a more curvaceous and feminine shape. It is highly dangerous and eventually results in a deformed appearance due to the silicone migrating to other parts of the body.

546 The reader may rest assured that, even in my darkest and most vulnerable moments I never had any intention of worshipping him!!

So it was that on the rainy winter evening of January 18th, 2011, I journeyed to the capitol. The first indication that this was going to be an unusual experience came from the taxi driver.

He was a bearded, tanned man of about forty who made conversation, as taxi drivers are wont to do, and somewhere within this conversation I casually mentioned that I was en route to a photoshoot. I do not know whether this inspired him or not, but as we pulled into the train station he told me he wished that he could kiss my hand. I offered it to him and he did so...reverently.

It was a shred of chivalry, or something like it. It was strange and beautiful to receive it here and now...and from the other side. I was reminded of the sort of thing I wrote about and practiced when I was a teenager, and of Alana's words:

> "I'm glad there are still men like you left in the world."

Picked up at the station by this 'bondage lord', I was then delivered...

> "...to a kind of...dungeon...in which was displayed everything the cruelest art and the most refined barbarity could invent... of a villain lawless and without religion...." (*Sodom,* pp. 39-40)

Nevertheless the photosession was performed tastefully, though we were not alone. Upon my arrival I was introduced to the owner of the dungeon (and also a place called *Subspace*), another professional photographer who was interested enough to remain throughout the shoot and take some pictures of me himself, and a young lady clad in the black leather and lace of the gothic subculture who described herself as "a service-oriented submissive." This last person was dedicated to the 'bondage lord' photographer, and she explained to me that this meant performing housework for him free of charge; it provided her with a thrill due to her having not had the opportunity to perform such activities when she was younger (would anyone believe this if it were not true?).

The shoot was to be conducted in the main room of the dungeon, on the bottom floor of a tiered chamber perhaps forty feet in height. An alcove in the far left corner of the room contained a refrigerator upon which was affixed a cartoon depicting Princess Leia (from *Star Wars Episode IV: A New Hope*), affixed to precisely the same cross to which I would soon be bound, being tortured by Stormtroopers. On the upper tier at the top of the stairs, the dungeon's owner sat watching *The Matrix* on a flat-screen television. (In retrospect, it seems amusing that both franchises deal deeply with concerns of faith, and that both present them in a post-modern pseudo-scientific manner so that they seem easier to believe.) As I changed my garb and my photographers prepared their equipment, I heard them discuss new torturous fetishes they might wish to introduce to the community; including one involving catheters, as I recall. I stated with some disgust that I was sure they "could find *someone* who was into that sort of thing!"

I still insisted on not being photographed nude, and I had earlier informed the 'bondage lord' that I did not enjoy S&M (despite singer/actress Rihanna's having begun to popularize it at precisely that time). After an agonizing Near-Death Experience I passed through at the age of sixteen, any possibility that I might receive pleasure from pain was well and truly burned out of me. Thus he had not gone to especial lengths to ensure the presence of myriad items that could cause such. Additionally, just as he had not hoisted me off of my knees or feet when subjecting me to strappado[547] in 2006, he did not now employ upon me any of the many adjacent instruments of torture immediately available to him. This was even the case when I was bound and/or chained to an armature which the Marquis de Sade mentioned on the 13th of January in his *120 Days of Sodom,* and what E. L. James referred to in *Fifty Shades of Grey* simply as "a large wooden cross like an *X*...."[548] For his part, the 'bondage lord' was more than happy to refer to it by its true name: a "Saint Andrew's Cross," upon which said Saint was martyred due to believing himself unworthy to be crucified in the same manner as Our Lord. It was I myself who had requested this device. It was for

---

547 A popular form of torture used by the Inquisition, strappado is the lifting of arms bound behind the back into a vertical position.

548 *Sodom*, 13th January, p. 336. *Fifty Shades of Grey*, Chapter 7, p. 98, Ch. 18, p. 322, 324 and Ch. 25, 484.

those who would do anything for love, even if in my case it was but a bright illusion, wet and cold upon the street above.

The 'bondage lord', who had fantasized about me for years, now at last had me helpless in his dungeon and then in his apartment, which despite his impoverishment (resulting from a messy recent divorce) was still adorned with the ropes and restraints that were the tools of the trade in his chosen double-life. Yet he did not touch me, for (as far as I'm concerned) a sort of miracle happened then.

He told me that he had planned to "use [me] hard and leave [me] on the floor for the night", as that was "standard breaking procedure" for a new submissive/slave, and that I "would have needed therapy" after the rest of the ordeal he had planned. Yet after seeing me "post-transition" and spending half an hour soul-searching on that rainy winter night, he decided that I was so "young and innocent" (which I pointed out was quite a feat at 31) that I "deserved better" for my first time. I found him to be by no means without religion, and in a manner far more reminiscent of *The Phantom of the Opera*[549] than the Marquis de Sade he also lamented his own life, telling me that he was weary of his kinky and overly sexually-active existence and that he wanted a good, Christian[550] one with a wife and children (which caused me to silently lament that I was unable to give him what he sought due to my lack of a womb). Just as I had felt unease at the threshold of the encounter, he had now become disillusioned by the crass shallowness of a sexually-indulgent life. He released me, with every element of my virginity quite intact, and paid for an earlier train ticket so that I might not tempt him with my mere presence any longer.

While we waited for the time of my departure, the 'bondage lord' offered to show me the numerous BDSM implements lining the walls of his little apartment, yet not willing to risk titillating him any further, I focused entirely on his collection of exotic weapons (besides, he had two different sizes of a blade I identified as a *kukri*[551]....) As snow

---

549 Especially that of the original 1910 French novel by Gaston Leroux.

550 No pun intended for all you Fifty Shades fans!

551 A curved blade wielded by the Gurkha warriors of Nepal, the kukri also has significance in the Nepalese Hindu religion. It represents the cow's-hoof, and signifies the fertility symbol "*OM*" and also the three most important gods

gently fell around us outside the station, I reached over to him, despite remembering his warning that so much as kissing him upon the lips would break my intangible protection and cause him to take me by force....

...Thus I kissed him upon the cheek and told him, "You deserve to be loved." Having an inkling of knowledge regarding the sort of life I had known, he replied with the same statement, this time directed at me.

(As a parting shot to libertine attitudes, his was virtue well rewarded; he has since remained true to his statements, and even come into some good fortune; power of a sort different than that which he might have held over me, and he has not turned from God.)

In the first story of this chapter, I had escaped through empowered self-respect. However, that was with regards to an industry and monetary gain. I had approached the above instance with the modern attitude of the kind I had seen from others and thought myself prepared to emulate. This was business – a simple photosession which would not even be nude – which could potentially become something more sensual. I also felt as though I "owed" the 'bondage lord' such service due to his being so accepting of and helpful to me at a time when it seemed noone else would be; a classic attitude through which one may fall into sexual entrapment.

Furthermore, being a woman of science, I assumed that any cultural or religious values placed upon virginity were really nothing more than attempts to assure men that any child birthed by their brides was guaranteed to include their own genetic information, and that due to my being such a sterile freak of nature my own maidenhood was not worth a...darn (perhaps not the best turn of phrase).

Besides, I was a "liberated" woman who assumed that we would use each other equally to satisfy our mutual – if disparate – needs. Why then did I emerge from the experience with the unshakable sensation *that I had just been rescued*?

Let me now affirm for those who wish to be especially religious that yes, remaining a maid has great value even among we who suffer

---

of Hinduism: Brahma, Vishnu, and Shiva. There is a legend that, in ancient times, if the kukri was drawn it could not be resheathed without having tasted blood.

the 'deformity' of being trans. For instance, my correspondent Roman Catholic Priest stated that my own vow to perpetual virginity was "a great gift for the Church!!!"

Now I have shared with you my darkest moments, for indeed had I not experienced such moments of seeming-abandonment and hopelessness myself and walked down that same path with you who may have had similar experiences, I would not be well-equipped to assure anyone that God, in fact, doesn't hate you. Mine was quite a journey to obtain something with which one half of the population was born...and which it is all-too-often encouraged to lament.

Elizabeth Cady Stanton, co-author of *The Woman's Bible*, describes the 'worst qualities' of the Jewish service (as she understands it) in two major ways. Firstly, that the Talmud states that during Purim's feast a man may drink until he cannot distinguish "cursed be Haman" from "blessed be Mordecai." Secondly and worse still, each man may apparently stand up in the synagogue every Sabbath morning and thank the Lord that he was not born a woman, as if having been so were the depth of human degradation.[552]

Yes, some degree of anti-Semitism was perhaps found even among suffragettes, yet in any case that is one prayer I cannot envision myself ever uttering! I would instead, if one will indulge me, attempt a "transwoman's prayer of thanks":

Dear LORD,

> I thank You for making me a woman, insomuch as I am and can recognize myself to be one, and for all of the unique experiences that have helped me to grow in wisdom and understanding.
>
> I thank You for taking me through the crucible of transition, both physically and spiritually, so that I might be made a new being in Christ.

---

552 *The Woman's Bible*, Part II, "Comments on Esther", Elizabeth Cady Stanton, p. 90. I am not certain how often this occurred in Stanton's time, but this phrase is used in the 1977 miniseries *Jesus of Nazareth*, directed by Franco Zeffirelli.

I thank You for comforting me in my moments of deepest darkness and doubt, like a Parent holding their daughter in the last hours of night.

I thank You for delivering me from evil and corruption and allowing me to return from such even as I stood in its final threshold, not fully understanding what lay beyond.

I thank You for being with me at all those times when I had noone else but You, and reminding me that You are all I truly need.

I thank You for teaching me that that which is of the flesh is only flesh, while that which is of the Spirit is eternal with Christ, and that I too have a soul and may have a place in Your Kingdom.

I thank You also for teaching me to love even those who persecute me, and reminding me that if the world hates me, I must know that it has hated Your Son first; even Jesus Christ our Lord.[553]

Amen.

The Two Perceptions of God

What took me so long to stop listening to the world more than to my own heart and soul? I found it easier to trust the world; it was so much more sure of itself than I. Most of my life was spent trying desperately to be something I fundamentally was not, and I was thus confused on the most basic level. It is here that the subconscious dwells, and thus it comes as no surprise that I have experienced intriguing dreams. There is one dream-vision in particular which I shall relate here, for it was the very reason I have written this book at all.

I was in the Garden of Gethsemane with Jesus and His disciples in the darkest hour of night. I sensed that there was very little time left before the soldiers came and the horror began to play out. I might have

553 John 15:18.

preferred to be merely an observer, yet I felt as though I were physically present at the scene.

However, rather than the Pharisees or temple guard, four Roman officers arrived, each holding a burning torch and carrying between them a palanquin with a golden throne upon which sat what appeared to be the Emperor of Rome in a scarlet cloak. The officers themselves were of daunting appearance in their crimson cloaks and golden armour, the plumes on their helms giving the impression of living flame, yet the presence of the Emperor was terrifying beyond description. Still, fearing that they were come to take Jesus away and inspired by Peter's example (in John 18:10), the Disciples and I took up arms to defend our Lord. I recall being angered at the thought that it must always be the same; that violence seemed ever-necessary in this world, for what else could I do in such a situation as this? A part of me wished that I might escape the notice of the Emperor upon the throne; that the pale robes and veils I wore might camouflage me well enough with the bark of the olive (or possibly birch or cedar; it was dark) tree next to which I stood that I would not be seen. As though reading my very thoughts, the Emperor then immediately turned his head to look directly at me and laid bare my past, my life, and my soul with seven words:

"What manner of weapon is that, woman?"

I did not know the answer myself; I was only dimly aware that I was even grasping a weapon of any manner; I knew that Peter wielded a blade, and though there is one other in the story, and "it is enough,"[554] I myself had not been given a sword. I thus looked down at my hands to determine what exactly I was holding. There I beheld a shepherd's staff.

To this day I am alarmed and amazed at what came over me at this point, for my fear was melted away and I was given a confident and unexpected response. I replied with another seven words:

"It is the weapon of a shepherd...."

554 Luke 22:38, KJV.

I continued to gaze upon the staff, and in an instant I received a dawning realisation of precisely what this gift meant:

"and yet it is not a weapon...."

As I said these seven words, the Garden faded away; replaced by an endless field of light. I would wonder later if I had been in Heaven, yet the light-grey nature of its illumination suggested that I was rather at its edge; at some manner of ethereal threshold, some alternate universe not affected by the laws of entropy which govern the dark one in which we now live. I lifted my head to stare directly into the eyes of the Emperor and gave my final statement:

"...for ours is no war."

The Emperor seemed bemused, or perhaps amused, at this and with a sweeping gesture and an empathic command bade that we all bow down in obeisance before him.

I was not about to render unto Caesar things which were not Caesar's[555]; not with Jesus Christ Himself standing silently ~20' to my left[556]!!! Still, my apparent approach of being ready to charge and beat upon the Emperor and his entourage with my shepherd's staff was unlikely to meet with success, even if the four armoured warriors had their hands full with the torches and the throne (and in addition to contradicting what I had just said, it would also have produced a rather comical image, for I am not exactly Gandalf from *The Return of the King*). Instead, I determined that while I was not intended to do battle this time, neither would I yield to the tyrant.

Not wanting to betray Jesus, my true Master, I planted my staff in the ground as I stood straight up and continued staring defiantly into

555 Mark 12:17.

556 The Disciples were directly in front of the Emperor; between myself and Jesus. Thus we were all on the right of Christ (thankfully, if Matthew 25:31-45 is at all symbolic in this case), but of course the Disciples were much closer to our Saviour than I!

the Emperor's eyes. Tactically speaking, I cannot recommend this as the best choice of response, either....

I boldly tried to stare the Emperor down for at least several seconds and possibly a minute or more, all the while in stark terror as my mind reeled with images of all the tortures which he had authority as Roman Emperor to inflict upon me; it was not like experiencing the "soldier rush" – the reason why the most effective attack is conducted as a single swift assault – wherein the presence of such overwhelming fear causes one to cease to be afraid. It was instead slow torture; truly a vivid nightmare within a vivid nightmare. As this transpired, I was filled with the sense that I had just challenged something infinitely more powerful than myself, and felt as if my blood were literally turning to ice. At last I glanced away to see how the Disciples were responding; I hoped that they had taken advantage of my distraction and escaped.

Instead and to my utter amazement, they were all kneeling prostrate! I didn't get it; this didn't seem to make any sense. Caesar was most assuredly the Bad Guy; my knowledge of the Scriptures at the time may have been less than impressive, but I was quite certain of that fact. What was wrong with my brain, that it would conjure such an image as this?!?

I looked back towards the Emperor enthroned upon the torch-bearing armoured warriors and saw a possible explanation for this: Jesus had moved so that He now stood just to the right of (and slightly behind) the Emperor[557], and looked far less helpless than He had a moment earlier. I was now quite confused indeed: there was One Being whom I knew Jesus to be seated at the Right Hand of, but I found myself unable to bow now; this couldn't possibly be Him....He was too ostentatious... too grandiose...too demanding that every dictated decree be obeyed....I couldn't kneel to the Emperor; but I could kneel to Jesus Christ. Then I considered that perhaps that was precisely the reason the Disciples had prostrated themselves; that they were really bowing to the Christ; He had given us a way out.[558] I angled myself to face Jesus and knelt prostrate as well, at which point the dream ended.

557 Ephesians 1:20, Mark 16:19, Luke 22:69, Matthew 22:44 and 26:64, Acts 2:34 and 7:55, 1 Peter 3:22, Psalms 63:8 and 110:1.

558 1 Corinthians 10:13.

So...what was I to make of this?!? I awoke after dawn sometime around Easter morning of 2010, shortly after my 31st birthday, and was not certain of what to think. I had little idea of what had just happened, but I certainly wanted to find out!

I described this vision to my gentle Dean of Theology, William Danaher. I told him that I was prone to spiritual visions and even had had a near-death experience when I was sixteen years old. Nevertheless, he was quite intrigued by this vision and even made it a major subject of his 2013 Saint Patrick's Day sermon, titled *Deeper Than Green*. Within this sermon he also related his response to me:

> "When she asked me what I thought, I told her that I could not tell her if it meant that she should study theology. The history of the Christian tradition is full of visionaries who had a profound effect on the church, in part because they were unburdened by theological education and stood outside of the normal church structures."

I actually did quite a lot of studying in the interim, and not only of theology. I endeavoured to explore all possible explanations for the vision, including the psychological ones. The Dean also took this approach in his sermon:

> "Psychologists have long debated the role dreams play in our lives. Sigmund Freud, the first modern psychologist to explore the meaning of dreams, felt that dreams were a cover-up for something else. In other words, another meaning is hidden underneath every dream, which for various reasons cannot be expressed directly. Carl Jung thought otherwise. Dreams, he argued, are clear expressions of our very own nature that mean exactly what they say. Both believed that dreams provide us with access to our unconscious, to a realm of ourselves that is hidden from the ordinary lives we lead. Dreams reveal to us our deepest desires and wishes, or deepest hopes and fears, and these affections – painful and pleasurable – make us who we are, in all our complexity."

To analyze this dream in the Freudian or Jungian sense – for the vast majority of dreams are merely a reexamination of recycled images and themes from one's personal subconscious mind – would reveal it to be reflective of deep-seated psychological concerns. Such is generally regarded as the most scientific approach to such things. This Harry Benjamin noted during a meeting with Sigmund Freud, gaining a brief laugh from the otherwise very serious and biologically-oriented man when he jokingly declared that...

> "a disharmony of souls might perhaps be explained by a **dishormony** of endocrine glands."[559]

Upon that issue of chemical balance, I cannot say exactly how important my gender-expression and identity may have been to this dream, however it does make objective sense that the Emperor would call me "woman". Even though I heard the words pronounced in English, they appeared to be said by a Caesar of Rome who would naturally speak Latin (and as I have noted previously, the Latin definition of female is connected to the breasts rather than the vagina or womb). Any connection between gender and the messages of the dream should become apparent as we continue to examine it. In any case, it is nice to know that the founding father of psychoanalysis and one of the founding fathers of transsexual studies conversed...and not about how crazy we "transsexuals" supposedly are! However, not everything can be explained by science, and not everything can be explained by sex.

The Wisdom of Sirach (also called Ecclesiasticus) predates Sigmund Freud by approximately two thousand years. It offers profound, yet similar, ancient insight into the nature of dreams:

> "What is seen in dreams is to reality
> what the reflection of a face is to the face
> itself.

---

[559] Erwin J. Haeberle's interview with Harry Benjamin on the occasion of his (Benjamin's) 100th birthday. Published in "*Sexualmedizin*", vol. 14, 1/1985. Retrieved from the *Archive for Sexology* http://www2.hu-berlin.de/sexology/GESUND/ARCHIV/TRANS_B5.HTM on September 21st of 2012. Emphasis mine (so Freud liked puns!).

> Can the unclean produce the clean?
> can the liar ever speak the truth?
> Divination, omens and dreams are all unreal;
> what you already expect, the mind
> depicts.
> Unless it be a vision specially sent by the
> Most High, [for God said that He would speak with people
> in dreams in Numbers 12:6]
> fix not your heart on it;
> For dreams have led many astray,
> and those who believed in them have
> perished.
> The law is fulfilled without fail,
> and perfect wisdom is found in the mouth
> of the faithful man.
> A man with training gains wide knowledge;
> a man of experience speaks sense."
> (Sirach 34:3-9, NAB)

It thus appeared quite wise to consult with those of experience regarding such visions; not only psychologists, but also ministers, priests, and theologians. There is much sense in analyzing a dream as the recycling of images and experiences already present within one's subconscious mind, yet one risks missing out on any higher meaning that might be present if one restricts their analysis to within those parameters. Fortunately, Dean Danaher provided more insight in his St. Patrick's Day sermon:

> "However, in the Christian tradition, dreams and visions do this and more. They tell us not only who we are, but they reveal to us the person we are called to be. They reveal to us our aspirations and hopes. Their purpose is not only to reveal knowledge, but to guide our decisions and actions in the present and future."

Whether the dream merely provides insight as to the state of my own mind or it possesses some deeper meaning, my attitude within the dream reflects one which I think many of my readers share. There appear to have been two major psychological themes flowing throughout this vision: Love and War.

I hadn't the foggiest idea as to why the latter would be of such importance to my subconscious essence – I am not exactly some former soldier abandoning her military past – yet I shall endeavour to address it first. Though your guess might be as good as mine with regards to the full implications of this dream-vision, it is certain that it delves into both matters of the Christian faith and of my own self.

Thus we address the matter of war a third and final time. The image of the Garden of Gethsemane reveals Jesus' ultimate position as the Prince of Peace. It was here that He uttered the immortal phrase, "all they that take the sword shall perish with the sword"[560]; a phrase which I myself did not even know to have been said by Jesus until the May of my 20th year. Why, I wondered, did those who first told me of the phrase not immediately associate it with Christ? Why, for that matter, have Christians been so unwilling to embrace the pacificism that Jesus demands of us?

I earlier mentioned His Blessed Eminence (Cardinal) John Henry Newman, the one after whom my high school was named. Instrumental in founding the Catholic University of Ireland and very recently Beatified by Pope Emeritus Benedict XVI, he had a style of preaching which was angelic in its androgyny. He also met with criticism (due to his celibacy) from the founder of what is known as 'Muscular Christianity'.

Muscular Christianity was an approach which combined energetic Christian evangelism with an ideal of vigorous masculinity; it was both described and praised as "the Englishman going through the world with rifle in one hand and Bible in the other." This writer also added that, "If asked what our muscular Christianity had done, we point to the British Empire."[561]

Though it may be a fine thing to be so, God did not will for all the world to be English. So it was that we received yet another example of Christians abandoning the ideals of the faith in their very attempt

560 Matthew 26:52, KJV.

561 Cotton Minchin, J. G. (1901). Our Public Schools: Their Influence on English History; Charter House, Eton, Harrow, Merchant Taylors', Rugby, St. Paul's Westminster, Winchester. Swan Sonnenschein & Co. p. 113.

to propagate it. Other motives, of course, were also present – if not dominant – such as that of the propagation of the aforementioned British Empire. Taking such an aggressive approach was of course what kept Gandhi from becoming Christian, and with him perhaps all of India.

The approach of Muscular Christianity reflects an attitude that certain aspects of God's and Christ's teachings must be sacrificed so that the faithful may survive in such a harsh world as this. It speaks monstrous volumes when we at last realize just how much we have come to rely upon such sacrifice. So it was in the vision: two thousand years later, despite the innumerable times this Passion has been portrayed, I could think of no manner in which to respond to it but by taking up arms.

Yet the LORD is a God of peace.

This is a confusion which stems from childhood, when mixed messages abound and when one has little or no means of properly sorting them out. As the transperson longs for liberation from their assigned casque of flesh, escapism is part of the very nature of the trans experience, particularly early in life. Thus we embrace whatever we are given so that we might be socially acceptable and try even to become fond of such things, no matter how horrible they truly are. For example, in my case when I was eleven, my friends and I would marvel over such things as the G.I. Joe Stealth Fighter[562] and actually become excited about the Persian Gulf War, and then we would hear Mass at Saint Agatha Elementary School and be told how horrible war truly is. I remember singing "God is watching us" while my classmate Martin sat at the back singing "Saddam Hussein is watching us" and feeling peer pressure to act as though that were somehow funny. If war were so wrong, why was it so glorified? Why was Jesus the one and only one to remind me that conflict was not the highest thing in which to strive for success?

---

562 The Phantom X-19, to be precise; though it bears it little physical resemblance, the Phantom was possibly inspired by the Lockheed F-117A Nighthawk, a near-supersonic stealth attack aircraft capable of delivering a nuclear yield. First flown in 1981, its existence became public knowledge the same year as the release of the G.I. Joe vehicle (1988) and it was widely publicised during the 1991 Gulf War (as a coincidence, the Phantom's pilot was code-named "Ghostrider" while the Nighthawk was dubbed *Shada* (Arabic for "Ghost") by the Saudi Arabians during Operation Desert Storm).

Thus we have before us the Demon's Question: Was it worth it? Was it worth what we have sacrificed to further the cause of Christendom?

> "That this tremendous, worldshaking process is taking place by causing suffering and pain corresponds to an eternal law of destiny, which states not only that everything great is gained by fighting but also that every mortal comes into this world by causing pain."
>
> – Adolf Hitler, January 30th, 1944.[563]

Hitler's operations had only the loosest association with Christianity, yet still I do believe a second opinion is in order. As in both of those things to which Hitler referred it is the women who suffer most, let us turn to them for a rebuttal....

> "We declare the doctrine that war is inevitable to be both a denial of the sovereignty of reason and a betrayal of the deepest instincts of the human heart."
>
> – "Preamble to the International Congress of Women," February, 1915. p. 35

This lovely counter provides not only stark contrast, but also quite a lot of cognitive dissonance when one considers that both speakers claimed Christianity as their faith.

Yet which one do we remember most? We remember the most famous one, the loudest one; the one which inherently disgusts those whose upbringing in a Christian environment has reached a subconscious level, merging with and establishing our inherent senses of right and wrong. Phrases such as "Love thy neighbour"[564] and "Stop judging by appearances, but judge justly"[565] are so deeply-ingrained in our culture that many of us forget that they came from Jesus Christ. Unfortunately, once Christianity has descended so deeply into our essences it can be

---

563 http://der-fuehrer.org/reden/english/44-01-30.htm Retrieved Thursday, October 4th, 2012.

564 Leviticus 19:18, Mark 12:31, Matthew 19:19, 22:39, Luke 10:27, Romans 13:9, Galatians 5:14, James 2:8.

565 John 7:24.

easily forgotten on the surface of our consciousness, so that external reminders of horrors committed in its name can seem to be the lingering face of the Faith. This causes it to become abhorrent to our sight, in the way that spattered blood stands out most upon a pristine white cloth.

I am not asking anyone to believe in the existence of demons or Satan or any sort of malignant and influential destructive consciousness; I do not know what the extent of such an influence is if it even is present. I must admit, however, that if this were part of some intentional scheme it would perhaps be the most diabolically-clever and fiendishly-satisfying one: to attempt to destroy Christianity...with its own goodness.

Let's play "Spot the Tyrant"! Here are several historical figures who have borne the title of Roman Emperor at some point in history. Despite the nature of the vision, the features of the enthroned Emperor were so vivid that he could be spotted even among this group. All of these images are from the Louvre in France save for Caligula (Ny Carlsberg Glyptotek in Denmark), Nero (Aphrodisias in modern-day Turkey), Charlemagne (the Palatine Chapel of Aix-la-Chapelle in Germany), and Napoleon (Palazzo Reale, Italy). Though the throne in the dream was virtually identical to the one in Andrea Appiani's "Apotheosis of Napoleon" shown here, the person upon it is all wrong.

Such ultimate villainy brings to mind another question: who was the Roman Emperor seated upon the golden throne? Prior to the dream I could not have picked a Roman Emperor (sans regalia) out of a police line-up, but this one's face was so vivid in the vision and so long did I spend staring at it that it left me with quite a clear impression; one which I might cross-reference with available historical material such as sculptures and coins. So it was that I studied in turn the appearances of every one of the sixty-seven Roman Emperors (and as many of the Eastern and Western Roman Emperors as possible, as even Charlemagne (a.k.a. Charles Augustus) and Napoleon claimed the latter title) to determine whether or not I had simply imagined the appearance of my own.

There was only one Emperor out of that whole crowd who had quite the same features – such as the pronounced cheekbones and deep, piercing eyes – as the one in my vision. Though the one I saw was much older than the man depicted by sculpture, his appearance was most certainly that of *Imperator Caesar 'Divi filius'* ('Son of God') *Augustus*, the 1st Emperor of Rome.[566] While it is nice to know that the being shown to me was real, this in itself renders the dream historically inaccurate, for as secular Roman Historian Tacitus noted in his *Annal*s:

"*Christus*...suffered the extreme penalty during the reign of Tiberius...."[567]

The Emperor of Rome at the time of Christ's death was *Tiberius Julius Caesar Augustus*; the 2nd Emperor of the Roman Empire, who ruled from 14 A.D. to the 16th of March 37 A.D.). Admittedly, it would not have been historically accurate for Tiberius to appear at the Garden of Gethsemane with only four attendants either, but why had I instead been shown Augustus, the Emperor of Rome at the time of Christ's birth?

Once again, the answer to this mystery would be revealed to me by a footnote in my Holy Bible which I had never before read. It was the 2003-2004 Edition which I have so often referenced, and it would offer profound insight into the dream's overarching theme of conflict versus capitulation. Regarding Luke 2:1's mention of Caesar Augustus,

---

566 Isaiah 48:6-12.

567 Book 15, Chapter 44, circa 116 A.D., translated by Church and Brodribb.

it points out that this emperor reigned from 27 B.C. until his death in A.D. 14, and that according to Greek inscriptions he was regarded in the Roman Empire as 'saviour' and 'god'. He was also credited with establishing a time of peace, the *pax Augusta*, throughout all of the Roman world during his lengthy reign. It was thus quite intentional that Luke related the birth of Jesus to the time of Caesar Augustus; the Emperor was thus contrasted with the *real* Saviour and Peace-bearer, the Child born in Bethlehem. Thus the great emperor is simply God's agent, like the Persian king Cyrus in Isaiah 44:28-45, who is used by God to accomplish His will.[568]

When interpreted literally with regards to it, light is shone upon a new facet of the dream-vision. During the vision itself I had understood why the Emperor had demanded that we kneel in absolute obeisance before him: I had stated that ours was no war. His response was clear: if we would not fight for our freedom, we would kowtow before him and accept his chains. This is not a thing easily reconciled; I was not meant to stand and fight him, so instead I chose simply to stand. Doubtless the Emperor had encountered many people willing to kill for their faith; how would he respond to those willing to die for it?

---

568 NAB, 2003-2004 Edition, p. 1095.

Here he is: Imperator Caesar Augustus, the 1st Emperor of Rome. I recall seeing this bronze statue years after having received this dream-vision and finding it quite fitting that it had no sculpted eyes; only empty eyesockets. It reminded me of how unfathomable the eyes of the one upon the throne were, and how looking into them was like gazing into unmade worlds. (Fragment of an equestrian statue of Augustus. 1st Century A.D., National Archaoelogical Museum in Athens, Greece.)

I shall close the issue of war-versus-peace by referencing the profound words of Mrs. Pethick Lawrence at the International Congress of Women. She stated that there are two kinds of peace from which we can choose. The first is based upon public justice and democratic liberty, it is a peace that is constructive and permanent, and a peace that can be brought about through negotiation with all and by mutual agreement. The second peace is formed upon exhaustion, the peace on the battlefield of misery and despair, the peace founded upon the victory of physical force.[569]

---

[569] "Resolution on Meditation." *INTERNATIONAL CONGRESS OF WOMEN. Report of Business Sessions.* FOURTH DAY, SATURDAY, MAY 1TH. (MORNING SESSION). p. 156. The motion was Carried unanimously.

The imperious image of the Emperor who addressed me simply as "woman"[570] was both terrifying and infuriating. In coming to claim Christ, he appeared to be playing the role of Judas the Iscariot[571], and in demanding that we all bow down and worship him, the one enthroned seemed to be playing the role of Satan[572]. He seemed to represent everything that was cruel and unjust in those with power.

However, consultation with a minister resulted in a suggestion regarding the Emperor which was most unsettling, due to the image of One Enthroned upon four fiery ones.[573] He was neither the Anti-Christ, nor Caesar, nor Zeus[574], nor Marduk. Perhaps my mind had cobbled together some sort of representation of a perception of the Old-Testament God.

How could my subconscious mind have ever thought of God in such a tyrannical manner? Perhaps it was easy in such a dark, "post-Christian" time as this, when He has become so vilified that there are those who would try to sink their venomous fangs into Him with the Seven Accusations. Perhaps it was too easy for someone like me who felt arbitrarily outcast by my fellow Christians simply because of how I was born.

---

570 It should be noted that being called "woman" was not a form of insult at that time of Christ. *Woman's Bible* Part II Comments on John, Elizabeth Cady Stanton, p.138.

571 John 18:9.

572 Matthew 4:9. Regarding my response to his order, I had not yet seen *300*, though it is just possible that Mordecai had some influence upon my rebellion as I had read the Book of Esther many years earlier.

573 Ezekiel 1. פרש *Saraph* or מיפרשה *seraphim* is generally translated from Hebrew simply as "burn" or "be burned" or more complicatedly as "fiery one" (specifically "fiery serpent"; ie. logographically *Hey s(h)in resh pey yad mem:* "ה Behold [the] ש fanged ר head(s) [/and] פ mouth(s) [of those who] י worship [the] מ Mighty").

574 This is despite the fact that the Imperator Augustus has been depicted in sculpture as a *Pheidias Zeus with the Nike* (modeled after the massive gold-and-ivory Zeus depicted seated and holding in his hand a winged woman referred to as a Victory) entitled *Pater Patriae* – Father of the Fatherland. http://www.mlahanas.de/Greeks/Arts/ZeusStatue.htm Retrieved October 22nd of 2012.

In any case, the dream showed a perspective which reflected Old Testament attitudes; I seemed to second-guess the actions/attitude of the Emperor because I fell into the snare of leaning on my own then-very-limited understanding.[575] I expected a hardened, intractable tyrant just as I expected the need to do battle with Him, and thus I was constantly forced to react instinctively when events did not play out as I had expected.

Yet Jesus, the perfect image of God's infinite compassion, was there as well. He seemed so helpless and yet so understanding as His agony again played out to remind me of those words whose roots run far deeper than their fragile flower would suggest: God loves you.

> "...the young woman...saw her visions as life-changing, inviting her to throw herself totally without remainder into a life of undistracted love and worship. When the young woman asked me if I believed that her vision was authentic, I told her that I recognized in it the same love that has animated Christian mysticism for thousands of years. Her vision not only oriented of her life as an individual, but it touched the most basic claim that Christians have given in every generation, at the deepest level possible, for thousands of years. Christianity lives by the claim that God knows us intimately and has invited us into a relationship of deep intimacy. We know this because we have been given the perfect revelation of God in the wounded figure of Jesus, whose vulnerability expresses in a finite way the infinite love of God."
>
> – Rev. Dr. William J. Danaher, Jr. Fifth Sunday after Advent. *Deeper than Green*

Whether there was more to the dream...I cannot say. However, there is something else I would like to reveal about myself. Despite its English spelling, my first name – Tiamat – is not truly Babylonian; it is Hebrew. In that language it means "the deep"[576]; that which knew only

575 Proverbs 3:5.

576 Douay Rheims 1899 American Edition (and many others). Logographically "ת Taw ה he ו waw מ mem"; "ה Behold [the] ת Cross, [the] ו Nail, [and the] מ Blood...(or Water)." See John 19:33-37.

frigid darkness until touched by God's Spirit in Genesis 1:2. I find this fitting, for in my 33 years of life I have experienced love as both a man and a woman, and both were immeasurably inferior to the love I feel from the LORD.

The One who could have conquered me because of His power, and to whom I surrendered because of His Love.

Thus the dream-vision in a sense displayed what I have endeavoured to do in this book: defend the understanding of the gentle, loving God from the image of the imperious, unapproachable, unrecognizeable One. We must remember that love is what the LORD truly wants from us; and as the infinitely-powerful Creator of all, love is all He could possibly ever need.